THE GOSPEL-DRIVEN CHURCH

THE GOSPEL-DRIVEN CHURCH

Retrieving Classical Ministry for Contemporary Revivalism

IAN STACKHOUSE

PATERNOSTER

First published in 2004 by Paternoster Press

09   08   07   06   05   04   7   6   5   4   3   2   1

Paternoster Press is an imprint of Authentic Media,
9 Holdom Avenue, Bletchley, Milton Keynes MK1 1QR, UK
and
P.O. Box 1047, Waynesboro, GA 30830-2047, USA

www.authenticmedia.co.uk

British Library Cataloguing in Publication Data
A catalogue record for this book is available from the British Library

ISBN 1–84227–290–X

Front cover image:
Gaugin, *Jacob Wrestling with the Angel, The Vision After the Sermon,*
The National Gallery of Scotland

Cover Design by FourNineZero
Typeset by Waverley Typesetters, Galashiels
Print Management by Adare Carwin
Printed and Bound in Denmark by Nørhaven Paperback

'Few books have stimulated me more in recent years than this penetrating analysis of present-day evangelicalism. Pastor-theologian Ian Stackhouse strikingly strips away many a charismatic shibboleth and in so doing points to what Christian ministry is truly all about. This book needs to be read by every evangelical church leader – as indeed by every student preparing for ministry.'

Paul Beasley-Murray, Chair of Ministry Today and
Senior Minister of Central Baptist Church, Chelmsford

'As both a significant contribution to pastoral theology and a personal manifesto for his own future ministry, I whole-heartedly commend this astute analysis of current trends in the charismatic evangelical scene by "Doctor Ian".'

J. David Pawson, International Bible Teacher

'Those of us who care about the church of Jesus Christ have been offered a plethora of rhetoric and programs for renewal in recent decades. They range from serious to silly and it is not at all easy to discern where to draw the line. Ian Stackhouse's book is a model of careful biblical and spiritual discernment, both appreciative and cautionary. I find him a most welcome ally in our "stay against confusion".'

Eugene Peterson, Professor Emeritus of Spiritual Theology,
Regent College, Vancouver B.C., Canada

'This thorough critique of so much contemporary revivalism and charismatic practice owes its power precisely to the fact that Stackhouse knows that movement from the inside, be its worship, its preaching or its ethos. This is no cynical observer from the margins, but a passionate pastor-scholar who knows the church deserves better. He has worn the shoes of revivalist Christianity and found they rub so much that they prove inadequate and crippling for the long journey of recovery of faith that this nation needs. There is a better way, and Stackhouse points us in the direction of an older tradition.'

Rev Paul Goodliff, Head of the Department of Ministry,
Baptist Union of Great Britain

'Uncomfortable. Hard-hitting. Ian Stackhouse mounts a powerful challenge against many fads to which the current contemporary church seems addicted. Unlike many other books, this one is not long on critique and short on answers. He provides some solid and biblical ways out of the current malaise in the church. Ian Stackhouse needs to be heard.'

Derek Tidball, Principal of London School of Theology

'This book is a fascinating and instructive record of its author's journey from what he increasingly sees as the impasse of charismatic revivalism to a thoughtful and inspiring re-appropriation of classic catholic Christianity and its gospel of grace.'

Canon Tom Smail

'Robert Burns made the point that "of all nonsense religious nonsense is the most nonsensical". Indeed it is the case that in the contemporary church sense and nonsense mingle cheerfully and frequently together and a large part of the pastoral office is to sort the wheat from the chaff. Ian Stackhouse pleads for a recovery of the tradition of the pastor-scholar and in the process draws on the thinking of some of the most valuable contemporary scholars who have the concerns of the church at heart.'

Dr Nigel G. Wright, Principal of Spurgeon's College, London
and President of the Baptist Union of Great Britain, 2002–3

'Too often the "ark of the church flies a 'flag of convenience', roaming the seas of modern world life but dangerously cut off from its 'home port'." To such a church, Ian Stackhouse's vision offers a fresh map and a new cargo manifest! The attentive reader will find here: a depth of respect for God's history in the Church, a breadth of reading and reflection, a high view of the gospel and of preaching, and a joyful advocacy of the "long obedience in the same direction" needed to sustain Christian discipleship today. It is "radical" in the true sense of the word, re-connecting us with the "deep roots … not reached by the frost". As an urgent and prophetic wake-up call to the contemporary evangelical/charismatic church, I warmly commend it.'

Philip Greenslade, CWR, Senior Lecturer,
Waverley Abbey House, Farnham

'Many sectors of the charismatic renewal movement have pinned their hopes on imminent "revival", but then substituted weakly based and short-lived fads – often under the name of "the new movement of the Spirit" – when the essential vision has not been realised. Dr Stackhouse offers a most welcome, searching, theological and pastoral analysis of this prominent problem. A "must" for all serious charismatic leaders.'

Max Turner, Vice-Principal and
Professor of New Testament Studies, London School of Theology

'This remarkable and immensely readable book combines the scholarly, the prophetic and the burningly relevant, in strong and equal measures. It acts as a thoroughgoing health-check for the "success driven" church and its leaders; a body-scan for potentially fatal and hidden tumours in the Body of Christ today.

We are summoned to seek out the "ancient paths", and called away from the seductive and passing fashions of a Postmodern Age, back to our biblical and historic roots. Stackhouse is a sympathetic and astute observer, a fine thinker who has succeeded in making us all truly think.'

Greg Haslam, Minister, Westminster Chapel, London

Contents

PART 3
CONCLUSION

Foreword

The Gospel-Driven Church is the first in a series of books that reflect the work of an ecumenical conversation, which, in the language of C.S. Lewis, is called 'Deep Church' (Letter to the *Church Times*, 8 February 1952). Deep Church, as the colloquium defines it, is a recapitulation and restoration of the historic Christian faith as reflected in the scriptures, creeds and councils of the early church, and in the lives of the community of saints. Deep Church, then, is neither specifically evangelical nor Catholic. It is best described as an adherence to the apostolic faith of the New Testament as it was received, expounded and explicated in the patristic tradition of the early Christian centuries. This tradition, beginning with the apostles and continuing with the Church Fathers, constitutes the dogmatic core of the gospel and is the common source – the deep artesian well – from which the three great families of Christendom – Catholicism, Eastern Orthodoxy and Protestantism – draw.

Deep Church is not, however, syncretistic: there is no pretence that Catholics and Protestants are the same under the skin, or that there are no fundamental theological disagreements between denominations, which, this side of heaven, will probably never be resolved. Nevertheless, like Lewis, in his letter of 1952, there is a sense that against the backdrop of theological liberalism, the differences between evangelical and Catholic sensibilities are not as great as the tradition they share in common. As Lewis, talking of the 'high' and low' wings of the Church of England put it, 'both are thoroughgoing supernaturalists, who believe in the Creation, the Fall, the Incarnation, the Resurrection, the Second Coming, and the ... Last Things. This unites them not only with one another but also with the Christian religion as understood *ubique et ab omnibus'*.

To retrieve and reconnect with the common Christian tradition once 'everywhere and by everyone believed' (to live in Deep Church) is not an archaeological or ante-diluvian exercise: it is a renewal of the historic givens of the faith for today's church. A conviction of the authors of this series is that while we are open to the new things God is doing, we must also be attentive to the 'old' things he has already done. Either through liberalism, pragmatism, or a capitulation to emotionalism, many of our churches have suffered from what the author of this book calls 'theological amnesia': we are not telling or indwelling 'the old, old story' because we have forgotten who we are. This is not intended as a dig at liberals, for even in the evangelical world there has been the emergence of what can only be called an identity crisis.

This is partly due to a crisis of confidence (almost amounting to a panic) as the hopes and yearnings for substantial church growth in the late twentieth century have not yet been realised in this the first decade of the twenty-first. But this identity crisis is also partly due to the re-emergent springs of ecumenism that first surfaced in the charismatic renewal of the 1960s and 1970s but subsided in the 1980s and 1990s. Now, increasingly, a significant number of the younger generation of charismatic evangelicals prefer to be thought of as 'mere Christians', sharing in a generous and open orthodoxy, rather than retrenching to a narrowly defined (albeit principled) biblicism. This openness to other confessions and constituencies that also draw on the common tradition can be seen in the influence of Eastern Orthodoxy on the theology and spirituality of evangelical scholars, the re-discovery of Celtic Christianity in new and old churches alike, and interest in the ascetic spirituality of the contemplative catholic traditions – notably, the spiritual exercises of Ignatius Loyola. Many evangelicals have also recently taken to Karl Barth: he has long been given close attention in the writings of Lesslie Newbigin, Tom Torrance and Colin Gunton, but has only been recently been taken-up by the evangelical mainstream on both sides of the Atlantic Ocean. P.T. Forsyth, the Scottish theologian, who in many ways is a forerunner of Barth, has also become a major theological resource for evangelicals, not least for the author of this book.

This brings us to *The Gospel-Driven Church* by Ian Stackhouse. For many years Ian was a leader in a well-known independent new church in the Home Counties. He is now the pastor of Guildford Baptist Church. Ian is one of the initiators of the Deep Church conversation. Like many of his Anglican colleagues, Ian is an evangelical with strong Reformed leanings, but he is, like others involved in the conversation, also a recipient of, and resource to, charismatic renewal. The *Gospel-Driven Church*, then, is written from pastoral experience and from theological reflection on participation in the renewal.

The first half of the book is unashamedly polemical. Ian knows from first-hand experience what is good about the renewal. However, he is critical of its recent obsession with church growth. He believes this obsession fuels a restless revivalism that is always following the latest fad in the relentless drive for measurable success. This critique is born out of Ian's conviction that the gospel itself – and the common tradition which carries it – has all the resources needed for both being church and doing mission.

In the second half of the book, Ian unpacks these neglected resources. He not only champions the return of powerful preaching but also argues for what we might call regular participation in the 'normal means of grace' – the sacraments of baptism and eucharist, and the receiving of the Word. Ian wants the people of God to be fed on solid food instead of the thin gruel of whim and fancy masquerading as the latest panacea for reviving the church. It would be fair to say that he favours the incarnational approach over the ecstatic – mediated grace rather than spiritual immediacy – not because he distrusts charismatic gifts or eschews genuine religious experience, but because he wishes to see them earthed in the natural and material world rather than floating off into the realm of fantasy, or a docetic denial of our humanity.

For me, the two most significant messages of this challenging and inspiring book are, first, that we must remember that the church is called by God to be faithful not successful, and, second, that we should always be wary of falling for the latest fads. This is not to say that they are bad in themselves – they may even be helpful or inspired – but it is to recognise that putting all our trust and energy into new revelations, innovative techniques, or pragmatic programmes as panaceas for the failure of the church, saps our confidence in the given resources of the gospel to fulfil the *Missio Dei*.

It is possible that some will interpret *The Gospel-Driven Church* as a turning away from both evangelism and charismatic renewal, and regressing to a staid liturgical fastidiousness and a discredited and discarded formalism, but I think this would be a misreading of the text and a failure to see the thrust of Ian Stackhouse's argument. *The*

Gospel-Driven Church is certainly a rebuke to the excesses of revivalism, but it is not a rejection of evangelism or charismata per se. Rather, it is a plea from a pastor for a more rounded and deeper understanding of renewal – one that is ever open to the Holy Spirit's leading, but also one that remembers all that God has already achieved for us on the cross and in his resurrection. This *anamnesis* connects us with the living heritage of the church, with the communion of saints, the heroes of the faith, and with one another. It restores us to health and stability, and provides the antidote to the culture of despair that comes from the bitter disappointment of so many false dawns, the personal sense of failure we feel, and the sheer exhaustion caused by frenetic and faddish revivalism.

In this book, Ian Stackhouse makes us only too aware of the 'sickness of hurriedness in the evangelical soul'. However, he lifts us from despondency to a measured hope: it's time, he is telling us, to adopt a more robust ecclesiology, turn to and gladly receive the means of grace already provided by Christ for his people, and enter again the ecumenical streams of blessing of the early renewal. If we do this, become part of the contra flow of a generous and open orthodoxy, we will be living in 'Deep Church'.

CANON PROFESSOR ANDREW WALKER

Series Preface

Many are exasperated with what they perceive as the fad-driven, one-dimensional spirituality of modern evangelicalism and desire to reconnect with, and be deeply rooted in, the common historical Christian tradition as well as their evangelical heritage – welcome to what C.S. Lewis called 'Deep Church'.

'Deep Church is far more than an ecumenical dream of coming together across the barriers of ignorance and prejudice: it is predicated upon the central tenets of the Gospel held in common by those who have the temerity to be "Mere Christians". This commonality in the light of post-Enlightenment modernism is greater and more fundamental than the divisions and schisms of church history ... Deep Church, as its name implies, is spiritual reality down in the depths – the foundations and deep structures of the Faith – which feed, sustain, and equip us to be disciples of Christ.'

Andrew Walker, series editor

Preface

Too much theology, Stanley Hauerwas has pointed out, is written by theologians for other theologians.[1] Though such theology contributes to the internal dialogue of the academy, it is, sadly, often detached from the realities of the church community and its mission. That being the case, I have wanted to reflect and write from the vantage point of being a pastor at the coalface, so to speak, and in the process recover, in a modest way, something of the pastor-scholar tradition.[2] After all, most theology until fairly recently was written in tandem with the pulpit; if Leander Keck is correct, the church pulpit is the route by which renewal will come about.[3]

My gratitude, therefore, goes to the Christian community of the King's Church, Amersham, who generously gave me space to combine studying and pastoring. Strange that we should have to defend or justify the combination of these two things – there was a time when the terms pastor and scholar were not nearly as precise and separate as they are now[4] – but given the fact that we do, I want to express my appreciation to the church for allowing such a marriage to take place. For my own part, I could not imagine being able to write anything of any significance without this weekly discipline of submitting to the often-messy business of the church; in my opinion, true theological reflection can only arise out of a commitment, in some form or other, to the communion of the saints. Theology is an ecclesial act.[5]

Because of this commitment to the church as the true location of theology, it seems appropriate to me that the primary theological interaction in this book is with theologians in the pastor-scholar tradition: theologians such as P.T. Forsyth, Dietrich Bonhoeffer, John Wesley, Martin Thornton, Eugene Peterson and Martyn Lloyd-Jones. Other voices such as Colin Gunton, Robert Jensen, Carl Braaten, Stanley Hauerwas, William Willimon, Walter Brueggemann, William Abraham and Lesslie Newbigin, share this same burden for theology in service to the church, and will be invoked throughout.

My instincts have led me to believe that this pastoral and theological tradition provides an important filter for the enthusiasm of charismatic renewal and, more specifically, contemporary revivalism. Not that I am alone. One of the great encouragements to me over the last couple of years is fellowship with other second generation charismatics, so-called, who are similarly convinced that the future of renewal lies in the retrieval of the classical tradition: what Andrew Walker has referred to as 'Deep Church', along the lines proposed by C.S. Lewis. But then others, from an older generation, have been saying this for years now. David Pawson, for example, has repeatedly encouraged the renewal to adopt a more robust theological approach to ministry, Christian initiation in particular. Thus, it should be no surprise to some that I interact in this book with some of these voices. Believe it or not, I have tried to write in a fairly irenic style; I have no personal axes to grind. Furthermore, this book does not presume to be the last word on the subject. It is best read as a proposal.

In terms of personal influences upon this work, my special thanks go to Stuart Reid, who first taught me to revere the pastoral office of the church and to preserve the gospel against all the various winds of doctrine that buffet the church. His wisdom has inspired me for two decades now and confirm to me that friendship and the sharing of books are very much intertwined. Such love of books leads me also to thank Philip Greenslade who similarly has sought to preserve theological integrity while remaining wide open to the Holy Spirit of God. Through such men, I have received a rich heritage.

Thinking about richness of fellowship, my thanks also goes to my friend Dave Hansen, whose timely book, *The Art of Pastoring*, probably did more than anything to keep me in the pastoral ministry, at a time when I had become so weary with the numbers game. Our three months as a family in Cincinnati with the church Dave pastors at Kenwood Baptist was truly a sabbatical break – one which helped shape this final version of the book.

This book began its life as a doctoral thesis, of significantly longer length than we have here; so I would like to thank my supervisor Graham McFarlane, for laughing and crying with me through the various stages of this work, and for ensuring that what is, in essence, a very personal piece of work did not remain just that. My hope is that this version of the thesis straddles the popular and the theological. Should it fail to do so, the responsibility is mine alone. I am particularly grateful for the support of John and Lisa Dawson who enabled me financially to carry out my studies at the Guthrie Centre, London Bible College, now London School of Theology. The Christian community there gave me endless encouragement and help during two extended periods of study.

My greatest thanks is reserved for my wife Susanna for loving me through all the joys and disappointments of

church ministry. Her stability, strength and simplicity of
faith have been a great balance to the frustrated mysticism
of her husband and have kept him practical; and if she
hadn't done that for me, our four sons surely would have.
To my best friend and to those dear boys I dedicate this
work.

Notes

[1] S. Hauerwas, 'What Would Pope Stanley Say? Interview with
     R. Clapp', *Books and Culture* (November–December, 1998),
     16–18.
[2] See E.T. Charry, *By the Renewing of Your Minds: The Pastoral
     Function of Christian Doctrine* (New York/Oxford: Oxford
     University Press, 1997).
[3] L. Keck, *The Church Confident* (Nashville: Abingdon, 1993),
     67.
[4] E.H. Harbison, *The Christian Scholar in the Age of Reformation*
     (Philadelphia: Porcupine, 1980 [1956]), 116.
[5] C.E. Braaten, *The Apostolic Imperative* (Minneapolis: Augsburg,
     1985), 179–85.

PART 1

THE PATHOLOGY
OF REVIVAL

Chapter 1

Revivalism, Faddism and the Gospel

From Refreshing to Revival

> Revival is a theme embedded in the evangelical psyche, and although most Christians know little of the actual history of revivals, they tend to have in mind images of mass conversions, of people being struck down in the streets as they become conscious of their sins and of pubs and brothels being forced to close down through lack of business. For as long as I can remember, there has been an underlying hope and belief that God will once again visit our land in this way.

Thus wrote former house church leader Dave Tomlinson in his somewhat controversial book *The Post-Evangelical*.[1] Although a good deal of his critique of the evangelical movement has inspired debate, Tomlinson's reflections concerning the almost obsessive anticipation of revival within the stream of the charismatic movement known as Restorationism are incontestable. To be sure, the Restoration movement in the UK was not, at its inception, an exclusively revivalist movement; for the main part, it concentrated on the promotion of new ecclesial structures, making a clear distinction between restoration and revival.[2] Nevertheless, the structural nature of Ephesians 4 apostolicity was soon eclipsed by the classical revival vision, as described by Arthur Wallis.[3] Though committed to the Restorationist model of church, Wallis' earlier vision of revival proved to be the most enduring.[4] In the nineties this revival theme intensified, embracing not only the Restorationist vision but also, as our discussion will make clear, various Baptist, Anglican and Pentecostal churches.

The impetus for this new wave of revivalism derived from what became known as the Toronto Blessing, which began in 1994, and which was described by advocates as a 'time of refreshing'.[5] The nomenclature is significant. Toronto most definitely was not a revival, according to its main protagonists, nor to be referred to as such; instead, it was to be understood as a harbinger of revival.[6] A cursory glance at the literature of the time, for example *From Refreshing to Revival*[7] and *Prepare for Revival*,[8] demonstrates the rapidity with which the connection was made between Toronto and revival, expressing a growing conviction that the phenomena experienced in Toronto were merely precursors to unprecedented evangelistic success. When this was quickly followed by news of the extraordinary events in Brownsville, Pensacola, where large numbers of people were coming to faith, the picture appeared complete.

The fact that Toronto was largely an internal church affair hardly seemed to matter to UK revivalists, nor the fact that Pensacola was a singularly North American phenomenon, with all the cultural and religious hallmarks peculiar to the American camp meeting. The fact of the matter is that the burden for revival, by which we mean large numbers of unbelievers coming to faith, has weighed heavily upon certain sections of the renewal movement, and in the nineties was ready for reinvigoration.[9] Both Pensacola and Toronto aroused this instinct for revival by providing classic examples of charismatic phenomena and conversions, leading, as seen in the revival meetings that took place in Marsham Street, London, to a direct attempt to imitate the sort of evangelistic success in the wake of Pensacola.[10] More generally, Pensacola and Toronto fuelled an anticipation of revival across a broad range of charismatic-evangelical events. Indeed, for a period of time in the mid-nineties, the desire for revivalistic growth seemed to be the sole rationale of the charismatic movement.

As we shall argue, the issue of size is not historically, or even biblically, the way revival has been conceived. The biblical verb 'revive' resonates more with prophetic criticisms of religion than with its popularity. Nevertheless, numerical growth is the way contemporary revivalists imagine revival, and it is the definition we shall attempt to critique here. Paul Oakley encapsulates this sentiment in his song 'All Around the World' (SF2 642),[11] where revival is used euphemistically for evangelistic success. Similarly, the song 'We Ask You O Lord' (SF2 1081) draws directly upon the notion of 'the Latter Rain': the end-time cleansing of the church and the turning of the nations to the Lord. For anyone who has inhabited the world of charismatic revivalism over the last three decades, these songs are standard fare, and are not without their appeal. We shall look more closely at the strengths and weaknesses of this hymnody in chapter two. At a number of levels, however, the hope for spectacular growth, expressed in songs like these, has proved injurious.

First, the aspiration for growth has encouraged competitiveness among churches – one that many leaders increasingly acknowledge. 'The second question we ask when we meet after "which church?" is "how many members?"' admits John Noble, of the Pioneer network of charismatic churches.[12] Secondly, and more significantly, the delay of revival success has encouraged a general weariness. To be sure, there have been claims of revival, but nothing matching the numerical expectations of the early pioneers of renewal has yet taken place, with the resulting pathology that arises from a 'hope deferred'.

Given the fact that there has been little self-criticism from within the charismatic movement, and certainly not criticism that has been in print, empirical evidence of this last point is hard to come by. John Wimber apologised for the false expectations generated by Paul Cain's prophecy that Britain would experience revival in the October of 1990, coinciding with a large gathering of charismatics at Docklands,[13] and thereafter remained somewhat ambiguous in his relationship to the prophetic; but his disavowal never took on the nature of an outright critique. What criticism there is within the charismatic movement remains largely anecdotal, and not by any means articulate. Indeed, if there is a sickness, tantamount to despair, it seems in many places to have been suppressed. Traces do appear, however, within the broad consensus of pro-revival groups of an increasing disquiet, or what might be termed an incipient protest. Ken Gott, for example, leader of the Sunderland Christian Centre, has confessed to a general weariness with the revival conference circuit,[14] whereas at St Andrew's, Chorleywood – a church that has played a pivotal role in Anglican renewal – the over-emphasis on revival prompted concerns, which led to a reassessment of basic ministry patterns.[15]

Gott's reflections on the development of his own ministry, from local church leadership to conference platform, are all the more compelling because Gott has been at the heart of the recent wave of revivalism, spanning the whole gamut of charismatic epicentres such as Pensacola, Toronto, Stoneleigh, Chorleywood, and, of course, Sunderland. Though his commitment to revival is unwavering, he accepts, nevertheless, that talk of revival has led to a number of false aspirations, not least of these being the obsession with size and numbers:

> Success cannot simply be measured by the size of our church, the number of meetings we can persuade people to attend, the church programmes we run … Success in God's eyes can be reflected only by our obedience to the command Jesus has given us: first, to *be* a disciple, then to go and *make* disciples.[16]

In the context of revivalism, such a comment represents something of a conversion: an admission that numerical increase has little spiritual import in and of itself. Mike Pilavachi, leader of the youth congregation Soul Survivor, notes something similar. He laments the obsession with the idea that revival will come on a certain date and notes his 'upset when we hear more about revival than we do about Jesus'.[17] Such a comment reveals his sensitivity to the way basic spirituality is subsumed by revival. Indeed, revivalism has a tendency to cultivate a sub-culture of its own, strangely detached from the person of Christ. In many places there is an increasing acknowledgment of the detriment to normal Christian living such revival expectation can produce, and an admission of the weariness that can set in when expectations fail to materialise. But, as we shall see, instead of encouraging a wholesale critique of the culture of revivalism, the disquiet expressed above has largely gone unheeded. If not unreservedly committed to revival any more, the general culture in the charismatic-evangelical world in the West is still waiting for a spectacular and unprecedented evangelistic breakthrough; and to this end many revivalists are seemingly prepared to try anything and everything to make it happen. It is this we call faddism.

The Rise of Faddism

Revival as an aspiration carries significant repercussions for those who engage with it, especially the temptation to abandon God in the pursuit of numbers. The temptation has many echoes in the biblical narrative and is well represented also in the classical spiritual tradition. From Austin Farrar[18] to Henri Nouwen,[19] Christian leadership has been consistently warned against the insidious lure of success. And where the warning has not been heeded, a psychology of despair has ensued. It is inevitable. The success syndrome, by definition, breeds perpetual discontent with the way things are; and it is this discontent, we shall argue, that is evident in so much of the revivalism that has attached itself to charismatic renewal.

To some degree, the present malaise in charismatic renewal can be located in its very origins. When one considers the heady rhetoric that was promulgated from the platforms of various Bible conferences in the seventies and eighties, as well as the growing anticipation that something akin to the South Korean revival was about to occur in the UK, despair, as an emotional response to the numerical plateau that the movement later experienced, is understandable.[20] To go further, as some have done, and regard the ensuing history of the movement, in particular the episode of Toronto, as a case of cognitive dissonance is a moot point.[21] Whilst charismatic renewal lends itself to sociological interpretation, and has undoubtedly evinced signs of routinisation along the lines described by Max Weber, the dismissal of Toronto as mere wish fulfilment, however, is to underestimate the authentically spiritual element in it.[22] But what is evident is that out of the despair concerning the minimal impact the charismatic movement has had, and despite the growing unease about the excessive use of the term revival, there has been a proclivity on the part of many to engage with various innovative strategies. In themselves these innovations have little in common with classical models of revival, but have been harnessed to the term as a way of realising its aspirations, in the hope of bringing about the revival in very tangible and practical ways.

The various initiatives or fads, as they might be termed, that have impacted the charismatic movement since the mid-eighties can all be explained, in varying degrees, in this way. From Power Evangelism to Willow Creek, or from Toronto to Pensacola, the various fads under scrutiny represent attempts from within the movement to maximise the impact of the gospel and realise substantial growth by mimicking success stories elsewhere; in short, they are attempts from within the charismatic movement to make the revival occur. Even though these stratagems and places express very different, sometimes contradictory, theologies, all of them act, or have acted, as panaceas for a movement desperately seeking to realise the early promise of its first pioneers. Appearing successively on the scene about every two to three years, they are often discarded as it becomes apparent that growth is not as straightforward as just following a fad. [23]

Faddism is not, of course, unique to the world of religion. The term was employed, for instance, during William Gladstone's administration in late-Victorian Britain to describe an ad hoc collection of policies based on no political ideology in particular, but simply upon the desire for popularity and electorability.[24] Translated into the world of charismatic renewal, faddism represents a similar pragmatism regarding theological and spiritual rigour, on account of a particular vision of revival. Of course, we might argue, there are only so many times revival can be prophesied about, or planned for, through successive innovations, without calling into question the credibility of those who foster such expectations. Speaking about New Zealand, Michael Riddell says,

> I have lost count of the number of revivalist movements which have swept through my homeland promising a massive influx to the church in their wake. A year after they have faded, the plight of the Christian community seems largely unchanged, apart from a few more who have grown cynical through the abuse of the goodwill, energy and money.[25]

Yet, in light of fairly depressing statistics and the widespread demise of denominations, there continues to be a concerted effort to arrest the process of atrophy by further activity. Not content to articulate and stay true to the contours of the gospel itself, and the means of grace by which churches are anchored in the gospel, charismatic renewal, under the pressure of its own revival rhetoric, has focused almost singularly upon issues of numerical growth. Clearly, numerical growth in the church is not an entirely illegitimate goal, but to make growth the primary rationale of churchly existence is to accept that the end justifies the means, and, as we shall argue in the case of the renewal movement, encourages theological innovation to an extent that undermines the basic tenor of Christian proclamation.

The alternative to the pragmatism that such growth aspirations has fostered is not pure religion, for, as David Bebbington reminds us, there is no such thing as undistilled religion.[26] Fidelity to truth and practical canniness are not mutually exclusive; they can, and often do, operate alongside one another. Indeed, with discernment, there is much one can learn from strategies that have worked elsewhere; fidelity to truth should never be used as a smokescreen for intransigence and inertia. In many places, an aversion to the language of the market is, in fact, an excuse for churches to carry on what they have been doing, without regard for the changing context of mission.[27] Nevertheless, success and growth criteria have forced, in some places, a rupture between these two organising principles, to the extent that theological pragmatism and relevancy, rather than fidelity to the gospel, is now the accepted hallmark of the movement: whatever can be done to avoid decline and stimulate growth. The fear of numerical decline, as we shall see, underlies many of the initiatives taken in the last couple of decades.[28]

The emergence of Strategic Level Spiritual Warfare as a major theme in charismatic renewal is a good illustration of the point that we are making: one of those 'fads' that have beset the movement at various points in its history. Its emergence and dissemination through various sections of charismatic renewal signals an abandonment, we contend, of serious theological engagement for a prayer strategy that promises unprecedented evangelistic success.

An example: territorial spirits

In terms of ethos, Strategic Level Prayer Warfare (hereafter Prayer Warfare) moves well beyond the evangelical notion of spiritual warfare by identifying not just the need to pray, but the need to pray strategically and aggressively against the various territorial spirits, so-called, which might prevail in a given area. Based on a tenuous exegesis of Daniel 10, where the Prince of Persia effectively delays the progress of Daniel's prayers, it is said by proponents of Prayer Warfare – most notably Peter Wagner – that such territorial strongholds need to be demolished before evangelism can be effective.[29] The March for Jesus campaign promulgates, albeit in attenuated form, the prayer strategy of Wagner.

The test case that is cited for this kind of prayer warfare is Latin America, in particular Argentina, where the non-Catholic churches have experienced remarkable growth.[30] Because the statistical evidence of growth appears to be incontrovertible in those areas where the technique has been used, it has given legitimacy to a technique that has as one of its aims the 'binding of the strong man' over a city or an area before a major evangelistic thrust. This legitimating of technique is not surprising. After all, if numbers are considered to be one of the major criteria by which the movement is judged, then automatically a method or strategy that can boost the statistics is self-authenticating; typically, there is not a little myth-making in the reporting of the revivals in South America, as well as a distinct missiological jealousy. But the purpose of the empiricism is clear: to promote Prayer Warfare as the key to unlocking the harvest in the West.

The fact that the cultural context of mission in the West is vastly different from that in South America does not seem to occur to the proponents of this method; nor does it seem to matter that the biblical support for their method is flimsy, to say the least. Indeed, Wagner admits his diffidence on this matter when challenged about the biblical basis of his approach, defending the method on the grounds that it has obviously worked.[31] Such an argument, of course, is not entirely remiss. After all, the inclusion of the Gentiles in Acts was based in the first instance on the experience of the Spirit and not on a careful exegesis of scripture. But there are limits to this approach. In the case of Wagner's approach to spiritual warfare, the fact that there is no explicit biblical reference to the technique is a fundamental weakness. And given that the method is offered as a guaranteed solution to the numerical demise of Western Christianity, the ramifications, as we shall see, are serious.

Of all the UK new church networks, it is only the Ichthus and Pioneer group of churches that have consciously embraced the teaching on territorial spirits – though, given the pervasive nature of Christian media, there is little doubt that Prayer Warfare has been widely embraced within charismatic circles in general. There is nothing that is particularly novel in the approach. Classic Pentecostalism, as Steven Land has shown, has a penchant for this kind of dualistic, apocalyptic spirituality.[32] Moreover, the positing of authority in a method is nothing new to evangelicalism either. The way Calvinistic theology ceded to Arminian theology during the nineteenth-century evangelical revival was by definition, as Mark Noll and others have argued, a capitulation of theology to a belief in method.[33] This eschewal of miracle in favour of rightly constituted techniques to bring about revival, epitomised in the revivalism of Charles Finney, has proved influential, and explains a good deal of the present predilection for methods, of which Prayer Warfare is one example. [34]

The significance, however, of such an organisational perspective on growth is that it has undermined confidence in the gospel itself as the organic centre of the church's mission. By accentuating awareness of spiritual warfare, certain sections of the renewal movement have brought into question, as Chuck Lowe has shown, the efficacy of the death and resurrection of Christ as the means by which God triumphs over evil in the world.[35] The dualistic worldview required by Prayer Warfare is of a kind that has negated, if not entirely overwhelmed, the traditional emphasis on the finished work of Christ as the victory of God in the world, and thereby has jettisoned, in the form of gospel preaching, a classical means by which this victory was implemented. In the scheme of Prayer Warfare, preaching the gospel, and the evangelistic success derived from gospel preaching, can only take place once the necessary demolition of spiritual forces has occurred. 'These are the powers,' argues Roger Forster, 'that we must cast out and overcome if we are to see captives released, especially in huge revival numbers.'[36]

Of course, theological sophistication is not absent among those who embrace this teaching. Martin Scott's embracing of this particular expression of spiritual warfare is countered, to some degree, by a robust doctrine of creation and a common sense biblicism in his overall theological vision. He retains a healthy understanding of the efficacy of Christ's victory over the powers,[37] as well as a belief that the most effective form of spiritual warfare is a church that has learnt to resist the prevailing culture.[38] As with the kingdom theology of Wimber, which affected the charismatic movement in the eighties, the metaphor of *Christus Victor* that underlies Scott's theology is a welcome supplement to the traditional forensic categories of the atonement that have predominated in evangelical theology. Nevertheless, Scott's commitment to what might be described as a charismatic hermeneutic, in which experience precedes theology, often negates this point.

Scott's hermeneutical method permits him to engage with a whole variety of techniques from Spiritual Mapping to Identificational Repentance that have, he admits, little textual basis,[39] and which cumulatively, we contend, undermines the efficacy of the victory of Christ by making proclamation of the gospel, and the inherent power of the gospel, dependent on a particular methodology of prayer. Prayer is, of course, essential to the effective implementation of the victory of Christ; at the very least, those who focus on prayer warfare have reawakened the church's commitment to pray for specific areas. Scott's prayer warfare, however, requires specific spiritual insight and knowledge of the demonic strongholds in an area, to an extent that, arguably, the gospel is displaced as the locus of evangelical authority.

As such, then, we have the strange and paradoxical situation of an overrealised eschatological vision, namely revival, resulting in a prayer warfare methodology that understates the gospel's own power to effect conversion. In effect, prayer warfare, with its associations with revival, has contributed to the demise of preaching as an effective means of grace by neglecting the theological grist that has underpinned preaching in the classical sense: namely, the announcement of a victory already secured. In Lowe's assessment:

> SLSW [Strategic Level Spiritual Warfare] minimizes what Paul maximizes: the victory which God has won over Satan. It counsels aggression whereas he exhorts steadfastness. It relies on innovative technique, but Paul urges the practice of spiritual disciplines. It promises great power to humans, while Paul warns concerning the abiding power of demons. It invents a new form of prayer: aggression directed against demons; Paul practices the only sort of prayer found in scripture: humble petition addressed to God.[40]

The emphasis on the victory of Christ explains, Lowe argues, why Christians are not called to go on the offensive against Satan in the manner encouraged by Wagner. The reason is that God has already won the battle. What Christians are called upon to do, however, is to stand and 'to hold the ground already taken in the face of an enemy counter-offensive. This is the appropriate stance for Christians: Christ has won the battle; we are to stand firm in the face of Satanic counter attack'.[41] We might object to this and argue that the exhortation to take up the sword of the Spirit, which is the word of God, proves that spiritual warfare has an offensive dimension.[42] Such is the basis, as we shall see, of a theology of preaching. But, in essence,

Lowe is correct. The overwhelming emphasis in scripture is not concerned with uncovering spiritual blockages to the gospel, but with the building up of Christian communities, who out of their moral and ascetical life hold out the gospel. The ongoing preaching of the gospel to believers, in order that they might continue to believe and act out of the dynamics of the gospel, is crucial, as we shall see, to this conviction.

Prayer Warfare has gained widespread appeal and promises results for those who use it, but a culture of despair as well as alarm has grown up alongside it: despair, because in the attempt to find the key to unlock the harvest, as it is termed, confidence in the gospel's own power to create its own institutions is lost; alarmist, because without a healthy understanding of what the Reformers called the finished work of Christ, understood within the broad categories of recapitulation, the evangelistic enterprise is vulnerable to a dualistic understanding of spiritual warfare – what Walker has described as a 'paranoid universe'.[43] Once the church no longer considers it important to evangelise itself in its own gospel, allowing the gospel itself to create its own hearing, then all that is left by way of theological discourse is anything ranging from bland moralisms to exotic excitement. Ultimately, the rhetoric amounts to the same thing: a church that must pray harder and work harder if it is to be effective. No longer fuelled by, or confident of, the power of the gospel itself, the Pelagian temper becomes all too apparent as the church wearies itself with yet another strategy. It promises itself to be the great panacea, the latest method to cure all ills and to bring in the harvest, but ultimately it reveals itself as a cheap substitute. As Greg Haslam observes, 'We are always looking for the alchemist's stone that will turn all our efforts into pure gold – instantly. It could be Power Evangelism, church for the unchurched, Alpha, Cell

Church, or even the New Apostolic Church movement.' For Haslam, Prayer Warfare, along the lines developed by Wagner, is yet another example. The real war, however, should 'be fought not with "new spiritual technology" devised by the advocates of SLSW, but with the older, proven and tested weapons', by which he means prayer, proclamation and acts of compassion.[44]

Haslam's comments and concerns about the particular direction spiritual warfare theology has taken represent a return to a more recognisably biblical and traditional position on the subject, and are all the more significant given his undoubted commitment to the charismatic movement in the UK. Moreover, his linkage of Prayer Warfare with other fads is evidence of an increasing awareness in charismatic circles of an endemic problem: a fascination with techniques and numerical success. Lowe's critique of Prayer Warfare, though more specifically missiological, is no less pertinent to our concerns. He helps us to realise that it resonates more with contemporary animism than with biblical notions of demonology. The warfare rhetoric that has proved so compatible with charismatic aspirations for growth is relativised by Lowe, who insists that 'Satan's authority was never derived from the geographical region where we lived, but from the way we lived. Now our sin has been forgiven in Christ, and we are free from his domain'.[45] This is no pietistic reduction of the gospel but a belief in the gospel's ability to save from the power of sin as well as the guilt of sin: to redeem as well as atone. Moreover, it represents a conviction that while evangelism is important, it derives its credibility from communities that inhere in the gospel tradition and its own intramural life.

It is surprising then, that popular Christianity appears to prefer the more exotic, irrational techniques of Prayer Warfare. That it does so is perhaps due to the ready explanation these techniques appear to offer for the lack of impact the gospel is having in the West, as well as providing an immediate antidote (although the perceived ineffectuality of many traditional prayer meetings also has a part to play, it must be said, in the attractiveness of this new prayer strategy). The popularity of Prayer Warfare can also be attributed to the way technique absolves one from the rigours of Christian discipleship in the context of the local church; indeed, we shall argue that fads have diverted attention away from the real challenges that face the church in the West, specifically the challenge of discipleship. Nevertheless, the empirical evidence of the South American context is a hard one to refute. With church growth as the priority in the declining West, vulnerability to this type of spiritual technology will be perennial.

Changing emphases: revivalism and relevance

Prayer Warfare, unlike some of the other strategies employed by charismatics, is directly linked through Wagner to the Church Growth Movement, as is the more recent emphasis on Identificational Repentance.[46] Pioneered by Donald McGavran,[47] and developed more recently by Wagner,[48] the church growth movement has as its basic conviction that there are certain principles upon which numerical growth can be achieved. But whilst in North America church growth methods have proved influential, in the UK renewal movement church growth principles such as strong leadership, lively worship, homogeneity and mobilising the laity have been loosely incorporated. In short, charismatic renewal in the UK is not synonymous with the church growth movement in North America.

Charismatic-evangelicals increasingly admit, however, to a tendency to adopt whatever method or strategy suggests itself for the sake of growth, usually from a context that has experienced significant growth itself. Stuart Bell's criticism of the increasing functionality of the charismatic movement, as it searches for this key to success, attests to the growing awareness within the charismatic movement that there is indeed a problem. 'It is so easy to say "what is the ingredient, the programme, the plan, the strategy that will bring about the breakthrough",' Bell remarks, as opposed to the more pertinent issue of the sort of church culture we are inculcating; but the reason charismatics are particularly susceptible to faddism, he admits, is because it promises so much.[49] With increasing regularity, various places and methods are upheld as models of success. Little attention is given to the contextual nuances of these locations and the appropriateness of a method for a particular place; there is simply the belief that by imitation of the method the same results can be reproduced.

The fact that these methods often subscribe, cumulatively, to different theological presuppositions hardly seems to matter. Thus, within the broad range of things tried by churches within this constituency one can find evidence of what we might term 'hard' and 'soft' evangelistic criteria[50] – confrontational as well as inductive evangelism – within the same place. Yet these seemingly contradictory positions can occur simultaneously, precisely because over and above the need for theological integrity is the desire for numerical growth. Theological incoherence in terms of methodology is not particularly a problem: if seeker-sensitive services with their inductive approach, or a toned down Alpha course, can achieve it, at the expense of overtly charismatic worship and confrontational preaching, the prevailing mood in many churches is that it ought to be tried.[51] Without any philosophy of ministry, confessional base, or any discernible notion of what exactly it is that the church is called to do apart from increasing its size, this is precisely what will happen. The coherence of these apparently contradictory methodologies lies in the overriding commitment to reaching out – an overt populism that, at times, seems to pay scant regard to the issues of biblical and doctrinal soundness. Soft and hard evangelism are merely two sides of the same coin.

Thus we find ourselves, in trying to develop a theology of renewal, interacting on two fronts: the raw fundamentalism of religious revivalism – embracing the motifs of holiness, warfare and intercession – and the soft evangelism of places like Willow Creek and programmes like Alpha, which, in effect, simplify the gospel for the sake of relevance and immediacy. The eclecticism of charismatic praxis in a local church context can embrace both, depending on what is deemed more popular at the time. The ambiguity, which results in numerous theological contortions, is often presented in terms of what the Spirit is presently saying to the church: a somewhat self-authenticating argument, but potent nonetheless in legitimating various techniques, soft and hard, in the cause of evangelism and revival.[52]

Curiously, it is this soft approach that has predominated in recent years, so that relevance as a criterion of church life and praxis is now universally accepted throughout the evangelical-charismatic constituency, posing an altogether different theological problem to that posed by the excesses of Pentecostal revivalism. 'Dynamically relevant' is the way Kathy Hasler describes the relationship of the Bible to the burgeoning field of lifestyle innovation.[53] The shift from fundamentalism to contextualisation can partly be explained in generational terms. Older revivalists resemble Pentecostalists in their unashamed commitment to biblical fundamentalism, whereas second generation charismatics are more prepared to engage culture, seeking to make the church more accessible to the unbeliever. Meic Pearse and Chris Matthews are illustrative of this shift in thinking among charismatics when they comment: 'If we're serious about revival, shrieking at the top of our voices may pay dividends in Tanzania or Tennessee, but in Tooting Beck and Tyneside we'll do better running an Alpha course.'[54] Similarly, Rob Warner introduces *The 21st Century Church* with an exclamation: 'Help I think my church is irrelevant',[55] and develops throughout a missiology determined primarily, though not exclusively, by contextualisation.

The root of this approach lies, once again, in the alarm that is felt concerning the limited impact the gospel is having in society. Because theology and tradition are deemed symptomatic of the unpopularity and irrelevance of the church, it ought to be abandoned. No supporting evidence is cited; in fact, research may conclude the growing popularity of things ancient and traditional.[56] What exists is merely anecdotal testimony of the wide-spread disregard for existing models of church; but because this coincides with the overall decline in church attendance, the argument is regarded as complete.

Among church futurists, Michael Moynagh epito-mises this new approach. Replete with references to post-modernity and paradigm shifts, Moynagh's critique of the relationship between gospel and culture blames traditional church structures for the numerical decline in the churchgoing population, made more tragic, he demurs, by the fact that spirituality is apparently on the increase.[57] Because of the failure of the church to connect with this experience-driven spirituality, as he describes it, Moynagh suggests alternative models of church that adopt the inductive approach. The language of classical revival is toned down somewhat, but it is the revival of Christianity that Moynagh aspires to through less intrusive, more flexible, methods.[58] It is a posture that is becoming commonplace.

Rather than denouncing Moynagh and others as mere pragmatists, we should admit there is much here that is wise. Cultural shifts require re-examination on the part of the church of its existing structures.[59] There ought to be nothing sacrosanct about the preservation of Sunday evening services, for instance, or the survival of a particular liturgy. Relevance, moreover, is clearly an important factor in the perpetuation of faith from generation to generation. In a similar way to Moynagh, James Thwaites' creation-centred ecclesiology introduces a much-needed critique of the gnostic worldview that infiltrates evangelical spirituality, and which makes it so disconnected from, and irrelevant to, the everyday and the mundane.[60] What is disturbing about Moynagh's approach, however, is the presumption that a church that reflects the existential longings of the culture is one that can adequately reflect the confrontational scandal of the gospel. When so much of the re-imagining of the church is predicated on the accessibility and convenience of the church to modern 'lifestyle', there is every chance that this scandal will be circumvented, and that what is left is a syncretistic faith. The Alpha course, emanating from Holy Trinity Brompton, London, raises this issue by virtue of its own commitment to accessibility, and it is to this we now turn.

The case of Alpha

Moynagh refers to Alpha as an example of how churches are re-imagining their mission.[61] It has been almost the first attempt within the charismatic movement at some form of catechetical procedure. Intentionally at variance with the proclamatory manner of evangelism, with its associated altar calls and crisis moments, Alpha conforms to the process model within which catechesis forms a crucial part in not only initiating but also sustaining faith.[62] It has achieved remarkable success.

Nevertheless, whilst Alpha has made a positive contribution overall, arguably it fails to match up to the rigours of essential catechism, and indeed evangelism, as it has been historically understood, precisely at the point where it has made accessibility, relevancy and popularity the fulcrum of its success.[63] The keynote address to the course, 'Christianity: Boring, Untrue or Irrelevant', expresses this desire for theological accessibility among its architects and those churches that have adopted it: the toning down of confrontational, obtrusive language in favour of a soft approach designed to maximise the appeal.[64] It is an intentional strategy on the part of those who designed Alpha, and one that is not without its own theological rationale. After all, very few evangelical conversions fit the Damascus road model. But such a strategy has left Alpha open to the accusation of 'dumbing down' the faith to a lifestyle option.

The issues here, of course, are by no means straightforward. On the one hand, Alpha can be commended for seeking to remove some unhelpful stereotypes that outsiders have of Christians. Moreover, the Alpha material is not entirely without the traditional evangelistic appeal. But it is the supposed strength of the course, namely small group discussion, that undoes this note of confrontation, for it is here that the summons to repentance is relativised by the need to include the opinions and beliefs of all. As an exercise in group dynamics, this inclusivity is essential; as a way of conducting apologetics, it is unavoidable (unless one interprets the offence of the gospel as an excuse for insensitivity); but as with many small group programmes that have proved so popular as a way of conceiving Christian discipleship in the contemporary church, it has serious limitations for inculcating the faith confession of the church. In many ways small group spirituality, as Robert Wuthnow has demonstrated, has been at the forefront of the demise of doctrine.[65]

In his largely sociological assessment of Alpha, Stephen Hunt connects this 'watering down' of the gospel to the overall floundering of charismatic churches after its initial growth – the watering down of the gospel being the way to increase the marketability of Christianity in what was, after all, the decade of evangelism.[66] The overall effect has been the promotion of an easy believism, or what Percy terms 'Join the Dots Christianity': a faith that ignores the baptismal summons of repentance and faith in Christ, due largely to the fact that these are deemed inimical to the initial consumer.[67] Indeed, John Peters, leader of St Mary's, Bryanston Square, London, admits to such a process in his own presentation of the gospel during Alpha. Contextualisation of the gospel, both in its original move away from Judaism, and now in the contemporary setting, he argues, requires us to suspend the language of repentance and the kingdom of God.[68]

Again, in terms of cultural awareness and sensitivity to the needs of the initial enquirer, such a commitment to contextualisation is to be encouraged. We should be reluctant to criticise anyone who displays such an enthusiasm for reaching unbelievers; after all, most Christians, it must be noted, are saved on a shred of truth, and spend the rest of their lives working out theologically what they have done. Nevertheless, such a willingness to accommodate the language of faith to the needs of the unbeliever over the long-term means that the faith commitments of evangelical-charismatic congregations in twenty years time will look quite different, one suspects, to what has been understood hitherto as typical evangelicalism.

Alongside these general concerns, it is possible to adumbrate more specific theological concerns, for not only does Alpha replay the docetic heresy by separating Christ and the Spirit (simply by demarcating a Holy Spirit weekend from the rest of the course), it also assumes conversion very early on, as evidenced by the fact that the material moves swiftly on from matters of receiving faith to reading one's Bible. For a course purporting to introduce the Christian faith, without the pressure of commitment, it is an odd move. More seriously, it engenders a faith that is without any true sense of crisis. This, of course, is intended. Crisis conversion is one of the things Alpha is trying to distance itself from. But conversion without any sustained note of confrontation and offence can only be a breeding ground for the very worst kind of apostasy. It will spawn churches that are growing, active, friendly and popular, but without any instinct for the gospel drama, proper conversion and, consequently, without any evidence of authentic spiritual discipline. As Pete Ward notes, 'Analysed at a cultural level, Alpha is successful because it has simplified evangelism to a predictable process ... Christian mission is a broader and probably a significantly more costly endeavour than participation in an Alpha course.'[69]

All of this is perhaps too critical of an evangelistic pro-gramme that has, at the very least, reawakened confidence in the churches' ability to evangelise. It will, no doubt, remain an effective tool for evangelism. We contend, however, that part of the success of Alpha can be located precisely within the mood of despair we have already noted. Its popularity may be attributable in part to the growing anxiety felt about declining numbers. Indeed, numbers, statistics and the declining church population are at the forefront of the Alpha rationale.[70] Hunt makes the comment that Alpha 'may be interpreted, if one wishes to be particularly cynical, as forcing the expected revival and fulfilling prophecy ... a way of dealing with the discord resulting from the unfulfilled expectations of the Toronto Blessing'.[71] In the wake of Toronto, it at least gave charismatics something to focus upon. But what Hunt does not point out is that this is how many initiatives in the charismatic movement can be interpreted: strategies that are designed to bring about the promised harvest, but which conceal an underlying despair.

Perhaps fad is rather too harsh a description for Alpha, for the reasons stated above. Even though it assumes a great deal about the participants and encourages rapidity of conversion, it has been a step in the right direction. The fact that Alpha is caught up, however, as Hunt points out rather cynically, in a wider agenda relating to church growth means that it has been allowed to progress uncritically. Again, if a method works, who is to stand against it? Such pragmatism has developed to the point that Alpha has now become something of a yardstick as to whether a church is really committed to evangelism. No mention is made of the fact that it is labour intensive, or that many people still become Christians apart from Alpha; on the contrary, in many places Alpha is regarded as something of a panacea.

The Numbers Game

It is essential we cite these popular initiatives, as well as the associated literature, because what we are examining, namely the renewal, is by definition a grassroots, popular movement. This is both its strength and its weakness. On the one hand, its populism has made it successful numerically, but precisely because it is a popular movement it is, on the other hand, vulnerable to the fluidity of popular ideas, if not the consumer market. What follows in response is not a defence of high culture versus popular culture; that would be a thesis too easy to construe.[72] Rather, we are seeking to buttress the populism of the renewal with a more robust theological framework.

This essentially theological work is not being done in isolation; there is a growing consensus, particularly among what might be termed second generation evangelicals, that experientialism and pragmatism in the cause of church growth cannot be sustained in the long-term without seriously affecting, and indeed distorting, our overall understanding of the gospel and the life it demands in response.[73] Indeed, the overtly pragmatic, faddist approach must be eschewed precisely because it is symptomatic of a crippling anxiety in the church about its place in the world, and therefore unfruitful as a source of renewal. 'Emphasis on models of church growth, church marketing, and entrepreneurial leadership,' observes Alan Roxburgh, 'reflect the uneasy, marginal consciousness of the churches.'[74] The comfort that comes from numerical increase is what makes evangelicalism so susceptible to church growth theories and the latest religious trends – tantamount in many cases to opportunism.[75] And it is this obsession with growth that many are now realising needs to cease if, paradoxically, the church is seriously to engage in the task of mission.

Church planting, as another popular method of evangelism, conforms, to some extent, to this same unhelpful psychology.[76] Indeed, in the last decade, church planting has emerged in its own right as a strategy that purports to guarantee growth, though, to be fair, it has not been without an underlying theological rationale, nor an awareness of its limitations. Wisely, Roger Ellis and Roger Mitchell agree that while 'church structures in and of themselves do not create growth … they can certainly inhibit it'.[77] This much we ought to concede to Church Growth strategists; there are plenty of occasions when church planting is exactly what churches should be engaged in, for reasons of context and mission. But what is absent in church planting literature, and, more generally, in the whole gamut of methods deployed by churches in their desire to realise growth, is an appreciation of the need for ongoing Christian nurture – nurture that is the basis upon which missionary congregations, so-called, can be sustained in the long-term. When church life – and indeed evangelism, which has for too long lacked a theological rationale – is detached from these issues of spiritual nurture, programmatic and manipulative techniques become commonplace, distorting the shape, as we shall see, of Christian self-understanding and Christian ministry.[78] When growth replaces qualitative Christian nurture as the rationale of the church, traditional notions of initiation into the gospel are sacrificed on the altar of expediency, and pastoral care of the saints, in the somewhat ambiguous and messy business of real life, is set in opposition, unnecessarily and unbiblically, to the call to evangelise.[79]

There is nothing particularly novel in this situation. Evangelicalism by definition has always had a strong evangelistic impulse – an inherent motivation to make more people Christian. And alongside this traditional impulse is a concomitant activism, an accepted hallmark of evangelical spirituality. As Bebbington reminds us, 'the evangelical concept of holiness did not retreat from the bustle of life except for temporary refreshment: contemplation was not its ideal. It was high praise indeed to describe a layman as a Christian worker'.[80] Where the charismatic movement has impinged upon this traditional evangelical ethos, it has not only left this activism intact, but has exacerbated it.

The reason for this is the particular nature of charismatic revivalism which conforms, it should now be clear, to the revivalism propounded by Charles Finney, who believed revival could be induced by methods, as opposed to the perspective of Jonathan Edwards, who understood revival as a free and sovereign act of God.[81] Due to the relative paucity of Reformed theology within charismatic circles, the movement has been dominated by this need to find the appropriate key to unlock the harvest. But what this amounts to is an unchecked activism as the church preoccupies itself with the next programme to bring it about. Meanwhile, however, evangelicals and charismatics suffer from an attenuated spirituality. Issues of spiritual formation are almost entirely subsumed by categories of functionality; theological inquiry replaced by sociological analysis. In the charismatic movement, it has meant the domination of the prophetic-visionary strand over and against the pastoral and the priestly.

The dialectical tension of what may be regarded in the sociology of religion as the prophetic and the priestly is in many ways the backdrop of this book.[82] In the renewal over the last thirty years it can be stated more colloquially: the triumph of vision over substance. This has bred an idealism concerning the church that, as we shall see, makes pastoral care in such a setting problematic. Ironically, it has meant the neglect of a theme that was at the core of the movement in its early years, namely personal discipleship in the context of the worshipping life of the church. In fact, we contend that this was a much more central theme of the early charismatic movement than revival. To be sure, self-consciousness concerning size and numbers was not absent, but the more important issue of discipleship and relationships overshadowed such concerns. Nevertheless, as the church became aware of its increasingly marginalised status, vision triumphed – and with it, prophetic rhetoric.

Visionary language and prophetic positivism has fed directly into the aspirations of revival by providing it, as we noted with the Docklands prophecy, with repeated assurances that success is on the horizon.[83] And to a degree it has provided sufficient stimulus and expectation for it to continue to inspire activity. Indeed, the prophetic is synonymous, in charismatic parlance, with outward – the centrifugal as opposed to the centripetal.[84] Martin Thornton reminds us, however, that covenant relation needs both a priestly and a prophetic dimension, a synthesis of stability and evangelism: 'Priest-plus-prophet spells synthesis of stability and evangelism, ordered discipline and spiritual freedom, corporate worship in place and "private prayer".'[85]

In the terminology of the charismatic movement, we might describe this marriage as a theology of the Word and the Spirit, in which spontaneity – euphemistic for the Spirit – is grounded in the fixity of confessional faith. Freedom requires form, vision requires substance, and outreach is dependent on the existence of a disciplined community that is the ultimate 'hermeneutic of the gospel'.[86] In the renewal, where numbers have become so important, this synthesis has struggled to emerge. Charismatic renewal lacks a distinct ascesis; thus, it forfeits the missionary power of the spiritual community, for, as Thornton points out, 'The body of Christ in microcosm, localised in place, localised in bread and wine, priest and remnant, in prayer and in place: this remains the pastoral norm of missionary power.'[87] Relevancy is not the only criteria by which we assess the effectiveness of ministry. In fact, the contribution of post-liberal theologians, most notably George Lindbeck, to the issue of relevance is to argue that 'religious communities are likely to be practically relevant in the long run to the degree that they do not first ask what is either practical or relevant, but instead concentrate on their own intratextual outlooks and forms of life'.[88] In short, instead of trying to recapture a lost Christendom, churches would better spend their time disciplining the few in order to incarnate the gospel, however successful numerically it might or might not be.[89]

Such a position should not be mistaken for defeatism, nor cultural retrenchment; nor should it be confused with the Anabaptist vision of the pure believers' church. This would lead to a form of 'ecclesiastical sectarianism' (a charge which, incidentally, has been levelled against Hauerwas, and to which he has forcibly replied),[90] and would not do justice to the vagaries and inconsistencies of Christian nurture. Instead, what is being described here is an attempt within the structures of the institutional church to cultivate discipleship, as well as fidelity to the basic shape of the gospel, as the primary way in which the gospel saves the world: a robust and confident celebration of the veracity of the gospel that has the ability to both embrace as well as transcend culture.[91]

Heal Our Nation

To argue for this position does not mean we have to abandon all notion of revival. Undoubtedly, the cry for revival is a legitimate one, indeed a biblical one, if one invokes it as a verb rather than a noun. In many parts of the world, revival is clearly not a spent metaphor. But the present revivalism that has beset the charismatic movement, as reflected in its praying and worshipping life, has taken its cue more from the sociologists and the statisticians than it has from the theologians. Commenting on the eighteenth-century revival in Northampton, New England, Robert Jenson makes the observation that 'revival was not in its founding beginning a means to promote religion; it was the surprising result of a critique of religion'.[92] Edwards experienced revival as a consequence of attending to a much larger frame of God's revelation of his Son Jesus Christ and the vitality of the Holy Spirit. That it led to what might be termed the original revival, a concert of prayer for the conversion of the world, was the reason why Edwards described it as a 'surprising work'.[93] His concern, however, was with the lamentable state of covenantal religion in second generation New Englanders.[94]

If the present revivalist enthusiasts would focus more on critiquing the *qualitative* rather than the *quantitative* nature of the church it could claim with more validity the New England revival as an antecedent.[95] Moreover, in a kind of irony, such a focus may encourage the type of spiritual formation that makes the church attractive to the outsider. The church becomes attractive, notes Alan Kreider, in proportion to the disincentives to join it;[96] worship as a means of attracting unbelievers did not feature. In fact, from the second century onwards, unbelievers were barred from Christian gatherings.[97] Nor was there any exhortation to evangelism; rather it was 'beauty of life', one of them contended, '[that] encourages strangers to join the ranks'.[98] In short, pastoral attention to the inner life of the church as a place of spiritual formation ensured the attentiveness of outsiders to the truth of Christianity. Strenuous communal lifestyle buttressed by a rigorous ethical standard for entry (spiritual formation that derives from the core drama of the gospel) ensured that the church grew so that by the time of the Constantinian conversion roughly 10 per cent of the Imperial population belonged to the Christian church. At present, such obsession with the internal life of the church could seem indulgent; moreover, such disregard of the missionary imperative seems almost rude. Yet it is precisely because the churches formed such tight knit, distinctive communities that they not only survived but also grew.

Although pre-Christendom conditions cannot be repeated, they do leave some clues as to where the contemporary church might lay its own stress: namely, the formation of a counter-cultural religious community, rooted in faith and baptism, which acts as the final 'detoxification from the dominant order'.[99] This is not, as some might suspect, a retreat to the ghetto, nor the promulgation of a sectarian form of Christian faith; rather it represents a realisation that in an increasingly diverse and secular culture the only way for Christian communities to thrive is to become 'resident aliens'.[100]

Churches that are committed to the programme of church growth cannot do this essential work, because the addictive character of the numbers syndrome effectively stifles any genuine attempt in spiritual formation. The most promising and likely source of spiritual renewal is the local congregation. Here the potential is enormous. The future is hopeful as long as pastors, says Richard Foster,

> keep their focus on the enduring work of the cure of souls and refuse to be distracted by all the religious fads which come their way … Pastors themselves must come to believe that to pour themselves into a hundred or so people growing their souls into Christlikeness is a ministry of immense value.[101]

That Christian leaders might not take Foster's advice is because the promise of revival and the possibility of growth remain a constant temptation. But what follows is an indication of the type of things one might attend to should one decide on the latter option. Unlike Kreider, we do not feel the need to dismiss revival completely as a phenomenon pertaining only to the lost world of Christendom.[102] Postmodernity is far too complex, and contradictory, for us to have to make that claim. In any case, revivalist spirituality has some healthy aspects, as have been acknowledged above, that may well help churches to remain open to the ever-surprising possibilities of

Holy Spirit activity. Furthermore, just because something is faddish does not mean it cannot be engaged with. But what we must not allow is for the current despair over church decline to set the agenda for what the church should be about, as if the moral state of a nation is always the blame of the church and of individual Christians. Nor should we allow revival to be packaged in the way that it has been in the charismatic movement as a panacea. That the identity of the church, as well as its mission, are forged in interaction with the circumstances of the time is, as Keck reminds us, a truism, 'but that the world sets the agenda is sheer capitulation'.[103] Regrettably, there are signs across the evangelical-charismatic constituency that the church has lost its nerve and has grown despairing, precisely because it has capitulated to the world's standard of judging success. It has led to an impoverished and undeveloped ecclesiology, and, strangely, has reduced the possibility of the church being of any relevance at all in society. 'The social form of the church must find its basis in its own faith rather than in its social environment', argues Miroslav Wolf. 'Only thus can churches function effectively as prophetic signs in their environment.'[104]

Notes

[1] D. Tomlinson, *The Post-Evangelical* (London: Triangle, 1995), 23.

[2] D. Lillie, *Restoration … Is This Still on God's Programme?* (Crediton: The Kyrtonia ExPress, 1994). On how charismatic renewal affected traditional Baptist structures see D. McBain, *Fire Over the Waters: Renewal Among Baptists and Others from the 1960s to the 1990s* (London: Darton, Longman & Todd, 1997), 75–86. See also M. Harper, *None Can Guess* (London: Hodder & Stoughton, 1973), 144–8, for its impact upon Anglican structures.

3   A. Wallis, *In The Day of Thy Power: The Scriptural Principles of Revival* (London: Christian Literature Crusade, 1956).

4   A. Walker, *Restoring the Kingdom: The Radical Christianity of the House Church Movement* (Guildford: Eagle, 1998[4]), 51–3.

5   For example, B. White, *A Taste of Revival* (Tonbridge: Sovereign, 1997), 19–28.

6   T. Gray, 'An Anatomy of Revival', *The Evangelical Quarterly* 72:3 (2000), 249–70.

7   T. Virgo, D. Holden, J. Hosier, *From Refreshing to Revival* (Eastbourne: Kingsway, 1995).

8   R. Warner, *Prepare for Revival* (London: Hodder & Stoughton, 1995).

9   See P. Dixon, *Signs of Revival* (Eastbourne: Kingsway, 1994), 292, who makes the connection between renewal and revival very explicit by stating that there has never been revival without renewal first.

10 See A. Read, 'Awakenings in Westminster', *Compass: The Journal of Non-Religious Christianity,* Walton-on-Thames, Pioneer Direct (Winter 1997/1998), 14–15.

11 *Songs of Fellowship 2: The Essential Collection* (Eastbourne: Kingsway Music, 2000) (abbreviated as SF2. SF1 refers to an earlier compendium of songs). We will be referring to this collection of songs, throughout, as illustrative of the theology of the renewal movement in Britain.

12 J. Noble, *The Shaking: Turning the Church Inside Out to Turn the World Upside Down* (London: Monarch, 2002), 226.

13 J. Wimber, 'Revival Fire', *Renewal* (September 1991), 26–9.

14 K. Gott, *Dismiss the Crowds* (Eastbourne: Kingsway, 2001), 33.

15 Alan Tweedie, former Administrator at St Andrew's, verifies this point in conversation, 25 March 2003.

16 Gott, *Dismiss the Crowds*, 33.

17 M. Pilavachi, 'What Revival?', *Renewal* (March 1998), 16–27.

18 A. Farrar, *The Triple Victory: Christ's Temptations According to St Matthew* (Cambridge: Cowley, 1990[2]).

19 H. Nouwen, *In the Name of Jesus: Reflections on Christian Leadership* (London: Darton, Longman & Todd, 1989).

20 See E. Vincent, *God Can Do it Here* (London: Marshalls, 1982).

21 See R. Howard, *Charismania: When Christian Fundamentalism Goes Wrong* (London: Mowbray, 1997), 116. Cf., P.J. Richter, 'Charismatic Mysticism: A Sociological Analysis of the Toronto Blessing' in S.E. Porter (ed.), *The Nature of Religious Language: A Colloquium* (Sheffield: Sheffield Academic Press, 1996), 100–130.

22 See M. Weber, 'The Nature of Charismatic Authority and its Routinisation' in S.N. Eisenstadt (ed.), *Max Weber: On Charisma and Institution Building, Selected Papers* (Chicago/London: University of Chicago Press, 1977³), 48–65.

23 M. Percy, *Words, Wonders and Power: Understanding Contemporary Christian Fundamentalism and Revivalism* (London: SPCK, 1996), 152.

24 See M. Pugh, *The Making of Modern British Politics 1867–1939* (Oxford: Blackwell, 1980), 36–7.

25 M. Riddell, *Threshold of the Future: Reforming the Church in the Post-Christian West* (London: SPCK, 1998), 14.

26 D. Bebbington, *Evangelicalism in Modern Britain: A History From the 1730s to the 1980s* (London: Unwin Hyman, 1989), ix.

27 See W.C. Wright, *Relational Leadership, A Biblical Model for Leadership Service* (Carlisle: Paternoster, 2000), 86.

28 See W.A. Beckham, *The Second Reformation: Reshaping the Church for the 21st Century* (Houston: Touch, 1997), 55–7. See also G. Coates, 'Forward' in R. Ellis and R. Mitchell, *Radical Church Planting* (Cambridge, Crossway, 1992), ix–x.

29 P. Wagner, *Confronting the Powers; How the New Testament Church Experienced the Power of Strategic Level Spiritual Warfare* (Ventura: Regal, 1996), 21–2.

30 See E. Silvoso, *That None Should Perish: How To Reach Entire Cities for Christ through Prayer Evangelism* (Ventura: Regal, 1994), and C. Annacondia, 'Power Evangelism – Argentine Style' in P. Wagner and P. Deiros (eds.), *The Rising Revival* (Ventura: Renew, 1998).

31 Wagner, *Confronting the Powers*, 80–8.

32 S.J. Land, *Pentecostal Spirituality: A Passion for the Kingdom* (Sheffield: Sheffield Academic Press, 1993), 65–6.

33 M. Noll, *The Scandal of the Evangelical Mind* (Leicester: Inter-Varsity Press, 1994). See also O. Guinness, *Fit Bodies Fat Minds: Why Evangelicals Don't Think and What To Do About It* (London: Hodder & Stoughton, 1995).

34 C.G. Finney, *Revivals of Religion, or Lectures on Revivals of Religion* (Cambridge: Harvard University Press, 1960).

35 C. Lowe, *Territorial Spirits and World Evangelisation?* (Fearn: Mentor/OMF, 1998), 58.

36 R. Forster, *Territorial Spirits* (London: Ichthus Christian Fellowship, 1991), 14.

37 M. Scott, *Sowing Seeds for Revival* (Tonbridge: Sovereign World, 2001), 44, 151.

38 Ibid., 137–43.

39 Ibid., 29–31, 147–50.

40 Lowe, *Territorial Spirits*, 65.

41 Ibid., 61. See also R.A. Guelich, 'Spiritual Warfare: Jesus, Paul and Peretti', *Pneuma* 13:1 (1991), 50.

42 G.D. Fee, *God's Empowering Presence: The Holy Spirit in the Letters of Paul* (Carlisle/Peabody: Paternoster/Hendrickson, 1994), 728–9: 'He [Paul] would simply not have understood the fascination with 'words' that one finds among some contemporary charismatics, as though what we speak against the devil is what will defeat him … Rather, as vv. 18–20 confirm, the "word of God" that is the Spirit's sword is the faithful speaking forth of the gospel in the arena of darkness, so that men and women might hear and be delivered from Satan's grasp.'

43 A. Walker, 'The Devil You Think You Know: Demonology and the Charismatic Movement' in T. Smail, A. Walker, N. Wright (eds.), *Charismatic Renewal: The Search for a Theology* (London: SPCK, 1995), 88.

44 See G. Haslam, 'Territorial Spirits and Strategic-Level Spiritual Warfare: An Assessment of Recent Thinking and Writing', Paper presented to New Frontiers International, Stoneleigh, 14 June 2000, 13. Interview 6 December 2002. See also D. Devenish, *Demolishing Strongholds: Effective Strategies for Spiritual Warfare* (Milton Keynes: Word, 2000).

45 Lowe, *Territorial Spirits*, 57.

[46] See J. Dawson, *Healing America's Wounds* (Ventura: Regal, 1994).

[47] D. McGavran, *Understanding Church Growth* (Grand Rapids: Eerdmans, 1970). For a more positive view of Church Growth see P. Cotterell, *Mission and Meaningless: The Good News in a World of Suffering and Disorder* (London: SPCK, 1990), 152–69.

[48] For an introduction to Wagner's extensive writing in this area see P. Wagner, *Church Growth and the Whole Gospel* (San Francisco: Harper Row, 1981) and P. Wagner, *Leading Your Church to Growth* (Harrow: MARC Europe, 1984).

[49] S. Bell, *Quality Control: Rediscovering a New Testament Church Culture*, Brighton International Leaders Conference, Brighton International Centre, 10 November 2000.

[50] W. Abraham, *The Logic of Evangelism* (London: Hodder & Stoughton, 1989), 77.

[51] For an introduction to Willow Creek in the UK see M. Hill, *Reaching the Unchurched* (Amersham: Scripture Press, 1994).

[52] See Wagner, *Confronting the Powers*, 142, for an example of this form of legitimation.

[53] K. Hasler, 'Doing the Lucozade Thing', *The Bible in Transmission: A Forum For Change in Church and Culture*, Swindon: The Bible Society (Autumn 2001), 6.

[54] M. Pearse and C. Matthews, *We Must Stop Meeting Like This* (Eastbourne: Kingsway, 1999), 116. See also L. Singlehurst, 'Revival: Fact or Fantasy?', *Renewal* (August 2000), 21–4.

[55] R. Warner, *The 21st Century Church: Preparing your Church for the New Millennium* (Eastbourne: Kingsway, 1999), 19.

[56] See R.E. Webber, *Blended Worship: Achieving Substance and Relevance in Worship* (Peabody: Hendrickson, 1998), and R.E. Webber, *Ancient-Future Faith: Rethinking Evangelicalism for the Postmodern World* (Grand Rapids: Baker Book House, 1999).

[57] M. Moynagh, *Changing Church, Changing World* (London: Monarch, 2001), 7–13, 18–34.

[58] Ibid., 106–38.

[59] See particularly the work of B. McLaren: *The Church on the Other Side: Doing Ministry in the Postmodern Matrix* (Grand Rapids: Zondervan, 2000), 19–26. See also L. Sweet,

Soulsunami: Sink or Swin in the New Millennium Culture (Grand Rapids: Zondervan, 1999), 15–42.

[60] J. Thwaites, *The Church Beyond the Congregation: The Strategic Role of the Church in the Postmodern Era* (Carlisle: Paternoster, 1999).

[61] Moynagh, *Changing Church*, 113–15.

[62] N. Gumbel, *Telling Others: The Alpha Initiative* (Eastbourne: Kingsway, 1991), 17–18.

[63] For a contrast to the soft evangelism of Alpha see A. Kreider, 'Worship and Evangelism in Pre-Christendom', *Vox Evangelica* 24 (1994), 7–40.

[64] N. Gumbel, *Questions of Life* (Eastbourne: Kingsway, 1995^2), 11–22. See also S. Millar, 'Preface' in Gumbel, *Telling Others*, 10.

[65] See R. Wuthnow, 'How Small Groups Are Transforming Our Lives' and R. Bird, 'The Small Group Takeover', *Christianity Today* (7 February 1994), 20–29. See also R. Wuthnow, *Sharing the Journey: Support Groups and America's New Quest for Community* (New York: Free Press, 1992).

[66] S. Hunt, *Anyone for Alpha? Evangelism in a Post-Christian Society* (London: Darton, Longman & Todd, 2001), 23–4.

[67] M. Percy, 'Join-the-Dots Christianity. Assessing Alpha', *Reviews in Religion and Theology* (1997:3), 16. See also M. Percy, *The Salt of the Earth: Religious Resilience in a Secular Age* (London: Sheffield Academic Press, 2001), 178–87.

[68] J. Peters, *The Evangelist's Notebook* (Eastbourne: Kingsway, 2002), 98–101.

[69] For a further analysis of Alpha and the resonance it has with the general McDonaldization of culture see P. Ward, 'Alpha – The McDonaldization of Religion?', *Anvil* 5:4 (1998), 286.

[70] See Gumbel, *Questions of Life*, 7, and Gumbel, *Telling Others*, 14. The preoccupation with numbers can be seen in various issues of *Alpha News*.

[71] Hunt, *'Anyone for Alpha?'*, 30.

[72] See K. Myers, *All God's Children and Blue Suede Shoes: Christians and Popular Culture* (Cambridge: Crossway, 1989), who is guilty of a certain degree of intellectual elitism in his critique of popular culture.

[73] See R.E. Webber, *The Younger Evangelicals: Facing the Challenges of the New World* (Grand Rapids: Baker Book House, 2002), 107–23.

[74] A.J. Roxburgh, *The Missionary Congregation, Leadership and Liminality* (Harrisburg: Trinity Press International, 1997), 20.

[75] The synonymy of success with increase in numbers, and failure with decrease, has been pernicious. As Gill notes 'little is as capable of engendering guilt among clergy as this'. R. Gill, *Beyond Decline: A Challenge to the Churches* (London: SCM, 1988), 69.

[76] Dawn 2000 as church planting initiative is perhaps the most vivid example of this particular strategy. See J. Montgomery, *Dawn 2000: 7 Million Churches to Go* (Crowborough: Highland, 1989).

[77] Ellis and Mitchell, *Radical Church Planting*, 113.

[78] See H. Young-gi, 'The Background and Characteristics of the Charismatic Mega-Churches in Korea', *Asian Journal of Pentecostal Theology* 3:1 (2001), 118, where the issue is raised of the effect of church growth on discipleship.

[79] See Peters, *The Evangelist's Notebook*, 66, who questions the wisdom of allowing pastors to lead churches when what is required is the visionary leadership of an evangelist. See also M. Robinson, *To Win The West* (Crowborough: Monarch/The Bible Society, 1996), 199–221 for an example of the mutual exclusivity of pastoral and missional language.

[80] D. Bebbington, *Holiness in Nineteenth-Century Evangelicalism* (Carlisle: Paternoster, 2000), 41.

[81] For a discussion of the difference, from a Reformed perspective, between revival and revivalism see I.H. Murray, *Revival and Revivalism: The Making and Marring of Modern Evangelicalism 1750–1858* (Edinburgh: Banner of Truth, 1994).

[82] See M. Weber, *Economy and Society: An Outline of Interpretative Sociology* (Berkeley: University of California, 1978), 439–68.

[83] For a helpful survey of the different prophetic strands in the UK charismatic movement see S.F. Latham, 'Is There Any Word From the Lord?: Schools of Contemporary Christian

Prophecy' (Unpublished PhD; King's College, London, 1999), 48–95.

[84] See R. Forster, *The Kingdom of Jesus* (Carlisle: Authentic Lifestyle, 2002), 84–5, for an example of this terminology in relationship to the March for Jesus; see also M. Bickle, *Growing in the Prophetic* (Eastbourne: Kingsway, 1995), 51–3.

[85] M. Thornton, *Pastoral Theology: A Reorientation* (London: SPCK, 1956), 35.

[86] L. Newbigin, *The Gospel in A Pluralist Society* (Grand Rapids: Eerdmans, 1989), 222ff. Not surprisingly, Newbigin has his own misgivings about the Church Growth movement. See L. Newbigin, *The Open Secret: An Introduction to the Theology of Mission* (London: SPCK, 1995), 126: 'There is no shred of evidence in Paul's letters to suggest that he judged the churches by the measure of their success in rapid numerical growth … this nowhere appears as either an anxiety or an enthusiasm about the numerical growth of the church.'

[87] Thornton, *Pastoral Theology*, 60.

[88] G.A. Lindbeck, *The Nature of Doctrine: Religion and Theology in a Post-Liberal Age* (Philadelphia: Westminster Press, 1984), 128. Lindbeck juxtaposes a Cultural-Linguistic model of religion alongside an Experiential-Expressive model, so typical of pietistic communities.

[89] Thornton warns against the addiction to numbers and conversion: 'The same body of Christ in the world, yet set apart from it, is the parochial pattern which grew and converted because it cared very little about conversion.' Thornton, *Pastoral Theology*, 64.

[90] S. Hauerwas, *Christian Existence Today: Essays on Church, World and Living in Between* (Grand Rapids: Brazos, 2001), 1–24.

[91] See A.B. Robinson, *Transforming Congregational Culture* (Grand Rapids/Cambridge: Eerdmans, 2003).

[92] R.W. Jenson, *America's Theologian* (Oxford: Oxford University Press, 1998), 63.

[93] J. Edwards, 'A Faithful Narrative of the Surprising Work of God' in *The Works of Jonathan Edwards Volume 1* (Edinburgh: Banner of Truth, 1979 [1834]), 344–64.

[94] See W.R. Ward, *The Protestant Evangelical Awakening* (Cambridge: Cambridge University Press, 1993), 273–95.

[95] See G. Chevreau, *Catch the Fire: The Toronto Blessing: An Experience of Renewal and Revival* (London: Marshall Pickering, 1994), 70–144.

[96] A. Kreider, *The Change of Conversion and the Origin of Christendom* (Harrisburg: Trinity Press International, 1999), 10–20.

[97] Ibid., 14.

[98] Minucius Felix, *Octavius* as cited in Kreider, *The Change of Conversion*, 18.

[99] W.H. Willimon, *Peculiar Speech: Preaching to the Baptised* (Grand Rapids: Eerdmans, 1992), 59.

[100] See S. Hauerwas and W.H. Willimon, *Resident Aliens: Life in the Christian Colony* (Nashville: Abingdon, 1989).

[101] R. Foster, 'Heart-to-Heart: A Pastoral Letter from Richard J. Foster', RENOVARE (November 2000), 2.

[102] Kreider, *The Change of Conversion*, 100.

[103] Keck, *The Church Confident*, 16.

[104] M. Volf, *After Our Likeness; The Church as the Image of the Trinity* (Sacra Doctrina/Grand Rapids: Eerdmans, 1998), 15.

Chapter 2

Worship in Revival

Worship for Effect

Worship is a subject that inspires passionate debate, particularly so in charismatic circles because worship, and what transpires in the act of worship, lies at the ideological core of the movement.[1] Without worship it is hard to envisage what charismatics would have left to contribute to the wider body of Christ. However, the propensity to sacrifice theological and spiritual integrity on the altar of contemporaneity, expediency and revivalism, and to allow vision to subsume content – expressed, as we saw in chapter one, in a growing preoccupation with fads – is especially true in the area of charismatic worship. Instead of conceiving worship as an event to participate in, as an end in itself, a more sinister note has been introduced, we shall argue, so that worship is now regarded, in many places, simply as a means to an end: the ultimate end being the increase of God's kingdom and rule in revival. As Jean-Jacques Suurmond deduces, 'The attitude of play seems to be the only right attitude to God ... as soon as God is used to achieve one purpose or another, we reduce the divine to an instrument.'[2] And what revivalism has introduced to our understanding is precisely that: an ulterior motive that robs worship of its essentially playful element.

We will begin our inquiry into the form and content of charismatic music on a more positive note, for there is, indeed, much to be positive about. Observing what he describes as the rituals of Pentecostal/charismatic worship, Daniel Albrecht observes a form of praise and worship among charismatics that is indeed celebratory: worship offered for no other reason than for the sake of giving praise to God.[3] In this mode of worship there is no ulterior motive, and utilitarian results are not sought. The atmosphere is one of playfulness where the symbolic and narratival world of Christian faith is enjoyed and experienced. Where it occurs, the combination of simple charismatic hymnody and congregational fervour is a very powerful combination: worship that is theologically robust as well as contemporary.

Recent hymnody in the renewal evinces this blend: 'All Heaven Declares' (SF1 110), 'All I Once Held Dear' (SF2 646), 'Come and See' (SF1 67), 'How Deep the Father's Love for Us' (SF2 780), 'Meekness and Majesty' (SF1 390), 'Thank you for Saving Me' (SF2 1015), 'You Laid Aside your Majesty' (SF1 631), demonstrate that contemporaneity and theological substance are not irreconcilable. Typically these songs focus upon the evangelical perspective of atonement – though Graham Kendrick is notable in that he also construes lyrics pertaining to the incarnation. Moreover, there are other songs in this collection that cluster around the image of God as shepherd (SF2 1030), shelter (SF2 894; SF2 935), and rock (SF2 652; SF2 807), thus providing a welcome complement to the triumphal songs that are so much a hallmark of charismatic worship. The legacy of this range of music has been felt across the denominations, so that there are few places in the evangelical world where this hymnody is not being sung.[4] In that sense there is little to be concerned about. Charismatic worship, as John Leach rightly points out, has introduced a welcome note of warmth, intimacy and optimism to traditional worship.[5] Charismatic worship gives expression to some of the best instincts for praise, thanksgiving and adoration.

On the other hand, given the nature of charismatic liturgy – which, as Albrecht points out, conforms basically to the tripartite ritual found in American frontier religion: the worship rite, the rite of the pastoral message and the rite of altar response – charismatic worship, despite the strengths noted above, and despite protestations that it is free of liturgical forms, is vulnerable to the pressure to provide within its worship patterns an opportunity for spiritual encounter. Though spiritual experience is in itself desirable, Albrecht notes a sinister development in the 'worship time', as it is popularly called, which he describes as 'transcendental efficacy': a view of worship that is as much to do with consequence as it has to do with meaning.[6]

The consequence may take on various forms. Most commonly it takes on the form of ministry time in which renewal, healings and transformation take place. For Pentecostals this is what constitutes harvest, once the preliminaries and the preaching have been enacted.[7] At other times, such efficacy transmutes into 'transcendental ecstasy'[8] – particularly among charismatics who are desirous for worship that might lead to supernatural encounter. In the context of worship such motivations are almost unavoidable, and not necessarily pernicious – indeed, in the right context, spiritual encounter of an ecstatic nature should be positively encouraged. But judged by more theological and doxological criteria, the desire for ecstasy may be viewed as somewhat susceptible to consumerist notions of exchange: put colloquially, 'getting something out of the worship', which contributes in its own way to the growing tendency for Christians to move from church to church on the basis of their personal preferences in worship.[9]

Albrecht's unease with this *overly* experiential dimension of charismatic worship is one that is beginning to be expressed in the UK charismatic movement too.[10] In the introduction to his album *What Grace*, Kendrick explains his concerns about the excessively experiential focus of charismatic worship. The album is itself a deliberate attempt to redress the balance by providing lyrics that project onto the person and work of Christ: 'It is too easy for our praise and worship,' he argues, 'to become experience centred ... we need a lot more songs that look at the Lord and his qualities and then we can respond to that.'[11] Similarly, Pilavachi registers his concern over the excessive use of the first person in modern choruses, preferring to see instead the reintroduction of music that focuses on God:

> Years ago at Soul Survivor we sang lots of the 'Jesus is my girlfriend' type of songs. They drip romance and intimacy. I love them and still believe there is a strong biblical justification for them. A while ago, however, we realised that they were almost the only songs we used. We were dying of intimacy. There are after all only so many ways you can tell Jesus you are 'falling in love with him' in half an hour.[12]

It is the prevalence of this 'me-centred Christianity', notes Pilavachi, which underlies the very pathology we are describing here, for it is a form of Christianity 'which always descends into hype and techniques and the latest quick fix solution to the problems of the church'.[13] It is easy to see why: once worship is detached from the main narrative and confessional stance of the gospel, it becomes a useful partner to a churchmanship that has itself neglected the strangeness of the Christian story in favour of a broadening appeal and increased numbers. What Pilavachi and Kendrick testify to is the demise of charismatic worship to a state that is tantamount to Albrecht's 'transcendental efficacy': worship that is only valued because of the interest it can engender or experience it can induce. Ward concurs, noting that the process of enculturation, by which charismatic worship has sought to appeal to popular music culture, has led to some unfortunate repercussions, not least the vulnerability of worship to musical trends and the burden of performance driven worship with its cult of worship leader.[14]

For worship to be hijacked by various other agendas, and to be used for a means other than that of offering praise and worship to God – whether it be to induce a particular experience, to bring about an ecstatic state to facilitate mission, or to induce revivalist fervour, as often happens in charismatic settings – is to be guilty of the manipulation Albrecht describes. It introduces a motivation that is antithetical to the worshipping life of the church. 'Powerful rhythms are not new in church music,' notes Brian Wren, 'yet when intense rhythms are amplified, relentlessly pursued, or both, they become compulsive.'[15] Such an intentional use of rhythm, he asserts, for the purpose of compelling a desired response, must be renounced, if worship is to retain its integrity.

Percy has pointed out this abuse of worship already in his own treatment of Vineyard worship.[16] The lack of a doctrinal and narrative trajectory in the charismatic repertoire, he argues, betrays the fact that worship is not regarded as didactic but existential. In the present climate this may be no bad thing. The postmodern sympathy for the ecstatic may well resonate with this emphasis. But in the process the indicative mood that ought to characterise a large proportion of church hymnody – worship that celebrates the gospel revelation in and for itself – is thereby swallowed up by the mood of intensity. The requirement for intensity in worship displaces traditional concepts of Christian assurance by becoming the dispenser of grace itself. Indeed, as Michael Horton points out, 'The contemporary style, in which music plays an important part, is now viewed by many as the only means of grace.'[17] Worship takes on an authority of its own so that only *in* and *through* the experience of worship, and the way we perform in worship, can grace be appropriated; hence, the pressure to make something happen. Worship as spiritual formation is sidelined in favour of worship as effect.[18]

It may be, of course, that the transmission of creedal and doctrinal content is reserved for elsewhere in the overall scheme of things. William Abraham speaks favourably of the eschatological, kingdom-centred teaching of the Vineyard movement as a welcome departure within the Church Growth movement from the soft evangelism approach of Wagner;[19] it certainly introduced a combative and possibly more robust theology compared to its theologically loose hymnody. But given the preponderance of interest focused on worship via conferences, tapes and CDs, this positive feature almost becomes an irrelevance. The fact is, as the early Methodists knew so well, many Christians imbibe their theology through what is sung rather than what is taught, which is why the issue, as Marva Dawn and others point out, is such a serious one.[20] No matter how orthodox our preached theology may be, worship and music are more than able to displace it by their potency.[21]

Of course, one has to bear in mind that different themes are accented at different times, depending on what the Spirit is saying to the church. This is no surprise for, doubtless, there is very little by way of hymnody that is not derived to some extent from personal testimony or historical context. In the case of the charismatic movement, however, the thematic clusters of songs mirror well the various fashions that have appeared throughout its history, and to this extent are expressive of the very faddism described in chapter one. This is not to say that every fad has a song associated with it, but it is to say that charismatic worship has tended to track closely the whims and vagaries of charismatic waves. Underlying many of them, however, are two dominant themes: namely, intimacy and revival, which carry also a number of theological ramifications.

Send revival

Songs focusing explicitly on the promised revival are a good place to start our inquiry. Although 1996 saw an intensification of the revival theme, they have been a feature of charismatic worship throughout its history. Charismatic worship is perhaps never more original than when it is singing about the church marching on the land in revival power.[22] Through prayer, intense fervour, and increased holiness, the worshipper calls upon the Lord to bring revival: for example, 'Restore O Lord the Honour of Your Name' (SF1 483), with its final prayer that God might bend the church so that the world might be saved.

Again, our purpose here is not to be so theologically precise that we miss the underlying authenticity of such songs for Christian spirituality.[23] Such lyrics are standard fare in a revivalist setting, and express a genuine and wholesome longing for God's kingdom to impact the church and the world. What is cause for concern, however, is the *cumulative* impact of this emphasis when it is sung to the detriment of all else. When that occurs – and for a time in the mid-nineties it seemed as if there was little else to sing about – some bold counter-plays are required lest the psychological anxiety created by such intensity leaves the congregation exhausted.

The reason for this exhaustion is quite simple. By focusing so much on the desperate state of the nation, the lukewarm state of the church and the relative quietness of the Spirit – as in the song 'Great is the Darkness (Come Lord Jesus)' (SF2 742) – a collective neurosis can occur as revival urgency displaces basic Christian assurance about the church, the Lordship of Christ and personal salvation. The revival song 'Father of Creation (Let Your Glory Fall)' (SF2 714) combines all these elements in its chorus. Expressing typical charismatic fervour to march upon the land, it could be accused of engendering a kind of anxiety, precisely because its triumphalism is detached from the historicity of the triumph of the gospel. With what mandate does the church implement the victory of God in the world? And outside of the gospel how might such a victory be sustained? Sadly, the desire for what is 'not yet' eclipses what has been secured already in the person and work of Christ. Statistics, numbers and the desire for revival success have relativised the legitimate note of triumph in the church's proclamation and mission in the world, based on the ultimate eschatological event: namely, the resurrection of Christ.[24]

The more recent song 'We Have Sung Our Songs of Victory' (SF2 1092) gives us a clue of the outcome of this revivalism, and could be read as an open admission of the very pathology described here. In the context of revival, it is one of those rare songs of lament, and in that sense should be commended for its realism; nevertheless, the reference to 'songs of victory' and 'prayers for rain', which, according to the songwriter, have amounted to nothing, could also be seen as evidence of the tiredness and disillusionment that is bound to accompany the rhetoric of revivalism. It is inevitable. The unrealism and mythology of revival spirituality, with its aspirations of exponential growth, can lead only in this direction.

The concern for rootage in gospel assurances, which forms the theological basis of what follows in our proposal, does not seek to eradicate the dissonance that will inevitably be felt within the eschatological now/not yet. Maybe this is all that these songs are seeking to express. And just because there is a theological imbalance, does not mean a song should not be sung. But one suspects the disappointment in the song is more attributable to, and illustrative of, the rupture that revivalism makes in basic Christian understanding. As we stated earlier, revivalism has the strange and ironic tendency of neglecting the substantial message of the gospel, precisely at the point where its own aspirations amount to an overrealised, almost utopian, eschatological vision.

In considering this type of worship, one wonders whether it is necessary to burden congregations in this way; cumulatively, this kind of revival theology has the ability to foster a guilt neurosis that is not only emotionally tiring but also threatening theologically to the foundation of Christian salvation. Theologically, Wolfhart Pannenberg locates this guilt neurosis in revivalist pietism to the separation of forensic justification and mystical participation in Christ. Without an understanding of continuous existence in Christ, initiated in baptism, a peculiar actualism occurs, he argues, whereby 'we must accept the promise of divine forgiveness again and again, because we slide back into sin again and again'.[25] In sum, revivalist religion has a tendency to foster a guilt neurosis at the point at which the requirement of continual repentance, in the cause of revival, is detached from a participationist and trinitarian understanding of grace. It leads to a number of ironies, as Percy notes, concerning the worship of the Vineyard movement. Essentially,

Vineyard worship stresses intimacy and immediacy; yet, the requirements of holiness as a precondition for revival create a gap between God and the worshipper: God can only move close, in reviving power, once the community of faith has been purged and cleansed.[26] Thus, the worship time takes on the extra burden for the worshipper of proving one's holiness and devotion.

This display of zeal and ardour may be typical of holiness traditions, but overall it distorts, as David Peterson has shown, the biblical doctrine of sanctification where holiness is not so much a process as an event.[27] Holiness is indeed something to strive for, but it is to be pursued on the basis of a definitive holiness already granted; it is understood as a way of being as well as becoming, a one-time event as well as a process. Once holiness is tied to the revival agenda, and becomes a matter simply of zeal and intensity, this assurance of God's possession of us in Christ is lost; henceforth, Christian living is diverted from its chief end, we might say, which is to live for the praise and glory of God who has called us in Christ, by becoming a means to an ulterior end which is the deliverance of the nation. Finding its expression in revival songs, Christian worship is similarly abused, albeit through laudable sentiments, to the point that many complain of its tiresome hold.

This may be an odd charge to make of a movement that has been credited with injecting liveliness into worship, but it is a charge that is not without basis. After all, the revival that has so often been sung about and prayed for has, until now, eluded the church. The logic of revivalism, therefore, permits us to conclude only one thing: our state of holiness and zeal is not yet adequate; hence, more intensity is required to bring it about. In short, a spiral of self-condemnation ensues as churches, under the burden of revival, consistently register that they are falling short of the mark. The actual experience of worship and ministry, and the altered states of approval and disapproval thereby induced by the oscillation of intimacy and holiness during this time, becomes a substitute for the holiness already secured and glory already witnessed to in the gospel. In the traditional model, worship is as much *about* God as well as *to* God; in revivalism, however, worship in itself becomes the final arbiter and dispenser of the truth of the gospel – a form of worship that can be addictive, even idolatrous.

We can see this revival consciousness at work in a number of other well-known songs that have appeared in the last decade. In 'Lord You Have My Heart' (SF2 912) there is an implicit belief that drawing near to God in worship will bring down the glory of God, and presumably the revival. This is not a celebration of the glory that already inheres within the gospel of Christ, but a further glory, encapsulating all the hopes of a revived land, that can only be uncovered by intensity: the community of feeling that charismatic spirituality has often been identified with. What is implicit here is made explicit in the song 'Lord, Let Your Glory Fall'[28] in which the numinous experience of the priests in the temple in 1 Kings 8 is retold. The tempo of the song reflects the fairly buoyant and upbeat mood that is the hallmark of charismatic musicianship; but what is problematic with this lyricism is the repeated discontentedness of the worshipper with the status quo and an inadequate understanding of the factualities of revelation. In the retelling of the drama, and in the expression of desire for more (again, an entirely legitimate desire), the song, nevertheless, inhabits a peculiarly pre-Christian hermeneutic that forestalls on the fulfilment of the promise of glory in the coming of Christ and the Spirit.

In reply, it may be argued that there is far more in the gospel to be appropriated than can ever take place at the point of conversion. The charismatic impulse towards this is vital for the wider church community. Moreover, the urgency to see 'revival in the land' is not entirely misplaced. What is at stake here, however, is the way in which the prerequisite fervour and longing for 'more' is so often detached from the eschatological fulfilment of the promise of glory that already has taken place in the gospel. Indeed a thesis has yet to be written about the way charismatic hermeneutics and homiletics tends towards an undue emphasis on the narrative world of the Old Testament, without recognition of the fulfilment of that narrative in the story of Jesus. It often leads to simple allegorical 'This is That' preaching.[29] Thus, congregations are pulled away from the traditional locus of Christian worship that is christological, to worship that is simply efficacious and expressive of what is 'not yet'. This way can only lead to tiredness and loss of hope, when, perennially, the gospel is sidelined and the revival never arrives.

The mood of intimacy

Revival songs contain language that is peculiar to that tradition. In these songs the stock Old Testament image of nation is transferred not to the church, but the nation of Britain itself – for example, 'Can a Nation be Changed' (SF2 682). They have been a feature of charismatic renewal from its inception. Nevertheless, there are other songs that resonate more overtly with cultural moods by virtue of their doctrinal lightness and the appropriation of the language of intimacy – so much a feature of cultural immanentism – whilst remaining wedded to the revival psyche. It is these songs that we shall now examine.

   This conjunction of revivalism and anti-intellectualism, whilst understandable, is not the only way of conceiving worship. On the contrary, in historic revivalist settings hymnody fulfilled a didactic role, instructing the saints in the major doctrines – particularly so in Methodist revivalism.[30] Contemporary revivalism, however, reflects at this point the cultural mood of immediacy: the function of its hymnody is experiential rather than didactic. The overall impact of these songs has been to renege on the more challenging themes of judgement and salvation in Christ, the basic *ordo salutis*, so as to identify with the cultural mood of romanticism. Spiritual immediacy, expressed in worship, is precisely what is required in postmodern culture. Revivalistic enthusiasm coheres well with what Harvey Cox describes as experientialism,[31] acquiescing, in the process, to the need for worship that is doctrinally light, but musically immediate nonetheless.

If music was theologically neutral as a medium, the situation we have described would not be serious; but of course, as Jeremy Begbie points out, music imprints its own theological meaning, separate to the theological content of the words. And in the case of the renewal, the simplicity of the music underscores the theological lightness of the lyrics. The standard four- and eight-bar choruses, he argues, were symptomatic of the culture of immediate gratification – the church's attempt to reflect the culture of immediacy.[32] Kendrick comments on the doctrinal weakness, not to mention musical ineptitude, of many of the songs: 'The disproportionate number of "subjective experience" songs being written begs the question of how much the world's agenda of placing existential experience and individual fulfilment at the centre of things has influenced our worship.'[33] 'My own view', he writes elsewhere, 'is that the proportion of personal songs is far too high and is at the expense of songs that are actually about God, who he is and what he has done.'[34]

Critics like Pilavachi, label these type of intimate songs 'Jesus is my girlfriend' songs, and in doing so highlight the emotionalism, if not mild eroticism, that have always been a feature of charismatic and mystical traditions. But what concerns us here, in songs such as 'My First Love' (SF2 930) and 'Holy Spirit, We Welcome You' (SF1 188) is not so much the theme of intimacy (after all, who wants worship without intimacy?), but the excessive plundering of it, to the point that these songs of intimacy often appear with relentless monotony, and often in complete ignorance of the deliberate emotional constraints of traditional liturgy, where sentiment is guided by the wider theological tradition. Undoubtedly, the love of God should be regarded as the predicate of all Christian theology, but the language of intimacy is so developed in songs such as 'Over the Mountains and the Sea (I Could Sing of Your Love Forever)' (SF2 975) that it forgets the essential backdrop to the doctrine of grace, which is judgement. The situation at present allows for the excessive use of the images of intimacy, precisely because the church is more concerned to contemporise and contextualise. Our argument, however, runs in the opposite direction: worship ought to evoke scenes of a strange world that challenges as well as resonates with the contemporary, lest the guiding motifs of familiarity and accessibility end up trivialising the great themes of biblical revelation.[35]

Again, it is important to remember the positive contribution that renewal music is making. To insist on doctrinal precision at this level is to miss the unique contribution music and song can make to an overall spiritual diet. Rightly so, Leach warns us against an overly critical posture on worship because there is validity in simply expressing one's love for God.[36] Nevertheless, the problem remains of cumulative impact. When intimacy is the only theme to emerge in our worship then the church is guilty of allowing one prominent, contemporary metaphor to 'overcome the checks, balances, and ballast that the whole catholic tradition provides'.[37] The consequence is sickness for the movement as a whole, simply because no one image can express the whole counsel of God and, thus, provide all that the worshipper needs for a fully developed spirituality. The pathology, in terms of worship, is equivalent to that described earlier when focusing on the very positive rhetoric surrounding new and latest strategies: an increasing and unnecessary dissonance between expectations and reality. As Kendrick appreciates, 'if we continually expect people to sing about experiences and feelings they are not necessarily having, we will empty the act of worship of reality and de-value its content to the level of a borrowed personal perspective'.[38] What is left, in consequence, is a certain blandness and weariness, as the church loses sight of the wider theological and pastoral perspective.

Although Methodist piety might be described, similarly, as 'heart religion' – like the Moravians who shaped their spirituality – Wesleyan hymns are not about the merits of experience per se. They are supremely about what God has done in Christ.[39] It is the grace of God in Christ that unleashes the lame to leap for joy, and not the mood of joy that provides access to the gospel. But without a resolute commitment to such a theological agenda, understood within a liturgical framework, however loose, the tendency is for the faith to 'sink into vulgarism or pure moralism'.[40] Contrast the doctrinal rigour of Wesleyan revivalist hymnody with the aversion of popular songwriter Matt Redman towards didactic: 'Personally, I'd never write a song just to teach something, but I am aware when writing a song that it could end up teaching somebody. I guess as a worship songwriter you're voicing what's in your heart.' [41] Under such criterion, it is possible that the Christian narration of grace will be eclipsed by the burden of romanticism, and God in Christ, redeeming and saving, reduced to an experience to be induced, precisely because faith in postmodern culture requires experience in order to legitimate it. Hence, communion with God in charismatic revivalism is not so much the result of recalling the theological inheritance of the grace of God in Christ, but of getting something from the worship experience itself. This can be done quite easily given the popular tone of the songs involved, but such an apologetic of spiritual experience – a striving after sentimental effect – is undermining of the gospel and represents, as Erik Routley noted, 'insecurity, competitiveness, and a lust for quick results'.[42]

As a summary of the problem we are seeking to describe here, Routley's perceptions concerning sentimental tunes in worship, which, incidentally, he argued would not be tolerated elsewhere, is most apt.[43] Competitiveness has become an insidious part of charismatic-evangelical churchmanship precisely at the point at which it has become aware of its shrinking market; and insecurity results because, of course, the worshipper, according to subjective criteria, is never quite certain whether the level of emotional intensity experienced in worship is sufficient to validate one's place in the body of Christ. The level of zeal and intimacy required, as a precursor, and indeed expression, of revival is burdensome in the extreme. As Oliver O'Donovan warns, 'The gift of subjective freedom must already be seen as an aspect of our being-in-Christ, not merely a precondition or a consequence of it.'[44] Otherwise, the charismatic insistence upon liturgical freedom and spontaneity can itself become a form of legalism: the intensity required in worship is unsustainable; furthermore, the language of intimacy, detached from the message of grace, and unhinged from the historicity of this message of grace, is vulnerable to hype and manipulation. Our instincts tell us that in certain cases this has become the case.

Historically, there is nothing unprecedented about the dilemma that contemporary worship finds itself in. Revival religion, by definition, is an attempt to break with convention and push the boundaries of religious experience. The motivations are not entirely ill conceived. But when the cry is for another Pentecost, as in 'O God of Burning Cleansing Flame (Send the Fire)' (SF2 955), it is legitimate, theologically, to question whether the quest for greater and richer experiences of God, as the basis of revivalistic religion, in actuality undermines the foundations upon which such a revival could thrive.[45] Once we depart from the givenness of the gospel tradition, whether for the sake of experientialism, aspirations of revival, or just raw emotionalism, the way is open for a spirituality of anxiety.[46]

Worship for God

Instead of reflecting the confidence of the movement, we have argued that the preoccupation with growth, the various strategies designed to bring this about, and a hymnody that strives for the next experience, betrays a loss of confidence: a growing nervousness about its future and a theological ignorance of basic Christian tenets that have historically safeguarded the gospel from activism, legalism or, conversely, mere sentimentality. It may be argued that the spate of revival songs in 1996 kept alive hope, but in fact the very opposite could be the case.[47] Because revivalism carries an unrealistic hope – though one that is tantalisingly believable – it inevitably results in, and is indeed expressive of, disappointment and disillusionment.

Rather than stemming the tide of ideas and innovations, however, the disappointment has only served to contribute to the growth of faddism, as the search for the harvest continues. This is, in summary, the pathology that faces the charismatic movement at this critical juncture in its history. It finds expression, as we have seen, in its worship as well as its programmatic structuring of church life, so that wherever we look, both in the new churches and in the wider evangelical community that has paralleled these features, there is a basic ignorance of historic, orthodox Christianity and a preoccupation, instead, with the statistical credibility of the church. This book is a modest attempt to retrieve for the evangelical-charismatic constituency such an ascetical community. Chan warns us that 'an enthusiastic spirituality that is developed in isolation from an ascetical spirituality cannot be sustainable for long, nor can it have universal applicability'.[48] It explains, he argues, why Quakerism, as an example of enthusiasm, has had historically only limited appeal. Without a true ascesis that is rooted in the tradition, it soon becomes bland and introverted. Indeed, the concern for cultural relevance in the revival tradition, Paul Westermeyer argues, means that the opposite occurs: they become churches that are isolated from the cries for justice so often found in ancient musical and liturgical traditions: 'The peculiar Protestant temptation is to become ingrown precisely in attempting not to be ingrown.'[49] Revivalists are in danger of speaking an in-house language known only to themselves: a degeneration of evangelical Christianity into a quietist, introverted spirituality, as predicted by David Pawson in the wake of the Toronto Blessing.[50]

The significant number of people who move on from their evangelical/charismatic moorings in favour of Orthodoxy or Catholicism, is just one symptom of that malaise, and ought to be taken seriously by those in the renewal. Significantly, these converts understand the move as a progression from adolescence to maturity, born out of a desire to retrieve lost artefacts of the tradition that were thrown out with the proverbial bathwater.[51] In response, revivalists, we are arguing, should attempt to couple the enthusiasm of their tradition to thoroughgoing catechesis: attentiveness to the revelation, training in the disciplines and commitment to the body of Christ, which, thereby, allows for faith to be sustained outside of revival. One of the deleterious features of a revivalist mentality is that short of what might be termed a surprising manifestation of God there is very little else to be getting on with. Whole sections of legitimate church activity are held in suspense, and, moreover, deemed a failure, simply because they fall short of revival criteria. Commitment to spiritual formation, on the other hand, takes seriously the fact that there are indeed seasons in the Christian journey, both personal and corporate, and that intense fervour is not sustainable, nor even necessarily required, in order for Christian living to occur. It is simply enough to commit oneself to 'the technique of going to church'.[52]

In the context of worship, where the main issues in charismatic theology converge, this would involve a number of bold liturgical moves, not least the reintroduction of the Christian lection as a way of rooting worship in the full trajectory of the Christian story. After all, all life is ordered by one rhythm or another, and liturgy helps the church to subvert secular rhythms with the narrative of the Christian year.[53] Moreover, worship as catechesis would require larger theological and musical frames that would include something more intentional in terms of the movement of worship: patterns of worship that would involve gathering, confession, praise, thanksgiving and benediction. To be fair, there have been attempts within the renewal to outline a theological pattern of worship. Vineyard, in particular, helpfully sought to describe worship as a movement from praise to intimacy,[54] though such a pattern can encourage an unhealthy expectation for climax, thus putting an intolerable strain upon both worship leader and congregation. Instead, revivalistic worship requires a concomitant theological and biblical framework that does not simply justify its enthusiasm but subverts it, lest its commitment to informality, liturgical freedom and spontaneity becomes itself a form of legalism. As Debra Dean Murphy shows, there is no such thing as worship, or indeed Christian knowledge, prior to and apart from the embodied traditions and liturgical instincts of the church.[55]

In the light of revivalist rhetoric, this new agenda sounds, one has to admit, hopelessly compromised. Church going on a Sunday and ordered patterns of worship smacks of *opere ex operata* – the very thing that churches in renewal seek to distance themselves from.[56] Rather than being seen as Pharisaic, however, which is a typical way charismatics caricature their non-Spirit-filled opponents, such worship could actually feature, in this second generation, as a crucial part of the overall ascetical vision. Indeed, as Rodney Clapp points out, in a culture where Sunday has been completely secularised, and where even Christians pay scant devotion to the weekly pattern of Lord's Day worship, going to church on a Sunday could actually be a radical statement of one's commitment to the gospel.[57] Far from being a retrograde step, the retrieval of such churchly practices and gestures could be central to a new radicalism that incorporates both old and new. Essential to the ascetical tradition, however, is the conviction that it is simply enough just to be there. Contrary to the pietistic instinct on these matters, it is God, not us, who is the main performer; conversely, it is we, and not God, who are the audience;[58]

therefore, it is sufficient, despite lack of fervour or zeal, to simply be present and participate in the givenness of the revelation. As Thornton reminds us, 'in bad and difficult times, we can turn everything upon the divine action of Christ, do our poor best, fail miserably, and stop worrying. "Being there" is a lowly yet efficient act.'[59]

In a tradition where fervour, growth and the perceived presence of God are often the only yardsticks by which we might monitor spiritual progress, such a lacklustre view of worship appears to compromise the radical revival tradition, holiness revivalism in particular. The alternatives of judgement or revival, as the only two options available to revivalist interpretations of the church (a view derived from Finney that 'a revival of religion is indispensable to avert the judgement of God from the church'),[60] does not permit such a sedentary posture. And, to be sure, there are times when mere attendance is tantamount to the kind of nominality charismatics are so keen to lambast. Even so, if congregations are to develop ascetical life, then worship, of necessity, ought to be less dominated by zealous performance or cultural relevance and more attentive to the Christian revelation; it should be less preoccupied with 'bringing God down' in response to the performance of our worship and more concerned with 'entering into' worship, contiguous with the revelation of God in Christ ruling and interceding. Obedience and disobedience, in dichotomous relationship, are not the only options available to a Christian congregation, despite the rhetoric of revival thinkers. Such a view produces discouragement and tiredness, for, presumably, the lack of revival success is a signal of prevailing disobedience; hence, more effort required in worship. A preferable alternative would be to retain a sense of liveliness in worship, all the while rooting this fervour in the historicity and factualities of the revelation.

In proposing this as a way forward for charismatic worship, Leach ponders whether these contrasting ways of looking at worship are merely a question of semantics.[61] After all, the language of 'entering in' and God 'coming down' could amount to much the same thing: a pressure that is widespread throughout the charismatic movement to provide encounter and immediacy in the worship experience, creating by its effect an impression of being contemporary, successful and relevant.[62] We contend, however, that the distinction is more than just semantics; it is a crucial difference between worship in which there is a pressure to perform (God coming down), versus worship in which the church submits to the peculiarities of the revelation (entering in), realising that worship is, at best, a thankful response. As one recollects the events of the gospel and participates in the communion into which Christ has co-opted us, worship becomes less a performance and more a case of celebrating what is given.

Such a theological approach would make a crucial difference to the way worship is understood in the charismatic constituency, for it would introduce a necessary ontology to otherwise experimental categories, thus freeing the liturgy from the burden to produce. Thanksgiving is the reflex action on the part of the church to the Lordship of Christ and the present situatedness of the believer in Christ – the theological axioms we are seeking here to restate. Thanksgiving, argues David Pao, is 'an act of submission when the performance of such an act is not aimed at coercing God to act, but is a way to acknowledge him to be the Lord of all'.[63]

James Torrance, using more technical language, describes this as the difference between a trinitarian and an existential model of worship. Trinitarian worship is a celebration of the mediation of Christ as our High Priest who himself is the worship leader and who brings us in the presence of God.[64] Such a conception of worship as trinitarian and mediated would confront that transcendental efficacy that we noted earlier and locate the real missiological task as an ecclesial task: the creation of faithful communities that are genuinely counter-cultural, alert to the veracity of the revelation and, moreover, prepared to be shaped by it. These are communities that are shaped definitively by the gospel itself and initiated into the kingdom by stringent catechetical procedures. The frenetic pace of the charismatic constituency, and charismatic worship in particular, would be replaced by serious discipleship. Whilst not unmindful of the task of witnessing, witnessing would be gathered up, under such a schema, into the notion of discipleship.

Such a model does not require music to engender an emotional experience, for, as liturgist Westermeyer points out, 'Music is not fundamentally an emotional phenomenon. It is sound ordered in time.'[65] As such, the main focus of worship would be that of rehearsing, celebrating and, furthermore, participating in the actualities and realities of the Christian revelation. This is no mere confessionalism. Precisely because the work of Christ is inseparable from the person of Christ, it is clear that trinitarian worship does not refer 'to the doctrine of the Trinity only, but to the knowledge that arises from participating in the very life of the triune God. We worship the Father, through the Son and in the Spirit'.[66] Yet, worship is never less than a good confession. Worship is not a performance by which the church seeks to access divine power; rather, worship is the way we pay attention to the magnitude and mystery of Christian truth, and through it bear unselfconscious witness to the kingdom of God in the world. Indeed, we were never called to build the kingdom; though such language features a great deal in modern evangelicalism, it is never used in the New Testament. Instead, we are invited to receive the kingdom and participate in God's own mission to the world.[67] For a churchmanship that has conceived worship in the context of revival, these churchly signatures might prove difficult to embrace. The loose structure is performed in the name of informality, relevance and immediacy, and is close to the centre of charismatic ideology; it is expressive – we ought to remember – of an understandable mistrust of ritual and form. But the irony is that the loss of distinctive liturgical space, transcending ordinary time, means in fact that no time is sacred. Immediacy and accessibility could mean, paradoxically, worship that is escapist and, strangely, irrelevant. Devoid of all theological ritual, alternative worship may be no real alternative at all, but a mimicking of the culture, and theologically insufficient to sustain Christian faith.

Notes

1   A. Brown, 'Charismatic Orientated Worship' in D. Carson (ed.), *Worship, Adoration and Action* (Carlisle: Paternoster, 1993), 178–88.
2   See J.J. Suurmond, *Word and the Spirit at Play: Towards a Charismatic Theology* (London: SCM, 1994), 29. See also G.S. Wakefield, *An Outline of Christian Worship* (Edinburgh: T&T Clark, 2000[2]), 227: 'Worship is not entertainment, though God is to be enjoyed. It should have no other motive than to glorify him and bring us into his presence.'
3   D. Albrecht, *Rites in the Spirit: A Ritual Approach to Pentecostal/Charismatic Spirituality* (Sheffield: Sheffield Academic Press/Journal of Pentecostal Theology Supplement, 1999), 181–3.
4   Charismatic songwriting is now a major industry, with new songs appearing at a rapid rate. See P. Ward, 'Evangelical Spiritual Songs 1966–1996: Production, Text and Audience' (Unpublished PhD; Kings College London, 2001), 134–5. The plethora of songs and worship conferences makes research problematic.

5   J. Leach, 'Renewal Worship', *Christianity and Renewal* (September 2001), 12–15.

6   Albrecht, *Rites in the Spirit*, 182.

7   Ibid., 165–9.

8   Ibid., 185–6.

9   See N. Scotland, 'Shopping for a Church: Consumerism and the Churches' in C. Bartholemew and T. Moritz (eds.), *Christ and Consumerism: A Critical Analysis of the Spirit of the Age* (Carlisle: Paternoster, 2000), 145.

10 G. Kendrick, *Worldwide Worship: The Source* (Stowmarket: Kevin Mayhew, 1998), 2.

11 G. Kendrick, *What Grace* (Make Way Music, 2001). The songs on this album borrow unashamedly from scripture, most notably the Psalms, as well as from traditional hymnody.

12 M. Pilavachi, 'Who Am I?', *Christianity and Renewal* (January 2002), 31.

13 Ibid., 31.

14 Ward, 'Evangelical Spiritual Songs', 134–5.

15 B. Wren, *Praying Twice: The Music and Words of Congregational Song* (Louisville: Westminster/John Knox, 1999), 160.

16 Percy, *Words, Wonders and Power*, 60–81. Percy's acerbic and often vitriolic style makes many of his insights difficult to embrace by those within the charismatic movement willing to critique their own tradition.

17 M. Horton, *In the Face of God: The Dangers and Delights of Spiritual Intimacy* (Dallas: Word, 1996), 157.

18 For a useful introduction to the debate surrounding contemporary worship see C. Plantinga Jr. and S.A. Rozeboom, *Discerning the Spirits; A Guide to Thinking about Worship Today,* Grand Rapids/Cambridge: Eerdmans, 2003.

19 Abraham, *The Logic of Evangelism*, 86–90.

20 M.J. Dawn, *Reaching Out Without Dumbing Down: A Theology of Worship for the Turn-of-the Century Culture* (Grand Rapids: Eerdmans, 1995). See also M.J. Dawn, *A Royal "Waste" of Time: The Splendor of Worshipping God and Being Church for the World* (Grand Rapids/Cambridge: Eerdmans, 1999).

21 Historically, worship has had its own role to play in the dissemination of truth, which is why the loss of liturgy in

worship, as Peter Jensen notes, is a severe blow to the cause of doctrine. See P. Jensen, 'Teaching Doctrine as Part of the Pastor's Role' in R.J. Gibson (ed.), *Interpreting God's Plan: Biblical Theology and the Pastor* (Carlisle: Paternoster, 1998), 87.

22 P. Ward, *Growing Up Evangelical; Youth Work and the Making of a Sub-Culture* (London: SPCK, 1996), 107–42. See also J. Begbie, 'The Spirituality of Renewal Music: A Preliminary Exploration', *Anvil* 8 (1991), 232–5. Most of our examples here will be taken from more recent songs.

23 S. Tippit, *Fire in your Heart: A Call to Personal Holiness* (Amersham: Scripture Press, 1988), 78–80, who locates such language in the Welsh revivalism of Evan Roberts.

24 See the sermon of James Stewart, who we shall quote later in reference to P.T. Forsyth, entitled 'The Shout of a King' in J.S. Stewart, *King For Ever* (London: Hodder & Stoughton, 1974), 9–16.

25 W. Pannenberg, *Christian Spirituality and Sacramental Community* (London: Darton, Longman & Todd, 1983), 20–22.

26 Percy, *Words, Wonders and Power*, 124.

27 See D. Peterson, *Possessed by God: A New Testament Theology of Sanctification and Holiness* (Leicester: Apollos, 1995).

28 Taken from *The British Worship Collection* (Stowmarket: Kevin Mayhew, 2000), 57.

29 For an example relating to Toronto see M. Stibbe, 'Four Waves of the Spirit: A Charismatic Exegesis of Ezekiel 47:1–12', *Skepsis: Anglicans for Renewal* (1994).

30 W.F. Lofthouse, 'Charles Wesley' in R. Davies and G. Rupp (eds.), *A History of the Methodist Church in Great Britain Volume One* (London: Epworth, 1965), 136–8.

31 See H. Cox, *Fire From Heaven: The Rise of Pentecostal Spirituality and the Reshaping of Religion in the Twenty-First Century* (London: Cassell, 1996).

32 Begbie, 'The Spirituality of Renewal Music', 238. See also J.S. Begbie, *Theology, Music and Time* (Cambridge, Cambridge University Press, 2000) for an expansion of his thinking about the theological significance of musical styles.

33 Kendrick, *The Source*, 2.

34 G. Kendrick, 'God and Groove', *Worship Together Magazine* (September/October 2001), 14.

35 Wakefield, *An Outline*, 228.

36 Leach, 'Renewal Worship', 14–15.

37 P. Westermeyer, *Let Justice Sing: Hymnody and Justice* (Collegeville: The Liturgical Press, 1998), 63.

38 Kendrick, 'God and Groove', 14.

39 See *The Methodist Hymn Book with Tunes* (London: Novello, 1933). Indeed, in the preface John Wesley claims of the hymnal that 'it is large enough to cover all the important truths of the most holy religion'.

40 R. Niebuhr, 'Sects and Churches', *The Christian Century* 52: 27 (1935), 885–7.

41 S. Adams, 'Praise Him Like We Should?', *Christianity* (October 2000), 21.

42 E. Routley, *Church Music and the Christian Faith* (Carol Stream: Agape, 1978), 95–6. Routley notes Vaughan Williams' comment that bad taste in music is a moral concern. Sentimentality in music, argues Routley, represents a loss of nerve.

43 For a thorough denunciation of the sentimentality that exists in modern culture see D. Anderson and P. Mullen (eds.), *Faking It: The Sentimentalisation of Modern Society* (London: Penguin, 1998).

44 O. O'Donovan, *Resurrection and Moral Order: An Outline for Evangelical Ethics* (Leicester: Apollos, 1986), 24.

45 For a useful survey of the differing revival approaches see I.H. Murray, *Pentecost – Today?: The Biblical Basis for Understanding Revival* (Edinburgh: Banner of Truth, 1998), 1–32.

46 The recovery of the drama of the gospel, in terms of the doctrine of sin and its theological and psychological resolution in the Reformed doctrines of justification and sanctification, form the basis of Richard Lovelace's renewal theology. See R.F. Lovelace, *Dynamics of Spiritual Life: An Evangelical Theology of Renewal* (Exeter: Paternoster, 1979), 95–144.

47 Leach, 'Renewal Worship', 15.

48 Chan, *Spiritual Theology*, 39.

49 Westermeyer, *Let Justice Sing*, 96.

50 D. Pawson, *Is the Blessing Biblical? Thinking Through the Toronto Phenomenon* (London: Hodder & Stoughton, 1995), 96–106.

51 See S. McKnight, 'From Wheaton to Rome: Why Evangelicals Become Roman Catholic', *The Journal of the Evangelical Theological Society* 45:3 (2002), 451–72; see also M. Harper, *The True Light: An Evangelical's Journey to Orthodoxy* (London: Hodder & Stoughton, 1997). In interview, Harper lamented the general progress of the charismatic movement from its promising beginnings as a renewal movement to what he describes as something approaching gnostic experientialism. Interview 23 September 1998.

52 M. Thornton, *Christian Proficiency* (London: SPCK, 1959), 19.

53 See E.H. Peterson, 'Eat This Book: The Holy Community at Table with the Holy Scripture', *Theology Today* 56:1 (1999), 15.

54 See B. Leisch, *The New Worship: Straight Talk on Music and the Church* (Grand Rapids: Baker Book House, 2001), 54–66, for a helpful defence of the Vineyard five-phase model.

55 D.D. Murphy, 'Worship as Catechesis: Knowledge, Desire and Christian Formation', *Theology Today* 58:3 (2001), 321–32. Interestingly, attitudes are changing in the way seeker sensitive churches, noted for informality, are planning worship. See R.R. Redman, 'Welcome to the Worship Awakening', *Theology Today* 58:3, 369–83.

56 See J. Leach, *The Spirit Comes (as part of the package): Why Being Charismatic is not an Option* (London: Marshall Pickering, 2001), 174, who accuses non-charismatics of hiding behind such terms as 'remnant theology' and 'search theology'.

57 R. Clapp, *A Peculiar People: The Church as Culture in a Post-Christian Society* (Downers Grove: Inter-Varsity Press, 1996).

58 For a useful discussion of this point in relationship to Kierkegaard's invective against passivity in worship see Leisch, *The New Worship*, 121–32.

59 Thornton, *Christian Proficiency*, 20.

60 Quoted, significantly, in Wallis, *In the Day of Thy Power*, 214.

[61] See J. Leach, *Living Liturgy: A Practical Guide to Using Liturgy in Spirit-Led Worship* (Eastbourne: Kingsway, 1997), 18–20.

[62] For a positive and informed view of the theological issues surrounding this see S. Morgenthaler, *Worship as Evangelism* (Grand Rapids: Zondervan, 1999).

[63] D.W. Pao, *Thanksgiving; An Investigation into a Pauline Theme* (Leicester: Apollos, 2002), 37.

[64] J.B. Torrance, *Worship, Community and the Triune God of Grace* (Carlisle: Paternoster, 1996), 11–31. See also C. Cocksworth, *Holy, Holy, Holy: Worshipping the Trinitarian God* (London: Darton, Longman & Todd, 1997), 3–22.

[65] Westermeyer, *Let Justice Sing*, 88–9:
> Worship and music are tied to deep emotions, to be sure, but not in the way we normally assume. Our attempts to stimulate emotions by short-circuiting the discipline of the cross are idolatrous. Genuine emotions come after disciplined singing of the songs of the faith, week after week, that lives through the cross to resurrection and does not seek shortcuts. This may mean worship may be boring at times, just like life … to assume everything in life always has to be glitzy and exciting at all times – especially our worship – is nonsense.

[66] K. Vanhoozer, 'Worship at the Well: From Dogmatics to Doxology (And Back Again)', *Trinity Journal* 23:1 (2002), 15. Experientialism and didactic are not mutually exclusive, as Rice correctly judges. See M.L. Rice, 'Pneumatic Experience as Teaching Methodology in Pentecostal Tradition', *Asian Journal of Pentecostal Theology* 5:2 (2002), 289–312. The biblical tradition, he argues, reflected in Pentecostal tradition, conceives worship as a vehicle of didactic.

[67] J.V. Brownson et al, *StormFront: The Good News of God* (Grand Rapids/Cambridge: Eerdmans, 2003), 40.

PART 2

MEDIATED GRACE:
THE PRACTICES
OF THE CHURCH

Prologue to Part 2:
Revival by Retrieval

In the evident despair about the seeming ineffectuality of the church and its practices, the concern of this book is for the church not to panic, but rather to recognise the unique missiological and historical setting it finds itself in. The assumptions upon which Christendom were founded have now gone, as Newbigin rightly pointed out.[1] Of course, the church should seek to maximise the impact of the gospel in new and innovative ways; but in no way should this missiological imperative undermine the church's celebration of the gospel and its growth therein. The growth of the church must never be allowed to take place artificially and at the expense of the gospel itself as the theological resource of the church. As Oscar Cullmann says, in the context of ecumenical debate:

> The Faith is faith in the victory of Christ. Our faith in the Faith carries also a certainty that the crisis we are going through, all of us together, has some special sense and meaning in the divine plan of the history of salvation. But what falls to hand for each one of us now, is to accomplish together the duty which God has given us, in the place and the time in which we find ourselves put by him.[2]

Hence, the most pressing challenge facing the evangelical-charismatic church is a confessional one: to have faith that the gospel is able to do its own work, create its own structures and fashion its own distinct community. Commenting on his experience of mainline denominational Christianity in North America, Keck complains of the way

> confidence in the gospel, and in the grand vision of a Christian humanism, was being abandoned, it often seemed, in favour of either narcissistic spirituality or frenetic activity. The churches' agenda seemed to be determined less and less by the resources of the gospel and their tested wisdom and more and more by extraneous agendas.[3]

The context in the UK is, of course, different, but the malaise is very much the same, born of a fear of becoming obsolete. And what these opening chapters represent is a response to the challenge set down by Keck in his introduction to write a comparable volume about this loss of confidence as it affects evangelical and charismatic parts of the Protestant family.[4]

This first section has been diagnostic. In what follows we shall attempt to prescribe an antidote to the current situation by focusing our attention back on to what might be termed more classical forms of ministry. Strategic Prayer Warfare – as well as its more recent expression, Identificational Repentance – is not what might be termed classical ministry; it has neither biblical nor historical support, but because the church has been ignorant of the wider tradition, such teaching has gained entry into popular consciousness through Christian media and popular publications.[5] Instead, we require forms of ministry, such as preaching, sacraments, prayer and the laying on of hands, that are effectual, yet redolent with biblical and theological integrity.

Our rationale for suggesting this recovery of means is as much historical as it is theological:

> If history is any indication ... the gift of renewal is most frequently given when the church places itself within the realm of possibility, in the context of those means of grace by which, according to the Old and New Testament, the Spirit works. Thus the renewal of the church begins, at least on the human level, with the recovery of those sources and practices that historically have enabled people to encounter and be encountered by 'the grace of our Lord Jesus Christ, the love of God, and the communion of the Holy Spirit'.[6]

In the trajectory of renewal there comes a point at which constant innovation is counterproductive; the history of renewal movements demonstrates that interaction with institutional processes is not just inevitable but responsible as a way forward, lest the enthusiasm of the early phase of renewal, with its attendant iconoclasm, eventually becomes implosive.[7] A return to classical ministry and the wider tradition is part of the overall progress of renewal spirituality: for renewal is best realised when we attend to those things – preaching, sacraments, prayer and pastoral care – that reconnect the church to the original gospel of what God has done in and through Christ. The church is most likely to be renewed not by the promise of programmatic change, or by some new wave of charismatic phenomena, though these will have their place, but by attending to those practices that are not so much guarantors of growth, but the given means by which God promises to sustain the faith of the church.

A tentative move in this direction can be found in *The Shaking*, where Noble, using Newbigin's various images of church, tries to re-imagine charismatic renewal as a meeting place of Reformed, Sacramental, Missionary,

Charismatic and Apostolic perspectives:[8] namely, preaching, communion, evangelism, charismatic gifts and trans-local leadership. To some extent, this book is an attempt to elaborate upon this speculation, showing how essential to the future of charismatic renewal some of these other dimensions are. Specifically, our hypothesis is that in the trajectory of renewal the continued process of innovation requires a complementary process of retrieval: a return to the wider catholicity of the tradition, coupled to a Pentecostal and Reformed theology, as a way forward. Retrieving these various dimensions is based on the conviction that knowledge of God cannot be achieved nakedly, be it objective rationality or subjective experientialism: 'Rather, Christian knowledge of God can only be gained by suffering God's saving activity as it engages us in word and sacrament as well as in the rest of the church's core practices.'[9]

Interaction with the givenness of the Christian tradition, based on a general confidence in the efficacy of the core practices of the church, is precisely what has been missing in the development of enlightenment epistemology, where the religious subject is regarded as antecedent to the church; accordingly, the church is seen as merely the provider of services, be it the modern denomination or the market consumption of church growth. When the church becomes the subject, however, of theological and spiritual activity, then the practices of the church become integral to the church being itself: the way the church attends to the promise of grace which it embodies as witness before the world.

This is perhaps claiming too much for those ministries and may be the cause of a good deal of negativity towards their continuing place in the church's life. It is because they have been understood as operating *ex opere operato*, without the need for personal faith, that charismatics and evangelicals have tended to distance themselves from such catholic sacramentarianism. The loss, however, is an immense one. Once ministry is practised in detachment from the main historicity of the gospel, and from the continual recollection and representation of the events of death and resurrection, the church has little else to offer except a spiritualised quietism or an evangelical activism. Neither alternatives are faithful to the very concrete, revolutionary power of the gospel itself, but given the shift of focus away from pastoral metaphors of ministry to missiological ones, are a present reality in some places, to the detriment of the church as a faith community.

Daniel Williams is critical of the faddism and trendiness of contemporary notions of ministry within North American evangelicalism. Being effective in ministry, argues Williams, has become more important than being able to act as interpreters of the historic faith. But the situation of theological and spiritual vacuity, created by a preoccupation with method, may be described as ironic, for it has meant the abandonment of means of grace that have, inherent within them, the power to bring about growth – growth that is intrinsic to the gospel and not extrinsic; growth that is organic and not simply mathematical.[10] In the end, of course, faithfulness in ministry may result in very little in terms of numbers. The main thrust of our argument is to suggest that there are other criteria for measuring success apart from numbers, alluring though the numbers game may be. But if there is to be growth – and there is no virtue in smallness per se – let us be sure that it takes its cue from the power inherent in the gospel itself, and the various means by which the gospel enacts its message.

Chapter 3

A Crisis in Preaching

To Preach or Not to Preach

It is in the area of preaching that we begin our attempt to retrieve elements of classical ministry, and thereby begin the process of redressing some of the concerns raised in part one. Some of the strongest attacks on traditional notions of ministry have been in this area. Criteria relating to notions of relevance and accessibility have attached themselves specifically to the ministry of preaching, and in the process have encouraged widespread criticism of the traditional sermon. The most recent and explicit criticism within evangelicalism emanates from Pearse and Matthews who, in the process of debunking the meeting syndrome within the evangelical and charismatic church, call into question the relevance and indeed efficacy of classical preaching. Indeed, Pearse dismisses preaching as a piece of cultural baggage: he parodies the proclamatory manner of preaching, claiming that in a postmodern world such a view does not cohere well with the hermeneutic of suspicion.[11]

Pearse's attack on preaching is of course by no means unique, or original. Many of his comments are traceable to David Norrington's *To Preach or Not to Preach*, which, in turn, is a restatement of a negative view of classical preaching put forward by Edwin Hatch at the end of the nineteenth century, who questioned whether sermons, in their traditional mode, are justifiable on biblical grounds, arguing that their form is more pertinent to the skills of the Greek rhetor.[12] Using similar arguments to Hatch, Norrington pursues a relentless attack on the central tenets and presuppositions supporting preaching in the contemporary church, deriding the sermon as synonymous with an overly institutional and anti-democratic posture.[13]

In many ways the vitriol expressed in the above publications is expressive of a wider negativity at the grass roots towards preaching; it has not survived well in the general development of charismatic-evangelical ministry. In contrast to the more immediate appeal of worship and prophetic ministry, it has come a poor second, relegated to the category of the cerebral. One notes a preference for the immediacy of the prophetic word over and against expository preaching in Jack Deere – a kind of in-house theologian for the Vineyard movement – precisely because it is able to deliver an effectual and decisive word that is not possible in the pulpit.[14] A similar contrast between the prophetic, meaning utterance directly inspired by the Spirit, and preaching, as routinised exposition of the scriptures, is set up by Graham Cooke[15] – a distinction that is commonplace in charismatic circles.

To some degree the dialectic is unavoidable, for there is indeed a difference between preaching and prophecy, but the sum effect is to render scripture-based preaching relatively innocuous. To be sure, the theological roots of both Deere and Cooke are too evangelical to permit them to disregard preaching altogether; their argument is simply that the church ought to be seeking fresh, immediate ways of hearing the voice of God. Norrington advocates a more dialogical form of communication that facilitates learning, rather than the largely passive form of discourse engendered by preaching;[16] whereas Gerard Kelly, in his analysis of postmodern culture and the challenges it poses to the church, advocates the visual medium of communication.[17] In a similar way to Deere and Cooke, though for different reasons, it requires Kelly to set up a dichotomy, this time between symbol and text, visual and word, thus positing a very bleak future for preaching.

In response, it is undoubtedly true that there are a whole plethora of ways of communicating the gospel, be it visual, liturgical, evangelistic, prophetic and apologetic, that have been stymied in certain quarters by an over-reliance on preaching. This book is itself an attempt to retrieve a number of various means by which the church, historically, has sought to proclaim and celebrate the gospel. Moreover, in defending preaching we are not denying the issue that Norrington raises of pulpiteering.[18] The impact of modern technology must inevitably force the issue of methodology for those seeking to communicate in a post-literate age. Sustained monologue no longer enjoys the status it once had, and the fact that it now needs justifying may be no bad thing.[19] What Norrington and others achieve overall, however, in their denunciation of the preaching event is the removal of a vital means by which Christians encounter Christ, namely through the sacrament of the word: 'The meaning of the proclaimed word' argued Dietrich Bonhoeffer, 'does not lie outside of itself; it is the thing itself ... it communicates that it is itself: the historical Jesus Christ.'[20]

We shall explore this sacramental dimension later. Our purpose in introducing the concept here is to show how odd it appears in the contemporary context; alongside the modern predilection for inductive, topical and thematic preaching it will appear somewhat overstated.[21] Even so, sacramental language is apt because at the heart of classical preaching is an appreciation of the gospel's own power in the act of preaching to create its own space – an awareness that regular celebration of the gospel itself, and our co-option into it, is essential for the sustenance of the church, including its witness to the world.[22] This is a view of preaching that includes, but also transcends, the modern obsession with application and relevance – transcending also the act of cajoling and exhorting from the pulpit. Bonhoeffer distanced himself from all such predetermined goals and intents, however laudable.[23] Instead, application, edification and inspiration are all subsumed under the free sovereignty of the Word as given in the Bible. The main intent of preaching is revelatory, allowing us to celebrate the gospel for what it has already accomplished, rather than what it might yet elicit in terms of practical application or heightened enthusiasm. But before articulating such a theology of preaching, we need to critique the reduction of preaching in this way, in order to demonstrate the inadequacy of informational or motivational language. It is to the revivalist model that we shall turn first.

Revival preaching

Pearse himself, in his preference for dialogical, inductive, and democratic discourse, makes mention of the revivalist form of preaching, seeing it historically as one of the two dominant strands of modern preaching, namely the pietistic strand. It has resulted in the familiar image of the 'rabid prophet' in the pulpit.[24] As we have already noted concerning revival worship, this kind of preaching is taken up with locating the spiritual and ethical blockages that hinder the promised harvest. The doctrine of grace, upon which all preaching ought to be predicated, is displaced by the message of obedience. The dominant theological language of this kind of preaching is that of surrender and repentance. It is this language, as Iain Murray points out, that forms the common currency of a very long-standing revivalist tradition, making revival conditional upon obedience.[25] The primary text is 2 Chronicles 7:14: 'If my people, who are called by my name, will humble themselves, and pray and seek my face, and turn from their wicked ways, then I will hear from heaven and will forgive their sin and will heal their land.'

This text is so deeply ingrained in the psyche of charismatic and indeed evangelical piety that it would be difficult to imagine the history of both movements without it. Indeed, it features in a number of worship songs: for example, 'We're Looking to Your Promise (Send Revival, Start with Me)' (SF2 1099). It found its way into the present day revivalism via Wallis, who saw in the text, along with a multitude of other biblical texts taken mainly from the Old Testament, a basic promise for revival for all who would consecrate themselves to the task. *In the Day of Thy Power,*[26] which encapsulated a great deal of this theology, became a basic primer for a whole generation of revivalists. From it derived not so much a form but a mood of preaching, in which the call to total obedience and surrender is so integral to the task of preaching – including the attendant revivalist altar calls – that to extricate it from the message would be to fundamentally distort, if not lose, the essential core of what charismatic revivalism is about.

As long as this is the case, it is difficult to see how anything else but exhortatory, anecdotal preaching will prevail. The events in Pensacola, backed up by the revivalist preaching of evangelist Steve Hill, and teacher Michael Brown, are only a recent version of what has been experienced by many as a staple diet: an overemphasis on obedience as the condition for national revival.[27]

Moreover, because of the numerical success of Pensacola, one suspects it will only exacerbate this type of theology: a brand of revivalist theology, in the case of Brown, that is reminiscent of the revivalism of Leonard Ravenhill.[28] Already Pensacola has been cited, in at least one popular treatment of the subject of revival, as paradigmatic of what happens when churches come to a place of brokenness. From the place of brokenness, in particular over lost souls, and from a position of complete surrender, 'God released his blessing on Brownsville, and a genuine revival has been born!'[29]

To be sure, there is a legitimate place for altar calls and preaching for decision. But what transpires in a culture of successive altar calls, which forms a large part of this particular liturgy, is a loss of memory about the central factualities of the gospel. Revival preaching encourages a pietistic devotionalism devoid of historicity, and a church culture driven by angst rather than by grace: in short, a loss of confidence concerning the main drama of the gospel narrative. It is this loss of confidence that is our main concern here, as well as the despair that attaches itself to a view of God contained almost exclusively within the notion of what happens in the large meeting.

This is precisely the problem facing churches that sought to replicate the Pensacola phenomena. It has exacerbated an already existing anxiety concerning results, leading, in consequence, to a growing pressure upon the church to fulfil the conditions of revival. But, as Richard Neuhaus points out, 'Preaching that aims only at that one big conversion, that decisive surrender, inevitably ends up exhibiting the signs of an exhausted teaching and a spent enthusiasm.'[30] In particular, such preaching represents an inability to come to terms with the varied and often messy nature of spiritual formation and may explain why many Christians begin life in a revivalist setting but do not finish their spiritual journey there. The language of total surrender simply does not do justice to the many quiet and daily decisions that constitute spiritual progress, often far away from the rarefied atmosphere of the revival meeting.

A further complication arises when we look at the exhortatory nature of revivalist preaching, for many times it fails to do justice to the true context out of which imperatives issue forth, namely, the indicatives of the Christian faith. Neuhaus states the issue thus: 'In our preaching we do not so much prescribe behaviour; rather we are midwives of the imperatives that issue from the indicatives of our proclamation.'[31] These indicatives of the Christian faith – salvation in Christ, the gift of the Holy Spirit and the coming of the kingdom of God – deliver their own imperatives, when they are preached faithfully and joyfully. Indeed, we may want to state it in even stronger terms: the imperatives of the gospel – forgiving one another, not stealing, avoiding sexual impurity – may be regarded not so much as prescriptive but descriptive: namely, of what it looks like to be truly living by the Spirit of Christ.[32] Making the reality of the indicative conditional upon the fulfilment of the imperative 'is not putting the imperative cart before the indicative horse; it simply emphasizes that new life (with the Spirit as its source) must become evident in the new conduct (under the Spirit's direction) and cannot exist without it'.[33]

Again, we may not want to go this far in our critique of the imperatival mood the New Testament features. Exhortation to holy living – the decisive surrender – is a valid form of gospel preaching and strangely enough one that is fondly remembered by those who have since moved on from such fundamentalism. We need to be careful, as Richard Mouw rightly warns, that our theological sophistication does not trivialise the call to radical obedience, so central to the revival camp meeting: the sawdust trail was not without symbolic and theological meaning.[34] However, when such preaching becomes the *only* message that is heard, it can soon sound shrill.

The confusion between the indicative and the imperative is more than just a theological issue. It has important pastoral implications. For once the imperative is divorced or uprooted from the nature of gift, as it is presented in the gospel, and set in isolation from the major doctrines of the church, worship becomes burdensome. Immediacy, which is so prized by revivalists, degenerates into tiresome repetition and subjectivity, fostering a spirituality of fear and even despair, for there are none who can live up to the decisive surrender except the few outstanding saints of Protestant hagiography. What it perpetuates, therefore, is the cyclical pattern of defeat, prayer and revival, which is so much a hallmark of revivalistic spirituality. Simon Chan critiques the spirituality of the higher life movement precisely on these grounds: 'Ascetically, reckoning on "letting go and letting God" entails a rather complex psychological process that only more spiritually proficient persons are able to perform.'[35]

Again, the irony in all of this is poignant. What is lost sight of in the abandonment of the indicative mood in preaching is just that mood that could enable true growth to occur, both congregationally and evangelistically. The mood one is describing is derivative of the indicative note of biblical spirituality: namely, a mood of confidence that something has actually transacted in the preaching of the gospel, something actually achieved in the death and resurrection of Jesus, and in the gift of the Holy Spirit, which in its retelling and appropriation can be a source of renewal.[36] When congregations actually come into an encounter with the message of the gospel itself, and draw strength from such encounter, they have more chance of producing spiritual growth, than if growth were attempted in a more direct and self-conscious way. Without this note of grace, as Neuhaus points out, Christian discourse is reduced to 'an amalgam of sentiment, nostalgia, psychic uplift and bland moralism'.[37]

We might want to call this process *natural* church growth: church growth that is intrinsic to the gospel rather than extrinsic, organic rather than mechanical.[38] In the realm of preaching, it represents a belief that as we faithfully expound the scriptures, the combination of good theology and the presence of the Holy Spirit will cause churches to grow. Certainly this approach is welcome as a way of avoiding the more impersonal aspects of the Church Growth movement. More importantly, it preserves the centrality of the doctrine of grace in the spiritual formation of the church, allowing the gospel to be celebrated and appropriated for its own sake, not simply, in utilitarian terms, as a vehicle of recruitment.

In a revival setting, however, where evangelism, as Walter Brueggemann observes, is tied so closely to church growth, this is difficult to do.[39] Preaching for decision and congregational growth is what counts in that agenda. But where this pressure to grow is relativised, the gospel can be heard more fully as a call to a particular way of life. Alan Lewis' understanding of the tension between the indicative and the imperative is germane to our argument at this point and is worth quoting in full:

Piously, or politically, we cripple ourselves with the need to bring about God's righteousness on earth, failing to hear what Jesus so vividly declares: that we need not shoulder that burden because the goal itself does not need to be accomplished. The goal is a fact, God's fact, the fact of grace and promise. No gap divides what God says from what God does; and the stories of the coming kingdom do not offer dreams and possibilities of what the Lord might or could do, but speak indicatively, and in the present tense, of what is happening, and of what the future is becoming. The kingdom need not – and cannot – be worked for; it may only be accepted and awaited. On the other hand this waiting for God's indicatives cannot be dispassionate or passive ... the gospel enslaves us again with its imperatives, demanding everything of us by way of repentance and discipleship.[40]

It is this we are advocating here: preaching where the gospel, in and of itself, is the fulcrum of the worshipping life of the church, and where the imperative arises out of the very substance of the gospel itself, rather than something additional to it. In this paradigm, the desire for large-scale revival is eclipsed by the more important task of evangelising the church in its own gospel – itself a missionary task – thus ensuring that whatever the church might become, it does at least witness to the drama and radicality of the gospel.

Of course, part of that radicality, as Darrel Guder reminds us, is the call as a disciple of Christ to enter into the missional purpose of the church.[41] But the point to emphasise here is that this is never done at the expense of personal reception of, and formation by, the message of the gospel; rather, evangelism, personal holiness and discipleship to Jesus Christ must be seen as an inevitable corollary of it – the authentic response to the grace of God effected by Christ and the Spirit. The repercussions of this approach in terms of preaching itself are immediate. At once it calls into question the hermeneutical bias of most revivalist preaching towards increased holiness, activity and intercession. Moreover, it challenges the predilection in contemporary homiletical theory with relevancy or application, and it is to this other end of the spectrum we now turn.

Relevant preaching

Preaching for relevance seems to stand in stark opposition to the more strident note that features in revivalist preaching. Coming as it does from a different theological presupposition, it could be said to stand in contradiction to it. Yet the fact that the two modes of preaching can often feature in the same setting confirms the observations made earlier regarding the juxtaposition of combative prayer warfare and seeker sensitive worship: ultimately it is not theological coherence that determines what constitutes ministry, but rather whatever contributes to the overall growth and indeed popularity of the church. Even within Pentecostalism – where typically preaching is of an especially combative, exhortatory nature – there is evidence that preaching has succumbed to the demand for relevance: 'In growing churches the sermons will be clear, relevant, simple, beneficial, and not too long!'[42] Apart from the presumption of relating growth to brevity of sermon, what Dye's comment amounts to is a weakening of the Pentecostal vision of gospel preaching.[43] Moreover, it represents a capitulation by the church to cultural expectations without any regard to the long-term ramifications of this position.

The same anxiety regarding the churches' relationship to culture can be found behind Norrington's derisory treatment of preaching: 'The prevailing culture, far from supporting the use of the sermon, points,' he argues, 'to its abandonment.'[44] Such a comment betrays Norrington's underlying cultural antipathy against preaching and the weakness of his overall methodology. Even if sermons were to be a proven, biblical form of communication, one suspects that the needs of the listener would override, for Norrington at least, the challenges that such gospel speech would require. And throughout the evangelical constituency one notes a bias to the needs of the listener: preaching that is communicable in everyday language and sensitive to the realities of modern living. Warner epitomises this approach when he insists on preaching that is accessible and pertinent to the needs of the twenty-first century. Jesus is the supreme communicator, whose parables are the prime examples of cultural accommodation and relevance.[45]

As an example of contextualisation, such attempts at cultural engagement are important; yet there is also something sinister about such a position on preaching: sinister because in the desire to make our preaching communicable and relevant something of the gospel's own inscrutability is lost. As William Willimon points out: 'If the gospel is so communicable why didn't the disciples understand it?'[46] Parables, contrary to popular preconceptions, are not there to make things simple; rather they are there to subvert our presuppositions and deliver to us a gospel that, in the final analysis, requires a miracle for us to understand it. As stated by this author elsewhere: 'if our congregations go away somewhat bemused, or even confused by the message, this may be no bad thing. The greater danger is that they will go away with everything intact'.[47]

In exposing relevancy as a false criteria upon which to base evangelism we ought to ask, of course, what is meant by the term, for what relevancy amounts to in many cases is a story or some anecdote that gives the sermon a whiff of immediacy. Genuine relevancy, on the other hand, will take more seriously the modern condition of alienation, seeking to address it directly as well as transform it.[48] Furthermore, we should be cautious about relevancy as a criterion for communication because in classical and biblical preaching there is an unashamed belief that the world of the text is relevant in itself. It is this biblical world, as Lindbeck reminded us earlier, that is interpretive of our world and not the other way around. To crave for relevancy at all costs, and to exalt the democratic speech of the small group, in the way that Pearse and others do, 'is a kind of slander against the text'.[49] Precedence ought to be given instead to the re-enactment of the gospel as it occurs in the text, so that what congregations receive in the regular preaching ministry of the church is a demonstration of why it is called gospel in the first place. The uninterrupted nature of gospel preaching is not a celebration of monologue; rather, it is the essential precondition of all serious reflection of the strange world of the gospel.[50]

Evangelising the Church

It should be clear that a philosophy of preaching, so described, is markedly different to current thinking in the technology of communication. At once, it stands over and against pious moralisms, exhortatory bullying, seeker spirituality and kitsch religion; indeed, this kind of preaching challenges the whole array of what takes place under the description evangelical preaching, which is eclectic, to say the least; for in classical preaching, the horizon is the eschatological future of sins forgiven, of a righteousness received and of adoption into the family of God, now realised in the death and resurrection of Jesus and the coming of the Spirit. Its announcement brings with it the drama of crisis and the mystery of event.[51] To that extent, preaching is not about numerical success, or congregational effect, anymore than worship ought to be about attracting new people to church. Instead of being absorbed by methods to get people to church, 'the more important question should be, does the church to which they are coming worship God truthfully?'[52] Fidelity to the basic metanarrative of gospel proclamation, for both

Christian edification and evangelism, should be primary, regardless of numbers.

This view of preaching, in which the church itself is the arena of evangelism, could be refuted, no doubt, with reference to C.H. Dodd's distinction between the *kerygma* and the *didache*: the argument that preaching, by definition, should be evangelistic, and that teaching should be towards believers.[53] Such a distinction is widely recognised and underlies popular beliefs about the difference between preaching and teaching. Pearse himself reverts to this formula in his own discussion about preaching, which explains why he sees gospel preaching as inappropriate and indulgent outside an evangelistic setting.[54] Partly, this can be explained by the fact that Pearse confuses bad preaching – manipulative preaching – with all preaching; but his antipathy to preaching is due also to the fact that his understanding of church ministry is more culturally than theologically determined. In Pearse's scheme of things – and in this he expresses a widespread view among evangelicals – preaching is culturally insensitive to postmodern Christians, while making the church, at the same time, an impenetrable subculture for the unchurched. It is to be used, therefore, only occasionally, presumably because it threatens to make the church obscure.[55] When it does occur, it should be more informational – what we might call homily – than kerygmatic.

Pearse's reflections on preaching as a form of communication represent a lack of nerve, if ever there was; both Pearse and Norrington have failed to understand the theological and pastoral presuppositions upon which good, expository gospel preaching takes place. Scripture posits no such distinction between *kerygma* and *didache*. The terms are interchangeable, and very often appear together with no attempt to be too precise concerning their distinctives. Indeed, in Romans 1:15, as Douglas

Moo points out, Paul's eagerness is to preach the gospel 'to you who are in Rome', the primary reference being the believing community in Rome.[56] The evangelistic mission of the church is clearly within Paul's wider horizon, but his first horizon is determined by the urgency of continually refreshing the church in the gospel itself. As Charles Moule states:

> If we maintain the familiar distinction between *kerygma* and *didache* too rigidly, we shall not do justice to the real nature of all Christian edification, which builds, sometimes more, sometimes less, but always at least some of the foundational material into the walls and floors.[57]

Given the mixed setting of a large number of Christian congregations in our present context, it is our contention that the need for kerygmatic foundations, as Moule describes, is especially urgent. The mutual exclusivity of preaching and teaching in the tradition assumes neat distinctions between the world and community of faith, in which *homilia,* was 'addressed to a congregation already established in the faith';[58] but as James Thompson points out, such a view of settled, instructed congregations, able to discuss various aspects of Christian life, 'was more plausible in 1936 than it is in 2000'.[59] Given the largely uncatechised nature of the contemporary church, gospel preaching to the baptised is entirely apt. Christian gatherings in the postmodern West present *the* evangelistic opportunity. Even so, our argument does not hinge on this growing reality. Gospel preaching – preaching that recollects and reconnects churches to the main drama of salvation – is crucial in and of itself, for the sake of believers, for it is in the retelling of the gospel that the dominant idols of the culture are brought to account. Through such preaching the essential awakening of the Christian imagination is made possible, which, as Paul Ricœur reminds us, is the bedrock of all biblical imperative, exhortation and application.[60]

Traces of such preaching ministry to the church are discernible in the New Testament; Norrington admits as much in the case of 1 Timothy 4:13 and 2 Timothy 4:2: the command to Timothy to preach the word. Norrington, of course, adds a disclaimer of his own at this point, namely that such a command in no way justifies a regular pattern of preaching in the church, both then and now. Because precise details about homiletic style are beyond recovery we cannot deduce from the texts, he argues, or project back on to them our own sermonic forms. Mark Strom agrees with Norrington in this regard. He insists that there is 'no evidence for anything like our conventions of preaching in the New Testament'.[61] We may equally well assert, however, that if precise details have been conveniently lost to us, there is nothing to suggest either that sermonising or regular preaching in the church was not an early church practice. Indeed, it may have been more widespread than we are suggesting here. And the rationale behind the continuation of such a practice lies not just in its biblicism, but in the conviction that salvation requires churchly re-enactment and reaffirmation if it is to prove transformative. As Andrew Lincoln notes concerning pastoral methodology in Ephesians:

> the writer is concerned to motivate readers, and he knows that a deeper sense of their corporate Christian identity and a greater desire to please God in wise and holy living will flow out of the sort of remembering of God's activities on their behalf that is accompanied by thanksgiving.[62]

The kind of community shaped by this word is the basis of all evangelistic endeavours.

This pastoral awareness concerning gospel preaching – and it is indeed an awareness that can only be felt fully where preaching intersects with pastoral ministry – justifies the whole theological enterprise that is being undertaken here. It displaces the obsession for growth to secondary status, because it sees the obsession for growth as part of the problem of a church that has capitulated to the world's criteria of success. Instead, the main business of the church is to ensure that the gospel finds a home within its worshipping life. It is this gospel, rather than the church's relevancy or contemporaneity, which determines its identity and mission.[63] The urgent task for preachers of the gospel is to reawaken the core memory of the church. As Willimon points out: 'amnesia appears to be the prelude to accommodation and compromise'.[64] And because the church has lost its memory, through spurious and misguided apologetics, the evangelistic task is in the first instance addressed to the church: the task of helping, to use Brueggemann's phrase, 'forgetters become rememberers'.[65]

Clearly, in the present climate, the recovery of the language of the evangel is apposite to the unbeliever. More importantly, it has value to the baptised who have heard the story, but in reality act as unbelieving believers. In fact, the urgent task of preaching is addressed precisely to this situation. Through preaching, the basic narrative of the gospel might be recovered and act as a catalyst for renewal. As early Restorationist ideology on the church was always keen to point out, the evangelist is first of all given to the church.[66] Guder concurs. The caricature of the evangelist handing out tracts, or preaching to the unconverted, is one definition, and a popular one at that, but 'if we understand the necessity of the church's continuing conversion, however, then the function of the evangelist is essential to the church's missional equipping'.[67]

Positive Preaching: The Preaching Theology of P.T. Forsyth

To the charge that such a high view of preaching represents nothing more than a wistful longing for the lost art of pulpiteering, it is worth noting that preachers in every generation have lamented the sorry state of preaching. Though Christian historiography is especially prone to such idealism, there never has been an ideal period in church history. It is not the onset of postmodernity that has brought into question the power of the pulpit, as Clyde Fant reminds us; even Charles Spurgeon regarded his own period – often perceived as the golden age of preaching – as apostate when it came to the reverencing of the word.[68] But in the midst of such decline, preaching has had its defenders who, by articulating the nature of preaching for their own generation, offer us something surprisingly contemporary by way of ministry in our present setting. P.T. Forsyth is one such proponent of preaching. His well-known theology of preaching, *Positive Preaching and the Modern Mind*, has proved so influential that it is worth spending some time here examining his understanding of preaching and the church's task.

Theologically, Forsyth was himself seeking to uphold the preaching of the gospel against the pragmatism he encountered within late Victorian Congregationalism, of which he was an ordained minister. In so doing, he articulated a theology of the atonement that stood in marked contrast to the liberalism of his early theology.[69] In that sense, he was fighting on a number of fronts: attacking liberalism, eschewing mere activism, but also confronting the romantic sensibility that engendered a faith that was far too subjective.[70] Forsyth focused his attack on the prevailing romantic mood on R.J. Campbell of the City Temple, whose *New Theology*, published in 1907, epitomised all that was wrong with the dominant theological tendencies of the time – specifically, its emotional pantheism. But Forsyth's basic objection to most modern theology was its anthropocentric inclination. It is this that makes him so contemporary. Indeed, the re-publication of many of his works in recent years is significant in that he provides, at an important juncture in the history of evangelicalism, an alternative way of construing the ministry and mission of the church.

In short, Forsyth perceives preaching as a legacy of the Hebrew prophet rather than the Greek rhetor.[71] This sets him against those in the present scene, including Norrington, who dismiss preaching, and more specifically sermonising, because of its associations with the style of rhetoric that quickly gained acceptance with the hellenisation of the gospel. The castigation of preaching, because of this perceived relationship, has become something of a fashion, and there is no doubt some truth in the association of the two.[72] Essentially, however, preaching takes its cue, Forsyth contends, from the gospel itself; indeed, it takes the form of sacrament: preaching as a prolongation of the events of the gospel itself, without which the gospel would prove ineffectual.

Such a high view of preaching may be rejected because it claims for preaching far too much: it demon-strates a reverence for preaching that substitutes for the gospel itself. Such is not Forsyth's view. What Forsyth means is that preaching can only be effectual in so far as it derives its energy from the actualities of the death and resurrection of Christ as the revelation of God's holy love, and, moreover, takes the proclamation of these events as its sole rationale: 'To be effective our preaching must be sacramental. It must be an act prolonging the great Act, mediating it, and conveying it. Its energy and authority is that of the great Act.'[73] This is how preaching is effective, and, furthermore, why preaching is so crucial, for it delivers to the church its own gospel. Preaching is 'the Word of the Gospel returning in confession to the God who gave it'.[74] The preacher's task, and the preacher's power therefore, 'lies not in initiation, but in appropriation. And his work is largely to assist the Church to a fresh appropriation of its own gospel'.[75]

Such a view differs markedly from what Forsyth saw as the modern predilection for experience as well as activism. In the event of preaching, the church is given opportunity to transcend such concerns and be confronted with Christ himself. Anything less than preaching as a celebration of Christ, such as we might find in preaching for decision, or preaching to evoke an experience, falls short of what preaching should be. Preaching is just that elongation of the gospel that makes it, in its most primitive form, an act of grace commensurate with the event of grace itself. Even faith, therefore, is the gift of God:

> It cannot be worked up by us, nor by anyone working at us. It is evoked by contact with Christ, who is the gift of God. That is why we must preach Christ and not about Christ; why we must set the actual constraining Christ before people and not coax or bully people into decision.[76]

It is this confidence in the very events of the gospel of grace, and the preaching thereof to effect that grace, that makes Forsyth so attractive for our purposes. After all, it is a loss of belief in the gospel as the primary resource for the church's own spiritual life and subsequent mission that lies, we have argued, behind the faddism that is now so much a feature of evangelicalism. But what Forsyth alerts us to is the futility of seeking to persuade the world by whatever strategy or experience, when the church itself has lost sight of, and ceases to enjoy, the gospel of Christ. Statistics concerning church attendance, and the interest in popular methods, was as much a part of Forsyth's purview as it is ours.[77] If embraced, however, as the main indicator of spiritual growth, the church is reduced to a going concern, even a franchise, rather than a communion of saints.[78] Only when the church returns to the gospel itself, however, learning 'not only to read the present situation' but also 'to read her own gospel before that', can we say, argues Forsyth, that true revival begins.[79]

In *The Church and the Sacraments*, Forsyth states this position more explicitly: 'A new baptism we need; meaning by that, however, not a new piety, a new subjectivity, a mere revival. We need a new Spirit, but in the sense of a recovered Word. For our present belief hardly supplies us with a Word.'[80] No wonder Forsyth has often been regarded as a forerunner to Karl Barth.[81] *Positive Preaching* is an elaboration of what the recovered Word might look like, and in the process he dismisses religious experientialism as being inadequate as a solution to human plight. 'At the present hour romantic religion has submerged evangelical, the religion of affection and temperament has obscured the religion of will and conscience.'[82] The gospel, for Forsyth, 'is an objective power, a historic act and a perennial energy of the holy love of God in Christ'[83] – holy love being shorthand for Forsyth's recovery of an evangelical doctrine of the atonement.[84] Reducing the gospel to an experience is to rob the gospel of its moral power and to play into the hands of optimistic liberalism and the culture of success that underpinned it. The gospel offers neither. It highlights, instead, the tragic proportions of the human situation and the drama of God's salvation in response, and as such throws us not into nice sensibilities or moods of faith, but rather into astonishment at the enormity of what was achieved on the cross.[85]

Behind Forsyth's invective is a relentless disdain for pietistic religion and the Pietists' way of religion, which was 'lapped in soft airs, taking a clique for the Kingdom, and sold to the religious nothings of the hour with all their stupefying power'.[86] Forsyth employed all the force of his paradoxical and antithetical style against such religion because it failed to deliver the gospel of the Redeemer. It was unable to do so precisely because it was 'unfit to cope with the moral case of the world, its giant souls and hearty sinners'.[87] Interestingly, Forsyth refers to this 'sympathetic' religion (meaning by that a religion without force or passion), as a 'suburban piety'.[88] The phrase is peculiarly Forsythian because all five of his appointments within the Congregational church were located in suburbia.[89] It was in suburbia that his theological vision was worked out. But suburban piety, for Forsyth, meant exactly that brand of effete Christianity that rendered the gospel ineffectual.

The theological root of the problem, for Forsyth, lies in a conception of God's Fatherhood at the cost of his holiness, resulting in the loss of moral poignancy. 'We have churches of the nicest, kindest people,' he laments, 'who have nothing apostolic or missionary, who never knew the soul's despair or its breathless gratitude.'[90] And with this, one detects a note of hopelessness in Forsyth: a grief concerning the ephemeral character of contemporary Christianity whereby 'imaginative greatness and moral poignancy' had been taken from preaching.[91] The gospel should not be reduced to an idea or a sentimental quietism. The gospel is historic, eschatological and efficacious, in and of itself.

The present antipathy towards preaching in certain sections of the renewal – particularly where accessibility has become the dominant concern – is derived, in our opinion, from this same failure of imagination: a pre-ference for mood rather than the moral; apologetic rather than apostolic; theosophic rather than theological; and practical rather than doxological. The reason for it lies in what Forsyth understood as the 'adjusting of the grace of God to the natural realm rather than interpreting it by our moral soul and our moral coil'.[92] In effect, it represents a loss of nerve in the gospel's ability to create its own agenda, to pose its own questions. Driven by the urgency of the evangelistic challenge, preaching has accommodated itself apologetically to the questions posed by the culture rather than to the crisis posed by the gospel. It has led to preaching that must fulfil, above all else, the criteria of relevancy and applicability to everyday life.

Without these twin motivators of contemporary communication, the inference is that numbers will continue to decline in a culture that will not tolerate anything that is too churchly. Mark Greene's conclusions about the priorities in modern communication, for example, exhibit a striking and somewhat astonishing antipathy to churchly discourse – such a position being necessary, he argues, if the church is to prove attractive to believers and unbelievers alike.[93] But his stress upon the need for relevance in preaching, addressing in particular the setting of the workplace, is so devoid of a churchly and doctrinal context that one suspects that it originates as much in the commuter individualism of the Home Counties as it does in genuine missiological concern. And in so far as this has been the case in the renewal movement, it will require some bold counter plays if the gospel is to be recovered.

The way to do this, we have already made clear, is not to revert to the raw fundamentalism of holiness preaching, with its stress on repentance. Sadly, contemporary preaching, in its despair about finding the right key to unlock the harvest, tends to resort to this default position. Within the wider evangelical-charismatic constituency, preaching tends to oscillate between the poles of confrontationalism and relevancy, thus missing the true gospel summons. Forsyth offers us a different way marked by the message of *holy love*: a conjunction that objectifies the introspection of holiness revivalism onto the doctrine of atonement. In *holy love* God reconciles to himself not the well-disposed but rebels.[94] The cruciality of the cross, as far as Forsyth was concerned, necessitated such stark descriptions of the human plight.[95] But salvation is of such magnitude and completion that it eradicates the anxiety of revival piety, for it is 'done *in* God and not *before* him, in his will and not in His presence'.[96] God is able to redeem as well as to bless and in God the great world-transaction over sin is done. As Forsyth rightly concludes:

> A faith wholly experimental has its perils. It varies too much with our subjectivity. It is not our experience of holiness that makes us believe in the Holy Ghost. It is a matter of faith that we are God's children; there is plenty of evidence in us against it.[97]

Such a full salvation carries its own demands, to be sure, for grace in the end, as Bonhoeffer points out, is costly if it is to be saving.[98] Nevertheless, the repentance that is so characteristic of revival faith, is not, in Forsyth, 'a thing possible by itself, or a condition effectual by itself without God, but only as that part or action of the complete work of Christ which takes effect through us'.[99] Hence, we should 'not tell people how they ought to feel toward Christ. That is useless. It is just what they ought that they cannot do. Preach a Christ that will make them feel as they ought'.[100] Forsyth's advice to preachers might equally well apply, in the light of our concerns in chapter two, to those who lead worship.

As preaching recovers its cruciform shape, so it could restate the gospel also for a church that has lost its intuition of wonder in a plethora of management techniques, vague romanticism and deeper life spirituality. It is this restoration of wonder that Robert Capon has in mind when he states:

> Of course there must be repentance. But even repentance is a celebration, not a bargaining session in which we work up enough resolve against sin to con God into putting up with us. It's not a turning from sin but a return to faith – a reawakening of our trust that all deeds, bad as well as good, have been done in God.[101]

Again, it is the loss of astonishment – or what we might term imagination – concerning the gospel itself that accuses evangelical-charismatic worship of its blandness. The cause of this blandness lies in the precedence given to converting the world and the numerical success of the gospel, to the detriment of celebrating the gospel. An attenuated spirituality will inevitably follow, as Forsyth understood so well, because eventually the church, in its appeal to the world, ends up speaking 'the language of our humane civilization and not the language of Christ'.[102] The dialectical tension that so many are fond of pointing out, between Christ and culture, at one level, is irreconcilable.[103] Ultimately, it is culture that will prevail: hence, the primacy of preaching, and preaching of a proclamatory kind, so that the church can once again find courage and joy in its own gospel as the true source of evangelistic zeal:

> It is only an age which starves the idea of revelation, by its neglect of the sacramental idea, that reduces preaching to evangelizing alone. It is only an age engrossed with impressions and careless about realities that could regard the preacher's prime work as that of converting the world, to the neglect of the transforming of the church.[104]

This means that evangelising the baptised becomes a central task in a churchmanship that has been overwhelmed by categories of relevancy and success. Ostensibly, such a project might seem an indulgent one. After all, should not the believing community have an adequate grasp of the gospel, sufficient to inform its worship? Pearse and others would have us believe so. In reality, however, faith needs constantly to be re-energised if it is to have any vital role in society – hence, the importance of recollection. It is the incubation of such faith in the church that ought to be the measure of whether the church is successful or not. Forsyth had his own quarrel with those who would measure the church by its numbers:

> Is the test of a Gospel the welcome it receives, the rapidity of its success? Is the distinctive note of the Church's Gospel that which immediately appeals to the democracy or the minor? Is Christianity to stand or fall by its direct effect on the workman or the youth?[105]

Rather, success is defined, as we have already argued, by fidelity to, and celebration of, the gospel, so that even though the church may not swell its numbers, and even though the gospel may not receive a wide hearing, it does at least have a true home.

Given the present situation in evangelicalism at large, with its desire for maximum impact, especially among the youth population, it is difficult to imagine how such an unashamed acknowledgement of the gospel's unpopularity could find credence. It smacks of defeatism and may be regarded as symptomatic of the very problem that has led to the present malaise: a churchmanship that is unconcerned with, and irrelevant to, the culture at large. But this is not doing justice to Forsyth. His was not a theology of retrenchment (in fact, Forsyth's ecclesiology was remarkably ecumenical).[106] Rather, his plea was for the recovery of a gospel that could make sense of the world in its sinfulness and would resist the process of sentimentalisation – a gospel, moreover, that could not be corrupted by utilitarian ends. Only this gospel had the power to effect transformation at both societal and personal level, and therefore needed to be preached once again in the churches as an agent of renewal.

Sacramentum Verbi: Preaching as a Sacrament

The recovery of preaching, in the manner described, is central to the recovery of the gospel. As we saw earlier, it is the neglect of the gospel that has made the renewal vulnerable to technique – the most recent expression of this being the spiritual technology of Prayer Warfare. Commenting on the Reformers' condemnation of speculative demonology, Lowe quotes Martin Luther who argues: 'God provided his church with audible preaching and visible sacraments.' Moreover,

> Satan resists this holy ministry in all earnestness, and he would like it to be eliminated altogether because *by it alone* is Satan overcome. The power of the oral word is truly remarkable. To think that Satan, that proud spirit, may be put to flight and thrown into confusion by such frail words.[107]

The reason Luther states this so forcibly is because he believed in the efficacy of the preached word as the means by which the church is sustained in its faith and witnesses to the world. Central to this understanding of preaching is the proclamation of Christ. This is not to deny, in homiletical terms, the place of apologetic; nor is it to deny the importance of didactic and moral exhortation.

These have their place in the way that Pearse and others describe. And it is undoubtedly true that preaching, in the way advocated here, is not the most efficient method of learning. To rely solely on preaching for that purpose is to ignore the many other ways the church historically has sought to catechise and disciple its members. What is under discussion here, however, transcends mere learning, and subverts the modern preoccupation with mere information. What we understand by preaching is revelation of the finished work of Christ, so that what congregations celebrate week after week is a fresh understanding of why it is called gospel in the first place. 'There are not nearly enough preachers,' Forsyth laments, 'who preach, nor people who take home, the reality of damnation, or the connection of liberty with it.'[108] Instead, the shape of the drama is reduced to a principle or a mood, thereby removing the note of evangelical crisis that is critical for authentic religious encounter. The importance of proclamatory preaching to the church – the evangelisation of the church, so to speak – is that it enables just that celebration of the gospel that Forsyth calls the 'organised Hallelujah of the church'.[109]

Again, this is not to deny the issue of pulpiteering, nor is it to dismiss the technology of communications – an ever-growing industry. But what Norrington and others achieve in their denunciation of the preaching event is the removal of a vital means by which Christians encounter the living Christ. Preaching is not just a word *about* Christ, argued the Reformers; it is a word *of* Christ. This conviction about preaching was articulated most clearly by Bonhoeffer in the last century: 'I preach because the church is there – and I preach, that the church might be there. Church preaches to church.'[110] In his lectures on preaching, Bonhoeffer describes the act of preaching, in typically Lutheran language, as a *sacramentum verbi*: a sacrament that actually ushers in the living Christ.[111] 'The preacher should be assured that Christ enters the congregation,' he argues, 'through those words he proclaims from the Scripture'.[112] Moreover, in the climb to the pulpit the preacher should arrive 'as a messenger from Marathon with his exultant cry – "the victory is won!"'[113] Anything less than this, despite protestations by its critics that this is mere theatrics, is not gospel preaching, according to Bonhoeffer, for it fails to be a word of Christ himself.

Because of the general misunderstanding and basic ignorance of this view of preaching, contemporary communication, consequently, is far more about the impartation of vision and motivation. This is acceptable in so far as vision is an important function within church leadership, but it is not the primary function of preaching. As Dave Hansen comments: 'My ideas for the church, even those inspired by the Holy Spirit, have no place in the pulpit; they are not the material of proclamation. Preaching our visions and ideas for the church is cheap leadership, and it is not preaching.'[114] On the contrary, pastoral leadership is concerned with keeping the person of Christ and the message of the gospel central.

The implications of this view of ministry for the way pastoral leadership arranges its time and study habits are, of course, numerous and will be left for the concluding chapter of part two. In terms of preaching, it requires, according to Bonhoeffer, competence and careful exegesis to ensure that it is the text, and not the personal preferences of the preacher, that determines what is said. 'When we ask ourselves, "What shall I say today to the congregation?" we are lost,' says Bonhoeffer. 'But when we ask, "What does this text say to the congregation?" we find ample support and abundant confidence. The faithfulness with which we enter the text makes this possible.'[115] In this regard, Bonhoeffer has been seriously misrepresented by some recent interpreters, who have seen in his idea of 'religionless Christianity' a disregard for textuality. To view Bonhoeffer in this way is anachronistic, to say the least. Even so, such a high view of preaching cannot be understood in a vacuum; it depends on a view of the church as the body of Christ: the church as the actualised presence of Christ. The word of the church is the word of Christ because its body is his also.[116] From this we deduce a very practical point: preaching not only takes place in the sermon but also via pastoral care and, as we shall see, through the sacraments. Preaching can only find its proper context within the overall pastoral care of the church, which is why a high view of preaching that is being upheld here requires, indeed necessitates, good pastoral practice and thoroughgoing discipleship.[117] Without it, preaching is guilty of homiletical positivism – of the sort Bonhoeffer criticised Barth for – that creates too sharp a dialectic between the Word and its recipient.[118]

Ultimately, however, it is the Word of Christ that the preacher brings to the congregation. As Bonhoeffer asserts, 'This proclamation of the Christ does not regard its primary responsibility to be giving advice, arousing emotions, or stimulating the will – it will do these things too, but its intention is to sustain us.'[119] Preachers must give themselves singularly to the word of Christ as it comes to us in the scripture.[120] Whether present models of ministry allow for such diligence in the pulpit is, of course, a moot point. It is certainly prerequisite of this agenda, and Thomas Long's image of the preacher as the one who bears witness to this gospel is supportive, because the preacher 'is one whom the congregation sends on their behalf, week after week to the Scripture'.[121] Here is an unashamed belief that the preacher's task of exegeting the word, of uncovering the promise of the gospel, is scriptural, historic and essential. For Long, the crucial activity of the leader is not running the church programme, nor trying to increase the size of church membership, but going to the scripture to listen for the truth; and the truth one is listening for comes ultimately in the form of promise.[122] Gospel preaching, by definition, is the recollection and retention of this original encounter with grace.

There are a number of obstacles in the way of a recovery of this understanding of preaching: not least, the bias towards anecdotal, testimonial preaching that, in the extreme, can undermine the centrality of the word. This reveals an ancient tension: the tension between the message preached and the lived experience of the preacher, between theologia and ethos. The present culture of suspicion certainly does require the preacher to earth the gospel in personal story. But if this is to equate to the criteria established by scripture it must take on the form, as Andre Resner points out, of self-effacement,[123] for the authority of preaching is not ultimately in the charisma of the preacher – although that too has its part[124] – but in the Christ whom the preacher proclaims.

In the context of experientialism, Forsyth's corrective makes sense: the need to create not so much a mood but a faith in Christ himself. Forsyth was relentless in his attack on sentimental, mood inducing spirituality:

> Faith then becomes a devout and altruistic frame of mind, a subjectivism, instead of an act diffused through life, a life act of self committal into Christ's hands and Christ's Acts of grace. Attention is withdrawn from the contents of faith to the mood of faith. [125]

In Forsyth's vision of preaching, the proclamation of Christ entails a response of nothing less than the will. It is the will, not the emotions, that is confronted in the preaching of the gospel. Bonhoeffer shares this view in his understanding of the task of preaching. In fact, it is only the Word that can achieve this: 'Only this Word keeps on being clear to us in its accusations and its promises. Only this Word makes us without excuse.'[126] Bonhoeffer's relativising of other things in the process, such as music, make interesting reading in the light of the current emphasis upon the worship experience. Bonhoeffer notes: 'Music and symbols (as the Berneuchen movement believed) do not make us without excuse; they are not unequivocal and do not break down the will.'[127] With the primacy given to music, however, it is difficult to imagine how such a high view of preaching could be retrieved in our context. The current fashion in homiletical theory with its stress upon the inductive, application and relevance is similarly antagonistic to such a view.[128] Even so, it is not alien to the biblical worldview. Paul refers to faith that comes by hearing and hearing through the word of Christ, whereby preaching takes on the characteristic of affective speech[129] – the word itself being the deed, achieving, in the Isaianic sense, that for which God has purposed it.[130] Gospel preaching is not just about the power of God, providing us with information about what he has done through Christ and the Spirit for our salvation. This is too small a view. Gospel preaching is actually in itself the power of God unto salvation.[131] It actually has the potential of delivering Christ to the congregation week after week.

Another obstacle to a recovery of preaching is the predominance of the visual in the present technology of communications. As we have already noted, recent publications surrounding the issue of postmodernity, and the ensuing relationship between church and culture, make the assertion that in a post-literate age preaching is obsolete. The communication of truth in postmodernity most definitely requires us to be visual.[132] But there are a number of things to be said in response. First, the sense of crisis for Christian faith that often comes in the wake of postmodern evaluations of the church may not be as serious as some claim.[133] We agree with Curtis Chang when he says that 'many existing treatments of the postmodern challenge manifest a certain ahistorical tendency, as if this latest epochal challenge represents some threat unprecedented in the annals of Western Christianity'.[134] Secondly, as Jacques Ellul reminds us, whatever the culture dictates to us regarding modes of communication has to be tempered by the overwhelming case that Christianity is essentially audio and not visual.[135]

Admittedly, this argument in itself does not justify preaching per se. As we shall see, there are other ways the church can commit itself to the notion of orality. Nor does it mean that we must jettison all forms of visual communication. Ellul's brand of Reformed theology is iconoclastic in the extreme and is shot through with unnecessary antithesis.[136] The rejection of the word is tantamount to a death wish, 'the key to the suicide wish and the real truth concerning the radical separation in a person's heart'.[137] But what Ellul does warn us against is the undiscriminating use of the visual, precisely because it fails so often, unlike the word, to confront. Whether it be the use of Christian television, or the prevalence of image in children's classes, 'by allying itself with images, Christianity gains efficacy, but destroys itself, its foundation, and its content. In reality nothing is left to say – not because the word is false, but because images have emptied it of meaning'.[138]

In the context of postmodern deconstructionism, such a restatement of the commitment to the word seems outrageously outmoded. More surprisingly, it runs counter to the trend among Protestants who, despite the Reformation, seem to have reached an agreement concerning the word's uselessness. 'What eager agreement with the idea,' notes

Ellul, 'that language is tyranny, that discourse is nothing but the expression of an undue, illegitimate superiority of the speaker over the person listening.'[139] This sentiment echoes throughout modern evangelicalism. Pearse's attack on the cult of the preacher speaks for a generation who are suspicious of the power plays behind preaching. Yet it is the word that is heard that is crucial to the survival of faith; anything less is entertainment, the mere gathering of a crowd, but not the delivery of truth, and as such represents the humiliation of the Word. For this reason, argues Eugene Peterson, the Hebrews and the Christians, over and against the Greeks, preserved the word-ness of their faith from the visual stimuli of the nude and drama: 'They knew how easy it was for the ardour of obedient listening to be diluted into amused watching.'[140]

We may not want to go that far in distancing ourselves from the new technology. As we have already noted, Ellul is guilty of so demonising the culture that he himself could be accused of paranoia. However, Ellul's theological vision, in which the word has been progressively humiliated, is invoked here to remind us that if the word, and preaching in particular, is to be retrieved for the church, it will require a re-education of the church regarding its historical place and biblical efficacy, over against the downplaying of language which is so much a feature of modern evangelism and its preference for the visual. Of course the church needs to avail itself of every available means of communication as it seeks to contextualise the faith in today's world; as Jolyon Mitchell warns us, 'Even if preaching is *sui generis* it cannot afford to ignore an audio-visual context.'[141] Nevertheless, 'to abandon now the pulpit's unfashionable and demanding mode of speech might be to stumble not over the cultural offence of an outdated medium but over the scandal of the gospel itself, of the crucified and buried Word'.[142]

Preaching is not just a medium for the gospel but is, in its very form and folly, an illustration of the gospel itself: a God who reveals himself and triumphs in the weakness of a crucified Messiah.

What we are proposing in this chapter, as a response to the present malaise in charismatic renewal, requires, admittedly, a high view of preaching, further than many are prepared to go in their appreciation of this ministry. Those who advocate it open themselves up to the quasi-magical charge that has often been levelled at the reformation view on preaching: a transference of power from the high altar to the pulpit. In preaching the Word of God, however, the Spirit does not transfigure our words to the status of canon, nor can we claim for them an immediacy with the divine. Rather, 'God adopts our words,' claims Hansen. 'He condescends, entering the congregation through the foolishness of our words, as we testify to Christ, expositing the scriptures, speaking the words which we must believe God provides, all the while knowing how profoundly flawed our best sermons are.'[143]

This is a necessary insight, introducing a note of modesty into the preacher's claims. But it also seems to make sense of the nature of sacrament, whereby through the event of preaching the receptive listener 'hears the words of God by not only attending to the preacher's claims and admonitions but also asking how in the mystery of providence these words may be the word of God for her'.[144]

That charismatics fail to exploit this understanding of preaching as encounter is surprising, for it comes out of the pietistic tradition – the notion that through the aesthetic sense the affective and the numinous element in religion might unite. This makes the preacher not just the interpreter of scripture; correctly exegeting scripture is only the foundation of preaching, as charismatics have been keen to point out to evangelicals. Instead, it makes the preacher the one who enables, in the actual event of preaching, the encounter to take place.

The possibilities of this in a charismatic setting ought to be manifold, but apart from one or two exceptions, hardly any time has been given to reflect on this. R.T. Kendall makes a helpful conjunction between the charismatic utterance of tongues in Acts 2:4 and the charismatic utterance of preaching in Acts 2:14. In an attempt to marry the Spirit and the Word, Kendall makes the point that 'what one hundred and twenty could do as the Spirit enabled them to utter – words in other languages – is what lay behind Peter preaching in his own language on the Day of Pentecost'.[145] Generally, however, evangelicals and charismatics have reneged on preaching. One of the reasons for this is the loss of what we are calling the *sacramental* dimension. Because encounter can only be understood as an immediate phenomenon (which is why the medium of music is so adaptable to this notion), the potentiality of traditional means, such as preaching, are overlooked. Preaching is perceived as a mode of ministry connected with an overall philosophy of ministry that is obsolete. Preaching the gospel, however, ought to be at the vanguard of the church's mission – the means by which the church is evangelised by its own gospel.

Notes

[1] See L. Newbigin, *Truth to Tell: The Gospel as Public Truth* (London: SPCK, 1991), 68–70.
[2] O. Cullmann, 'This, Our Common Crisis', *Faith IV,* 1972 as cited in E.L. Mascall, *Theology and the Gospel of Christ: An Essay in Reorientation* (London: SPCK, 1977), 30.
[3] Keck, *The Church Confident*, 16.
[4] Ibid., 9–10.

[5] For a very helpful and responsible critique of this teaching see P. Orchard, 'Breaking the Cobwebs of History', Payback Conference, Central Hall, Southampton, 10 March 2001.

[6] W.M. Alston and W.H. Lazareth, 'Preface' in W.H. Lazareth (ed.), *Reading the Bible in Faith: Theological Voices from the Pastorate* (Grand Rapids: Eerdmans, 2001), ix–x.

[7] See J. Finney, *Fading Splendour? A Model of Renewal* (London: Darton, Longman & Todd, 2000), xi, 34, 177.

[8] Noble, *The Shaking*, 79, drawing on the work of L. Newbigin, *The Household of God* (London: SCM, 1953).

[9] R. Hutter, 'The Church: The Knowledge of the Triune God: Practices, Doctrine, Theology' in J.J. Buckley and D.S. Yeago (eds.), *Knowing the Triune God: The Work of the Spirit in the Practices of the Church* (Grand Rapids/Cambridge: Eerdmans, 2001), 26.

[10] D.H. Williams, *Retrieving the Tradition and Renewing Evangelicalism* (Grand Rapids: Eerdmans, 1999, 9–39). Thus, 'it does not matter whether a given congregation is growing numerically at a fantastic rate or barely hanging on; the vacuum created by the absence of theological awareness and guidance provided by the church of previous ages is being quickly filled with a hankering after new techniques and gimmicks in the exercise of ministry' (11).

[11] Pearse and Matthews, *We Must Stop Meeting Like This*, 100–101.

[12] D.C. Norrington, *To Preach or Not to Preach?* (Carlisle: Paternoster, 1996). See also E. Hatch, *The Influence of Greek Ideas and Usages Upon the Christian Church* (Edinburgh: Williams and Norgate, 1891), 105–15.

[13] Norrington, *To Preach or Not to Preach?* 20–41.

[14] J. Deere, 'Being Right Isn't Enough' in K. Springer (ed.), *Riding the Third Wave: What Comes After Renewal?* (Basingstoke: Marshall Pickering, 1987), 92–4. See also J. Deere, *Surprised by the Voice of God* (Eastbourne: Kingsway, 1996).

[15] See G. Cooke, *Develop your Prophetic Gifting* (Tonbridge: Sovereign World, 1994), 17–19. See also Bickle, *Growing in the Prophetic*, 83–4.

[16] Norrington, *To Preach or Not to Preach?*, 42–68; Also Pearse and Matthews, *We Must Stop Meeting Like This*, 99.

[17] G. Kelly, *Get a Grip on the Future Without Losing Your Hold on the Past* (London: Monarch, 1999), 113–27.

[18] On the dangers of pulpiteering see M. Lloyd-Jones, *Preachers and Preaching* (London: Hodder & Stoughton, 1971), 14–15.

[19] See M.D. Atkins, *Preaching in a Cultural Context* (Peterborough: Foundery, 2001), for a helpful introduction to some of the concerns raised on both sides of the debate, as well as G. Johnston, *Preaching to a Postmodern World* (Leicester: Inter-Varsity Press, 2002).

[20] D. Bonhoeffer, *Worldly Preaching* (Nashville/New York: Thomas Nelson, 1975), 128.

[21] See F.B. Craddock, *As One Without Authority: Essays on Inductive Preaching* (Enid: Philips University Press, 1971).

[22] R. Capon, *The Astonished Heart* (Grand Rapids: Eerdmans, 1996), 105.

[23] Bonhoeffer, *Worldly Preaching*, 137–40.

[24] Pearse and Matthews, *We Must Stop Meeting Like This*, 95–6.

[25] Murray, *Pentecost – Today?*, 8–13.

[26] See Wallis, *In the Day of Thy Power*, 30, 105, as examples.

[27] Note here the prophetic ministry of popular writer Rick Joyner who, as Latham points out, 'Is There Any Word From the Lord?', 76, espouses a Restorationist eschatology. Joyner condemns the retreat mentality of pre-tribulationists, seeing his own task as that of stirring up the lukewarm 'Laodicean' last days church. For an example of Joyner's eschatological brand of holiness see R. Joyner, *The Final Quest* (New Kensington: Whitaker House, 1996), 78–122.

[28] For an introduction to Brown's popular writing see M. Brown, *Holy Fire, America on the Edge of Revival* (Shippensburg: Destiny Image, 1996). See also *High-Voltage Christianity: Sparking the Spirit in the Church* (Lafayette: Huntington House, 1995), where he seeks to protect the term revival from the twin enemies of sensationalism and complacency.

[29] M. Stibbe, *Thinking Clearly about Revival* (London: Monarch, 1998), 178.

[30] R.J. Neuhaus, *Freedom for Ministry* (Grand Rapids: Eerdmans, 1992), 195.

[31] Ibid., 195.

[32] T. Schreiner, *Apostle of God's Glory in Christ* (Leicester: Apollos, 2001), 264. See also P. Greenslade, *God's Story: Through the Bible Promise by Promise* (Farnham: CWR, 2001), 325.

[33] R.Y. Fung, *The Epistle to the Galatians* (Grand Rapids: Eerdmans, 1988), 282–3.

[34] R.J. Mouw, *The Smell of Sawdust: What Evangelicals Can Learn from Their Fundamentalist Heritage* (Grand Rapids: Zondervan, 2000), 7–13. See also M.C. Barnes, *When God Interrupts: Finding New Life through Unwanted Change* (Downers Grove: Inter-Varsity Press, 1996), 28.

[35] Chan, *Spiritual Theology*, 108.

[36] D. Coggan, *New Day for Preaching: The Sacrament of the Word* (London: SPCK, 1996), 50.

[37] Neuhaus, *Freedom for Ministry*, 195.

[38] See C. Schwarz, *Natural Church Growth*, British Church Growth Association, 1996. Note also R. Warren, *The Purpose Driven Church: Growth without Compromising Your Message and Mission* (Grand Rapids: Zondervan, 1995).

[39] W. Brueggemann, *Biblical Perspectives on Evangelism: Living in a Three-Storied Universe* (Nashville: Abingdon, 1993), 45–6.

[40] A.E. Lewis, *Between Cross and Resurrection: A Theology of Holy Saturday* (Grand Rapids: Eerdmans, 2001), 23–4.

[41] See D.L. Guder, *The Continuing Conversion of the Church* (Grand Rapids: Eerdmans, 2000).

[42] C.W. Dye, *It's Time To Grow: Kick-starting a Church into Growth* (Harpenden: Gazelle, 1997), 108.

[43] See J. Gordy, 'A Theology of Pentecostal Preaching', *Journal of Pentecostal Theology*, 10:1 (2001), 81–97.

[44] Norrington, *To Preach or Not to Preach?*, 103.

[45] Warner, *21st Century Church*, 65–6.

[46] H.W. Willimon, *The Intrusive Word: Preaching to the Unbaptized* (Grand Rapids: Eerdmans, 1994), 22.

[47] I.R. Stackhouse, 'Negative Preaching and the Modern Mind: A Crisis in Evangelical Preaching', *The Evangelical Quarterly* 73:3 (2001), 247–56.

48 B. Zink-Sawyer, '"The Word Purely Preached and Heard": The Listener and the Homiletical Endeavor' *Interpretation* 51: 4 (1997), 342–57.

49 G.O. Forde, 'The Word That Kills and the Word that Makes Alive' in C.E. Braaten and R.W. Jensen (eds.), *Marks of the Body of Christ* (Grand Rapids: Eerdmans, 1999), 9.

50 On this last point see the Introduction by C. Schwöbel in C.E. Gunton, *Theology For Preaching: Sermons For Brentwood*, Edinburgh: T&T Clark (2001), 1–20.

51 See A. Gilmour, *Preaching as Theatre* (London: SCM, 1996), for an elaboration of this point.

52 S. Hauerwas, *A Better Hope: Resources for a Church Confronting Capitalism, Democracy and Postmodernity* (Grand Rapids: Brazos, 2000), 157.

53 C.H. Dodd, *Apostolic Preaching and Its Developments* (New York: Harper Row, 1964 [1936]), 7–8.

54 Pearse and Matthews, *We Must Stop Meeting Like This*, 98.

55 Ibid., 99–101.

56 D. Moo, *The Epistle to the Romans* (Grand Rapids: Eerdmans, 1996), 162–3.

57 C.F.D. Moule, *The Birth of the New Testament* (London: Adam & Charles Black, 1966²), 130.

58 Dodd, *Apostolic Preaching*, 8.

59 J.W. Thompson, *Preaching Like Paul: Homiletical Wisdom for Today* (Louisville: Westminster/John Knox, 2001), 38.

60 See P. Ricœur, *The Rule of Metaphor: Multi-Disciplinary Studies of the Creation of Meaning in Language* (London: Routledge & Kegan Paul, 1986²), 6, where Ricœur contends for the heuristic power of fiction, and introduces the idea of metaphor as the power to re-describe.

61 See M. Strom, *Reframing Paul: Conversations in Grace and Community* (Downers Grove: Inter-Varsity Press, 2000), 206.

62 A. Lincoln, *Ephesians* (Dallas: Word, 1990), lxxxvi. For a development of the theme of Christian identity in the letter to the Ephesians as that which is already constituted in Christ see D.F. Ford, *Self and Salvation; Being Transformed* (Cambridge: Cambridge University Press, 1999), 117–20.

[63] See A. Walker, 'Into the Future: Some Notes on the Cultural Context of Mission and Gospel Hope', *Ministry Today: The Journal of the Richard Baxter Institute for Ministry* Issue 8, (October 1996), 38–46.

[64] Willimon, *The Intrusive Word*, 135.

[65] Brueggemann, *Biblical Perspectives*, 71–93.

[66] P. Greenslade, *Leadership: Patterns for Biblical Leadership Today* (Basingstoke: Marshalls, 1984), 171–2.

[67] Guder, *The Continuing Conversion*, 163.

[68] C.E. Fant, *Preaching for Today* (London: Harper Row, 1975), 4–7.

[69] T. Hart, 'Morality, Atonement and the Death of Jesus' in T. Hart (ed.), *Justice the True and Only Mercy: Essays on the Life and Theology of Peter Taylor Forsyth* (Edinburgh: T&T Clark, 1995), 21.

[70] J.H. Rodgers, *The Theology of P.T. Forsyth: The Cross and the Revelation of God* (London: Independent Press, 1965), 9.

[71] P.T. Forsyth, *Positive Preaching and the Modern Mind* (London: Independent Press, 1964 [1907]), 1.

[72] See Strom, *Reframing Paul*, 210–15.

[73] Forsyth, *Positive Preaching*, 57.

[74] Ibid., 66.

[75] Ibid., 61.

[76] Ibid., 46.

[77] P.T. Forsyth, *The Church and the Sacraments* (London: Independent Press, 1947 [1917]), 43.

[78] Forsyth, *Positive Preaching*, 117.

[79] Ibid., 234.

[80] Forsyth, *The Church and the Sacraments*, 19–20.

[81] J. Thompson, 'Was Forsyth Really a Barthian before Barth' in Hart (ed.), *Justice the True and Only Mercy*, 237–55. Indeed, Barth's theology of the Word would have supplied us with a similarly high view of preaching. See K. Barth, *Church Dogmatics* Volume 1:1 (Edinburgh: T&T Clark, 1963 [1938]), 1:4.

[82] Forsyth, *Positive Preaching*, 111.

[83] Ibid., 3.

84 See P.T. Forsyth, *The Cruciality of the Cross* (London: Independent Press, 1948 [1908]), 11–39, where he expounds the theological basis of holy love. For specific references see also Forsyth, *Positive Preaching*, 145, 173, 236–40.

85 See G. Hall, 'Tragedy in the Theology of P.T. Forsyth' in Hart (ed.), *Justice the True and Only Mercy*, 77–104.

86 P.T. Forsyth, *God the Holy Father* (London: Independent Press, 1957 [1897]), 14–15.

87 Forsyth, *Positive Preaching*, 244.

88 Ibid., 244.

89 C. Binfield, 'P.T. Forsyth as Congregational Minister' in Hart (ed.), *Justice the True and Only Mercy*, 177.

90 P.T. Forsyth, *Positive Preaching*, 244. Quoted, significantly, in J.S. Stewart, *A Faith to Proclaim* (London: Hodder & Stoughton, 1953), 54.

91 Forsyth, *Positive Preaching*, 243.

92 Ibid., 245.

93 M. Greene, 'Is Anybody Listening?', *Anvil* 14:4 (1997), 283–94.

94 Forsyth, *The Cruciality of the Cross*, 30.

95 Commenting on Romans 1:18–32 Moo writes: 'All therefore stand under the awful reality of the wrath of God, and all are in desperate need of the justifying power of the grace of Christ. We will never come to grips with the importance of the gospel, or be motivated as we should to proclaim it, until this sad truth has been integrated into our worldview.' Moo, *Romans*, 98.

96 Forsyth, *The Cruciality of the Cross*, 33. See A.M. Hunter, *P.T. Forsyth: Per Crucem ad Lucem* (London: SCM, 1974), 60–64, for an elucidation of this aspect of Forsyth's theology.

97 Forsyth, *God the Holy Father*, 101.

98 D. Bonhoeffer, *The Cost of Discipleship* (London: SCM, 2000 [1937]), 35–47.

99 P.T. Forsyth, *The Atonement in Modern Religious Thought* (London: James Clarke & Co, 1902), 77. Tom Smail concurs with this stress. T. Smail, *Once and for All: A Confession of the Cross* (London: Darton, Longman & Todd, 1998), 37–57.

[100] P.T. Forsyth, *The Work of Christ* (London: Independent Press, 1938 [1910]), 41.

[101] R.F. Capon, *The Foolishness of Preaching: Proclaiming the Gospel against the Wisdom of the World* (Grand Rapids/Cambridge: Eerdmans, 1998), 22.

[102] Forsyth, *Positive Preaching*, 113.

[103] Note, however, the important contribution of Mary Hilkert to this issue. Using Karl Rahner's sacramental understanding of creation, Hilkert offers an important check to the dialectical, crisis theology of Barth by showing that preaching can also appeal, on occasion, to the signals of grace in creation. M.C. Hilkert, *Naming Grace: Preaching and the Sacramental Imagination* (New York: Continuum, 2000).

[104] Forsyth, *Positive Preaching*, 54.

[105] Ibid., 233.

[106] See Forsyth, *The Church and the Sacraments*, 104–29.

[107] M. Luther, *Luther's Works* as cited in Lowe, *Territorial Spirits*, 96.

[108] P.T. Forsyth, *The Justification of God* (London: Independent Press, 1948 [1917]), 87.

[109] Forsyth, *Positive Preaching*, 66.

[110] Bonhoeffer, *Worldly Preaching*, 138.

[111] Ibid., 116.

[112] Ibid., 130.

[113] Ibid., 123.

[114] 'While the people of God want desperately to flock to the spiritual food of the Word of God, pastors flock to seminars on how to run church boards, administrate programs and raise up volunteers.' D. Hansen, *The Art of Pastoring: Ministry Without all the Answers* (Downers Grove: Inter-Varsity Press, 1994), 152–3.

[115] Bonhoeffer, *Worldly Preaching*, 158. For a fuller treatment of Bonhoeffer's theology of the Word and its implications for understanding his concept of 'religionless Christianity' see F de. Lange, *Waiting for the Word: Dietrich Bonhoeffer on Speaking about God* (Grand Rapids: Eerdmans, 1995).

[116] Bonhoeffer, *Worldly Preaching*, 127.

[117] Ibid., 177.

[118] For a discussion of this point see A. Resner, *Preacher and Cross: Person and Message in Theology and Rhetoric* (Grand Rapids/Cambridge: Eerdmans, 1999), 58–65. See also G. Wingren, *The Living Word: A Theological Study of Preaching and the Church* (London: SCM, 1960), 209–14, for a critique of the Barthian aversion to personality, as well as to natural theology in general, 89–94.

[119] Bonhoeffer, *Worldly Preaching*, 127.

[120] See R. Lischer, 'The Interrupted Sermon' *Interpretation* 50:2 (1996), 169–81.

[121] T. Long, *The Witness of Preaching* (Louisville: Westminster/John Knox, 1989), 44.

[122] See Forde, 'The Word That Kills', 10.

[123] See Resner, *Preacher and Cross*, 1–7, for an introduction to the issues at stake.

[124] Fee, *God's Empowering Presence*, 90–3.

[125] Forsyth, *Positive Preaching*, 45.

[126] Bonhoeffer, *Worldly Preaching*, 129.

[127] Ibid., 129.

[128] See R.L. Lewis and G.G. Lewis, *Inductive Preaching: Helping People to Listen* (Wheaton: Crossway, 1983).

[129] Romans 10:17.

[130] Isaiah 55:10–11.

[131] Romans 1:16.

[132] In addition to Kelly, *Get a Grip*, 113–27 see also B. Draper and K. Draper, *Refreshing Worship* (Oxford: The Bible Reading Fellowship, 2000), 36–44.

[133] See D. Smith, 'Junction or Terminus? Christianity in the West at the Dawn of the Third Millennium', *Themelios* 25:3 (2000), 55–69, for an example of this kind of alarmism.

[134] C. Chang, *Engaging Unbelief: A Captivating Strategy from Augustine and Aquinas* (Leicester: Apollos, 2000), 24–5.

[135] J. Ellul, *The Humiliation of the Word* (Grand Rapids: Eerdmans, 1985), 48–111.

[136] Ibid., 91: 'Images are incapable of expressing anything at all about God. In daily life as well, the word remains the expression God chooses.'

[137] Ibid., 195.

[138] Ibid., 203. For a stimulating defence of orality as the basis of Christian communication and its implications for homiletics – in particular the use of notes in the sermon – see W. Ellsworth, *The Power of Speaking God's Word: How to Preach Memorable Sermons* (Fearn: Christian Focus/Reformation and Revival Ministries, 2000), 39–67.

[139] Ibid., 201.

[140] E.H. Peterson, *Working the Angles: The Shape of Pastoral Integrity* (Grand Rapids: Eerdmans, 1987), 79.

[141] J. Mitchell, 'Preaching in an Audio-Visual Culture', *Anvil* 14:4 (1997), 272.

[142] Lewis, *Between Cross and Resurrection*, 376.

[143] D. Hansen, 'Preaching Cats and Dogs', *American Baptist Evangelicals Journal* 7:3 (1999), 20.

[144] S.I. Wright, 'An Experiment in Biblical Criticism: Aesthetic Encounter in Reading and Preaching Scripture' in C. Bartholemew, C. Greene, K. Moller (eds.), *Renewing Biblical Interpretation, Scripture and Hermeneutics Series Volume 1* (Carlisle: Paternoster, 2000), 263.

[145] P. Cain and R.T. Kendall, *The Word and the Spirit* (Eastbourne: Kingsway, 1996), 61.

Chapter 4

On the Importance
of the Sacraments

Eucharistic Instincts

In referring to preaching as the sacrament of the word, we are deploying fairly unfamiliar terminology. In many traditions the ministry of the word simply does not match this designation. But whatever we permit, or do not permit, within the definition of sacrament – and it is, of course, an ambivalent term – it is the loss of the concept of mediation, inherent in a sacramental understanding of religion, that is central to the diminution of Christian identity we are seeking here to expose.[1] An emphasis upon spiritual immediacy, embracing the holiness revivalism epitomised by Pensacola, the passive spirituality of Toronto, as well as various other 'waves' so-called, has meant the weakening of convictions concerning mediated grace, and what it has led to is a general amnesia concerning the central drama of the gospel – the very thing that makes Christian communities so compelling and distinctive in their varied cultural settings. Having examined the place of preaching in the recovery of sacramentality, we shall continue our exploration of means of grace, in this chapter, by focusing on the sacraments of communion and baptism, the latter being the fulcrum of all ecclesial existence, giving shape to the type of community where preaching and communion makes sense.

Such means of grace – communion and baptism – are, of course, entirely congruent with the doctrines of creation and incarnation. As Wainwright comments: 'Given this utterly corporeal character of the human life lived by the Word of God for the redemption of the world, it is entirely congruous that he should choose to keep coming to his church by material means for the sake of our salvation.'[2] To the preaching, observes Wainwright, are joined the sacraments: a commitment to the ministry of the word and the sacraments that has been commonplace in the historic Christian faith.

That certain Christian traditions place themselves outside the theological consensus of sacramental worship – eucharistic worship in particular – is what constitutes, in the typical sociological paradigm, a sect as opposed to a church, though the attempt by Michael Thompson to include within the definition of church non-sacramental, yet christocentric worship, is a convincing one.[3] There are, after all, other ways of safeguarding and defining orthodoxy apart from sacraments. Nevertheless, the absence of any discussion concerning the nature and significance of communion, and indeed baptism, is one of the most remarkable occurrences in the current fascination with worship in renewal circles, and as such demarcates the new churches from the more historic denominations. Most recent charismatic-evangelical treatments of the subject of worship mention hardly anything about it.[4]

To be fair, this may reflect the fact that most books on contemporary worship are written by songwriters, not liturgists. When it is evident, however, that charismatic-evangelical worship is conceived increasingly by its musicianship – which, as we have seen, has been doctrinally diffident – this observation ceases to be important. Musicians rather than pastors and theologians are constructing worship, and its hallmark is worship that is immediate, intimate and most definitely non-sacramental (indeed immediacy and non-sacramentality are two ways of saying the same thing); but the result has been the loss of transcendence. The collapse of the theological notion of mediation means that God is all too near.

In contrast, sacrament respects not just the notion of transcendence but also immanence by its appeal to theological aesthetics.[5] Through the instrumentality of mediated grace, true encounter is allowed to take place, without this ever violating the notion of the other: through means of grace, God is allowed space to be. Conversely, through sacrament human freedom is protected from the possibility of being overwhelmed by the Spirit, understood non-christologically. This often happens in charismatic worship: language of power in worship – the Holy Spirit's power – often negates human freedom, so that Christian living, as Percy points out, is conceived as the art of becoming *not what we are*.[6] Such language encourages an *ecstatic* rather than *incarnational* view of religion and can, at times, negate the human and material dimension of Christian spirituality.

The gnostic movement away from the human, with all spiritual pressures associated with anti-institutional spirituality, has been the tendency, notes Philip Lee, of Protestant spirituality – revivalist spirituality, in particular – with its emphasis upon knowing: 'Whereas classical Calvinism had held that the Christian's assurance was guaranteed only through Christ and his church, with his means of grace, now assurance could be found only in the personal experience of having been born again.'[7] In many places it has cultivated a hyper-spiritual view of Christian existence. Sacrament, on the other hand, as Irenaeus demonstrated in the second century with reference to the eucharist, addresses such gnostic features by rooting Christian experience in material things, and thereby demonstrating that the primary movement in the gospel drama is not some flight of spiritual fancy but, rather, God's enfolding of humanity in the condescension of Christ.[8] The sacrament of communion provides a *christological* meeting place for encounter, witnessing to the continuity of creation and redemption,[9] and respecting both divine transcendence as well as human personhood. Eucharist is the very means of subsistence,[10] which the Lord offers the church, wherein Christian existence is both incorporated and sustained, thus enabling us to posit a faith expressing salvation *of* the world rather than salvation *from* the world.

Without such mediation, the polarity between the divine and the human, standing in stark opposition to each other, can only be resolved, as Douglas Farrow points out, by a collapsing of space between the two.[11] In the absence of mediation, we are left with a 'laser beam' theology,[12] which appears to offer direct access and intimacy, but, in fact, offers no such thing, for it is offered only on the basis of continued progress in holiness in the 'community of feeling'. Ironically, as we have already noted, this can only encourage dualism, tantamount to escape – both theological and anthropological – as worshippers attempt to purge themselves of sin, intensify their zeal or have a worship experience in an attempt to access the divine. It is a form of spirituality that is prey to manipulative techniques.[13] Communion, on the other hand, centres our worship on the revelation of God in Christ as the necessary counterpart to our experience in worship: a model of worship that transcends the category of the phenomenal, positing a faith that is rooted in ontological and trinitarian categories.

An important benefit of this approach to worship is that it counteracts the plethora of impersonal metaphors that so often attach themselves to the lyrics of religious revivalism, such as 'There's a River' (SF2 1042); 'Fire' (SF2 718); 'Don't Let My Love Grow Cold' (SF2 702); 'Days of Heaven (Lord Send the Rain)' (SF2 699); 'O God of Burning, Cleansing Flame (Send the Fire)' (SF2 955); 'There's a Wind a-Blowing (Sweet Wind)' (SF2 1044). The impersonal nature of Spirit language has been one of the most disturbing aspects of revival culture, and has undoubtedly fostered an unhealthy interest in power. More importantly, however, the sacramental dimension ensures that the predicate of Christian worship is grace and not anxiety. Such an evangelical catholicity need not be in opposition to experience, or the desire for greater intimacy; rather, it should be the necessary forerunner and context. Communion counters the paradoxical angst that is created between the worshipper and God in some revival settings by insisting that holiness, prayer, and intimacy are located *within* the realm of grace and not external or preconditional to it. In many ways, it achieves this more naturally than preaching, as Hans Urs von Balthasar argued.[14] The eucharistic movement of death and resurrection transcends the predilection in evangelical spirituality of conceiving salvation only as soul-making and kingdom-building, and provides, instead, ecclesial and eschatological space – a *perichoretic* dimension – in which Christian existence is conceived, along Irenaean lines, as both an act of grace and a reaffirmation of creaturely existence.[15] Irenaeus, Farrow asserts, was able to challenge the two expressions of gnostic thought – withdrawal and assimilation – by upholding a eucharistic eschatology that both affirms and challenges the world.

It is here, in communion, that both expressions of immediacy that we have uncovered in revivalism, namely fundamentalism and contextualisation, are subsumed by a theology of grace that is neither hurried nor bland. Far from representing a slavish repetition – a holding on to an irrelevant past – the eucharist is a way, as Kenneth Stevenson reminds us, 'of seeing a fragmented world, yearning for what it was always meant to be'.[16] It is a means of grace as well as an intimation of the costliness of discipleship.[17] The repeated and habitual event of eucharistic worship means the inculcation of what Ford calls 'the eucharistic self':[18] an identity that is 'placed' in Christ, 'timed' in the intersection of the new world in the old, and 'commanded' to live faithfully to it, never 'as the prerequisite for us being there, but rather the purpose for which we are sent out'.[19]

The impact of this eucharistic dimension upon revival-istic spirituality is potentially dynamic, for communion locates Christian existence as first and foremost an ecclesial identity – something, Farrow points out, that not even Barth's theology of the word could fully achieve, tending as it does towards abstraction.[20] It resolves the dilemma that many revivalist churches face by countering the neurosis of penitential piety, as Pannenberg describes it,[21] that is redolent within certain strands of present day revivalism, while at the same time protecting the peculiar and distinctive nature of Christian worship from reduction to consumer faith. Christian faith is both grace *in* Christ, but it is also conformity *to* Christ – salvation and Lordship combined. And what communion and baptism achieve, as signs of the central narrative of the gospel, is the convergence of both these themes: what might be termed 'cruciformity'.[22] Cruciformity, as a description of Christian spirituality, is a helpful conjunction of revela-tion and vitality – a conjunction so often broken by hyper-spirituality on the one side, and dead orthodoxy on the other. Such a spirituality is pivotal to the future of charismatic renewal, for it puts things in the right order: the creation of a robust Christian identity, a consequent discipleship in imitation of the cruciform pattern, integral to which is the movement outwards to the world.

Remembrance and Revival

The retrieval of this sacramental dimension, focusing in this first instance on communion, ought to make sense in a highly sensate and sensual culture: means of grace that appeal to the aesthetics of sight and taste as well as sound. The appeal, however, is not only in the area of aesthetics. Though there might be a certain trendiness in the recovery of ancient liturgies, the real importance of retrieving a sacramental dimension to revivalistic spirituality is found in its ability to keep central the gospel narrative, of what God has done in and through Christ and the Spirit. Sacramentality is rooted in the notion that the most important factor in the delicate but necessary tension between the church and the world is the distinctiveness and peculiarity of Christian worship, in which the core drama of Christian faith is re-presented week after week.[23] Just so, the church avoids the latent tyranny that can often attach itself to the immediacy of revivalistic enthusiasm, too dominated by questions of knowing,[24] while, simultaneously, presenting to the world the peculiarity of the Christian story that includes within it progressive and ascetical formation in the life of the believer. In the initiatory rite of baptism, and through the repeated act of communion, the church celebrates the incarnation movement of grace, within which 'all the practices of Christian faith are present in crystalline form',[25] and to which Christian living is a lifetime of reorientation to these new realities.

To be sure, Christian worship, understood as singing, can achieve this same narration, but we have already seen that, for all the positive features of worship in charismatic renewal, it cannot be relied upon wholly to transmit the faith in this way. Indeed, in various ways, as we argued in chapter two, it has displaced, through the overuse of particular revival motifs, the theological indices of grace; hence, the importance, in the overall trajectory of renewal, of reintroducing a robust sacramental dimension alongside existing patterns of worship in this critical second phase. Without it Christian discipleship, ecclesiologically and evangelistically, attenuates into mere activism, mood, or, worse still, paranoia. As T.M. Moore states forcibly:

> For all the indications that evangelicals are enjoying great success, we are not fulfilling the mandate that has been given to us to go and make disciples in all the nations. While a number of explanations could be proffered for this as-yet-unacknowledged failure of mission, certainly the sad state of the sacraments among congregations of evangelical convictions must not be overlooked. The sacraments were intended to establish, strengthen, and distinguish the church and to equip her for kingdom life and mission in every age and context.[26]

The church can only fulfil its function in the world, to be salt and light, if it is distinctive; it can only begin to be distinctive if it ritually traces the contours of the Christian faith as presented in word and sacraments.[27] Contrary to the anti-ritualistic instinct of Protestant faith, this view requires us to see ritual – both communion and baptism – not so much as an interpretation of previously held convictions, but rather as actualisations of Christian understanding. Holiness, then, becomes an exercise in faithfully reflecting and retracing the core drama of the gospel – an absolute necessity for grace to be seen as authentic, but most definitely not a precondition of grace. Only as the church remembers, can it imitate Christ and progress.[28]

A theology of remembrance has a very different theological presupposition to that associated with revival. Arguably the terms are incompatible, predicated as they are on widely divergent agenda.[29] Whilst a theology of remembrance has an ecclesial focus – rooted in an appreciation of the ontological basis of the church – contemporary revivalism, on the other hand, has within its sight the disjuncture that exists between the church's life and the unfaith of the world – an essentially evangelistic, if not populist, focus. With the awareness that so many are outside the church, what business does the church have of retreating to the ghetto of its own in-house rituals? Thus runs the argument.[30] Invariably, however, commitment to revival, in both the strands we have located – classical holiness revivalism, and contemporary evangelicalism, with its emphasis on relevance – overwhelms the language of faith, thus leaving the church bereft of its major dogmas.[31] In the case of holiness spirituality, prayer warfare and charismatic worship in general, the matrices of grace are undercut by an excessive emphasis upon the deficiencies of the church's faith; in the case of such initiatives as Alpha and seeker-sensitive worship, grace is conceived without any real note of repentance and regeneration.

We have discussed already the thinking behind the latter approach: the concern to make the church accessible to outsiders, and to reflect the felt needs of the culture. The neglect of sacrament, in certain quarters, whilst reflecting a kind of Protestant gnosticism, most certainly has this missiological and cultural predicament in mind also: 'When people come to our church,' says one pastor, 'we want them to leave feeling like they have not even been in church.'[32] However, it is as well to reconsider the effectiveness of this approach. To a large extent, it is driven by an activist mindset that seeks to redress the decline of the church in the West. As such, it fails to recognise the unique opportunity, now delivered from the burden of maintaining Christendom, of re-conceiving its identity vis-à-vis the world in the particularity of the church's own faith convictions.[33] It is precisely this identity that has been lost in the growing secularisation of culture, for in the process the church has too often mimicked rather than acted as an alternative to the culture, thereby creating the possibility of being a church that is relevant, but without theological and spiritual weight.[34]

Signs of renewal in the church, therefore, such as the growth of Alpha, are not as trustworthy as we might think because, as Klaus Bockmeuhl observed, it is entirely possible for churches 'to add to their numbers even when the overall state of Christianity deteriorates'.[35] Indeed, it is our contention that this is what has happened. The general despair about the size of the church and its marginal existence in society is symptomatic of this spiritual deterioration, for it is an anxiety that is driven by an overtly secular agenda, namely growth, which at the same time has fostered neglect of the central themes of the gospel. Bockmeuhl once again:

> Secularisation of the church takes place when the church lets itself be determined by what happens to be the most venerable or newest or strongest factor in its environment (ideological, political, economic) or by what its environment announces to be the most pressing or most sacred aim or need of the moment.[36]

Therefore, prior to any further strategising and theologising concerning the success of Christian mission via Cell Church, Liquid Church, Alpha or otherwise, the constraints of the wider tradition requires there to be serious reflection about what the church is, both theologically and ontologically.

The recovery of the sacraments and the word – the power of remembrance as the way in which the gospel can be retold and reappropriated – is one way of attending to that challenge; a way that is entirely congruent with the nature of biblical faith. Since Christian faith is grounded in history and event, remembrance is the reflex action of the church that tells the story of the *magnalia Dei* in history.[37]

More pertinently, the act of remembering is critical because it ensures that the mission of the church to the world is energised by the gospel itself and not any other agenda, however laudable in terms of what the culture dictates, or what seems to be working elsewhere. Rather than being seen as an indulgence, the practice of remembrance is a vital resource the church possesses for awakening mission. Recollection of God's movement towards us and for us in Christ is the spiritual basis of all missiological activity by the church, because it is only out of the church's awareness of the gospel's power to initiate and sustain its own inner life that it can go forth into the world confident of the efficacy of its message. At the heart of revivalism ought to be a healthy regard, therefore, for the distinctive creeds, worship and social embodiment of Christian faith, lest the exhortation to greater obedience, or holiness, as so often occurs in revivalistic preaching and singing, acts in hostility to the doctrine of grace, and, conversely, lest membership of the church is diluted for the sake of growth.[38] A church celebrating and witnessing to the gospel's claim upon its own life is an anticipation – a necessary one at that – of the gospel's challenge to the world.

Communion in the History of Revival

Paradoxically, for we might imagine it otherwise in charismatic renewal, the Holy Spirit is pivotal in the churchly act of remembering, for it is the Spirit, in Johannine understanding, who 'will take what is mine and declare it to you'.[39] To consign the Holy Spirit simply to the execution of God's activity in mission, which occurs, as we shall see, in some Pentecostal theology, or to denigrate the work of the Spirit simply to that which is immediate, is to miss the important liturgical function the Holy Spirit has in the business of remembrance – a point that perhaps only a charismatic within the Catholic tradition can fully appreciate. Based on the understanding of the Holy Spirit in the Catechism as 'the Church's living memory', Hocken makes the assertion that 'the Holy Spirit will always remind the Church of the life, deeds and words of her Lord, and will make these present and efficacious in her midst'.[40]

Issues of pneumatology aside, however, and returning to our main theme, 'eucharist, in particular, helps us to remember God's decisive action in Christ,'[41] by rooting worship in the main drama of the gospel story. As the term eucharist implies, it is an understanding of worship that is instinctively a reflex action of thanksgiving – in response to the movement of God towards us in Christ – and as such, it would provide an important check upon a movement that, out of its despair concerning its limited success, can often, as we have argued, neglect this celebration of the gospel. 'The weakness of much current work and preaching,' commented Forsyth, 'is that it betrays more a sense of what has yet to be done than of what has already been done.'[42] Such has been the charge that we have levelled against the renewal movement at this particular juncture in its history. Sacramental worship helps to allay some of that despair by anchoring revivalistic zeal and aspiration in a present enjoyment of the victory and Lordship of Christ. A crucial question in this, however, is whether a predominantly non-sacramental renewal movement can now retrieve this dimension of Christian worship without believing it has betrayed its spiritual vision.

Part of the reason for the bifurcation in sacramental and charismatic spirituality at this point is a misunderstanding of terms. According to certain preconceptions, the language of remembrance is inert, dead language that stultifies spiritual growth, in contrast to the vital and pressing language of revival. However, as Fee points out, *anamnesis* is not the recalling of past events for the sake of nostalgia;[43] rather, in the light of the resurrection, it is the recalling into the present the very real and substantial events of death and resurrection, in order that they might be celebrated, enjoyed, even participated in.[44]

Transparently, there are differences in historical theology about the exact nature of what transacts in the sacrament; and these differences are by no means irrelevant to the issues being discussed here.[45] Transubstantiation is a position that, with the exception of Catholics, most in renewal will want to avoid; but an understanding of sacrament as prophetic sign is one that is increasingly being employed at the popular level to register dissatisfaction with a merely symbolic, or memorial, view of communion. Something approximating to this position is what we offer here: an understanding of sacrament, which moves beyond the Zwinglian memorialism of frontier revivalism to embrace the notion of sacrament as instrumental in the transmission of grace to the church.

Exegetically, such a position is tied to the etymology of *anamnesis*, which implies present enjoyment of, and encounter with, the living Christ in whose name it is done. Drawing upon Hebrew designations in the Psalms and elsewhere, where the remembrance of a name makes it alive, Marjorie Sykes elaborates on its meaning for our understanding of eucharist: 'The celebration of the Eucharist as a "memorial" is the releasing of Christ's

power and personality afresh.'[46] This should not be confused with the medieval notion of a repeated and actual
sacrifice; on the contrary, *anamnesis* should be viewed as
the 'perpetual recalling and energizing of the church of
that one sacrifice'[47] – just that re-energising in the gospel
that we are claiming lies at the heart of the present malaise
where faith has been eroded to the level of feeling or
rationality.

For revivalists to pass by such an obvious possibility
of liminality seems short-sighted, as well as unhistorical.
The history of revival – the Great Awakening in particular
– shows that communion has a central place in revival
historiography. The converting power of the communion
services at Cambuslang, Scotland,[48] is well attested to,
and may come as something of a surprise to charismatic
revivalists who have almost no instinct for such occasions.[49]
Indeed, the roots of North American revivalism can be
traced back to these Scottish Presbyterian 'sacramental
seasons', even if, eventually, the centrality of communion
diminished, in favour of the altar call.[50] Indeed, Edward's
sacramental position, often understood as a reaction to
Solomon Stoddard's belief in communion as a 'converting
ordinance',[51] was, in fact, influenced, as William Danaher
has shown, by the Scottish Presbyterian communions,
resulting in a view of the Lord's Supper which was both
memorial as well as a means of grace that satisfies the
spiritual appetite.[52] Similarly, among revivalists in the
Great Awakening, John Wesley held to the importance of
communion in the midst of revival.[53] Like Calvin, Wesley
understood the Holy Spirit as effecting the sacrament[54] – a
view carried over, as Lester Ruth has shown, into American
Methodism[55] – so that he too could speak of it, at times, as
a converting ordinance.[56]

When one considers that there were other legitimate
options available to Wesley, such as the religion of ecstasy

of the French prophets,[57] then it becomes clear that Wesley in fact retained the centrality of eucharist precisely because it rooted the revival in the actual and the tangible, though it was a means itself of encounter. In this respect, one notes Wesley's disquiet about the doctrine of 'stillness', purported by the Moravian Philipp Molther. This doctrine encouraged the abstinence from all the ordinances, particularly the Lord's Supper, and to 'be still', until true, saving faith, without doubt or fear, was attained. It was a doctrine of immediacy no less, in which Christ and not any ordinance is the only true means of grace. Wesley was appalled at such a doctrine. The sacraments were God-given and helpful both to the seeker and to the Christian wanting to grow in sanctification.[58] Indeed, Wesley's understanding of communion deepened rather than lessened after his renowned heart-warming experience at Aldersgate. In the history of charismatic renewal in the UK the opposite trend has often prevailed; sacramentality reduces in proportion to experientialism.[59]

In summary, classic holiness revivalism, and, more recently, charismatic experientialism are both expressions of spiritual immediacy.[60] But what is removed in a spirituality of the immediate, often by way of neglect rather than by deliberate disavowal, is an appreciation of the way Christian faith has typically, and traditionally, been sustained by a sacramental dimension. Indeed, the whole range of ecclesial activity, from pastoral care to missionary endeavour ought to be predicated on such a spiritual and theological agenda. This is not to say the church is only the church as it gathers around the word or the Lord's Table, but it is to recognise the importance of sacrament for the ongoing sustenance of the church. Aiden Kavanagh has stated the matter, concerning the place of eucharist and indeed baptism, which we shall examine below, in the following way:

The whole economy of becoming Christian, from conversion and catechesis through the eucharist, is the fundamental paradigm for *remaining* Christian. The experience of baptism in all its paschal dimension, together with the vivid memory of it in the individual and the sustained anamnesis of it in every sacramental event enacted by the community at large, constitute not only the touchstone of Catholic orthodoxy, but the starting point for all catechesis, pastoral endeavour, missionary effort, and liturgical celebration in the church.[61]

Coupled to proper catechesis, and careful preparation – what amounted in the early Christian communities to a period of up to two years – communion and baptism could be the missing sacramental dimension to a churchmanship conceiving its theology and praxis out of despair. It is by staying faithful to the basic narrative of Christian faith that the church is edified, as well as dynamically energised, in its call to be a witnessing community. This pertains to baptism, no less than the eucharist, as Kavanagh reminds us. The public act of baptism in the church is not just a cause for celebration that another member has been added to the church; something more is happening in the baptism, which pertains to the edification of the church: 'In the one being baptised, the church sees herself, sees her conversion, sees her own paschal faith, and thus the church is edified.'[62] It is to baptism we now turn.

Believing Before Belonging: The Politics of Baptism

Baptism represented in the early church the culmination of the catechetical procedure, during which instruction was given and exorcism was performed.[63] Through this process a candidate was truly initiated into the faith life of the church. Nor did it stop there. Baptism presupposed but also prescribed instruction, thus reflecting the injunction in Matthew's Gospel to baptise and teach. Post-baptismal Christian faith deepened through mystagogy, and 'renews in the reception of eucharist, in prayer, in ascetical struggle, so that the baptisand's whole life reflected his faith – the church's faith – in God's saving power'.[64]

At present in our contemporary scene, for reasons discussed above, no such rigorism exists. Where it has been pursued, as with the shepherding movement, it has been subject to abuse and has therefore been rejected.[65] One notes, therefore, the diminution of models of discipleship within the charismatic movement because of the failures of the past. Thus, we have a general commitment to baptism, but without the catechetical, pastoral and evangelistic apparatus that ought to support it. Given the potential that the renewal evinced in the early years for developing a thoroughgoing catechesis, such a state of affairs is disappointing, to say the least, and has not been fully overcome through Alpha. In fact, Alpha may be accused of adding to the general malaise by hardly mentioning baptism at all. Courses such as Alpha achieve this reduction of faith by way of a very popular and deliberate missiological ploy: the notion of 'belonging before believing'.[66]

This slogan lies behind a large number of evangelistic drives in recent years. The phrase is referred to explicitly in Emmaus Way,[67] is implicit in Alpha,[68] and is also a feature of Cell Church.[69] Reference is also made to the concept of 'belonging before believing' in an Evangelical Alliance magazine article endorsing an advertising campaign run by St Thomas' Church, Crookes, Sheffield – something of a flagship of Anglican charismatic renewal – seeking to attract young people to the church.[70] The campaign is expressive of the pathology that we were seeking to describe in part one, for it is about how one church set about advertising 'as national church attendance hits an all time low'.[71]

In the postmodern setting of social dislocation, such an approach has a number of advantages, not least the accessibility of the church to the outsider, free from dogmatic and ethical prerequisites, yet relationally strong. Nevertheless, the theological problem with 'belonging before believing' is that it circumvents the scandal of the cross, as symbolised in baptism – an offence that must be negotiated if true conversion and true *belonging* to the community of faith is deemed to have occurred. It is here that the epithet 'belonging before believing' breaks down. At its most pernicious it equates to an easy believism for the sake of recruitment, the pastoral and evangelistic ramifications of which are, one hopes, obvious. Jensen's comments about the retrieval of baptism in this context are germane:

> If baptism as interpreted at a time and place is puny or speaks inappropriately to the gospel, it is most likely the actuality and self-conception of the church that are antecedently puny or remote from the gospel. And when we perceive such sickness, reshaping of baptism must be and often has been a chief means to reform the church.[72]

If 'belonging before believing' represents a crisis of confidence in the churchly nature of Christian faith, then a renewed understanding of baptism must seek to reawaken the instinct for the dramatic and narratival base of the church's existence – a narrative focused on judgement and grace. The recovery of baptism, as the initiation into the Christian community, is central to the recovery of gospel identity as it relates to a churchmanship and a Christian movement that has diluted, for spurious reasons, the terms of its membership.

Among charismatic renewalists, it is David Pawson who articulates this position most clearly. Baptism is what Jesus refers to when he says, 'Unless a man is born of water and the Spirit, he cannot be born again.'[73] Indeed, so central for Pawson is the sacrament of baptism in the trajectory of Christian faith, that it becomes the crucial component of his four-stage salvation-initiation complex.[74] Too often, he opines, Christian conversion amounts to nothing more than a sinner's prayer, a one-time decision, which falls short of the initiation complex where baptism is vital.[75]

Crucial to this initiation complex is baptism as immersion. Not only does the biblical language *baptizo* demand as much, the nature of saving faith we are upholding here, as being constitutive of Christian discipleship, requires it to be so. Appealing to Hippolytus and the baptismal rites prescribed in *The Apostolic Tradition*,[76] Willimon notes: 'The physical inconvenience of the bath signified so well the renunciation and risk involved in discipleship. The politics of baptism is a politics of renunciation, and our rites must be strong enough to signify the cost.'[77] What the church recalls and celebrates in the baptism is just that awareness, which was referred to earlier, of a life that has died and has risen with Christ – the indicative of the faith that becomes the touchstone for all the ensuing imperatives. And in the fresh appropriation of that indicative in the event of baptism, the church is also able to articulate the nature and costliness of Christian living arising from identification and participation in Christ.

Again, it is important in the interests of revivalist spirituality that we understand the relationship between the indicative and the imperative this way round. As we follow the trajectory of baptismal theology in the New Testament, we see that the call to holiness, expressed in the imperative to 'not let sin reign in your mortal body',[78] is predicated on this prior reckoning that life has indeed passed, through baptismal obedience, from death to life, more specifically death to sin and alive to Christ Jesus.[79] Holiness is the logical outworking of a baptised life. As George Beasley-Murray notes concerning Pauline baptismal theology, 'the exhortations in his epistles simply repeat what has happened in baptism'.[80] To distinguish between the ontic and the ethical in baptism is simply fallacious; Christianity is a particular way of living made possible and determined by the ontological new existence that comes to pass in baptism.[81] The ethical note of sanctification derives its power and legitimacy not from the perfectionism or even legalism that so often feature in revival circles, but from the regenerative power of grace itself. Certainly the moral imperative needs to be heard – not to properly articulate what a baptised life might ethically look like is to render the baptismal formulae of 'putting off and putting on' innocuous[82] – but throughout there is an awareness that it is the act of grace itself, expressed in a sacramental view of baptism, that contains the *imprint* of what life looks like, as well as the power to effect it.

Evangelical Sacramentalism

The issue of the sacraments is, of course, part of the on-going conversation between non-sacramental revivalism and high-church orthodoxy. If orthodoxy is critical of the experientialism of pietistic religion, non-conformists have often derided their opponents for their dead ritualism. For this reason, notes Christopher Ellis, Baptist theology has often avoided the language of sacrament to describe baptism, for the idea that salvation is tied to any one means of grace threatens, so it is perceived, the belief in the free sovereignty of God.[83] Resolution of the antipathy for renewalists ought to be found, however, not in a weak view of sacraments, but rather in a more intense one: in the case of baptism an instrumental, and not just symbolic, understanding of the event.[84] Baptism as ordinance flattens the dramaturgy of Christian worship,[85] whereas, sacramentally, baptism in water 'can become a "rendezvous" with the crucified and risen Christ'.[86] The Petrine assertion that 'baptism saves you' may well confirm this view, without being confused with baptismal regeneration: namely, that in the actual event of baptism the forgiveness of sins effected on the cross becomes actualised, so that what one receives in baptism is a fresh assurance of forgiveness, and an immersion into that eschatological life which Christ himself has passed into by virtue of his filial obedience. Wayne Grudem supports this view by reading *eperotema* in 1 Peter 3:21 as 'appeal' rather than 'pledge': that is, in baptism we make an appeal for just that assurance of sins forgiven that makes baptism a celebration of the gospel.[87] The rite is pivotal to Christian living and, as with our comments on preaching, confirms to us the full drama of salvation. It takes seriously both the human predicament and the gospel response, thus keeping alive the atmosphere of crisis. That the notion of crisis does not sit comfortably alongside a consumerist culture need not deter the church from following this practice. Instead, the church ought to regard it as paramount to create a sense of crisis where none exists, thus acting in a truly prophetic way as a sign of a different kingdom,[88] for the loss of baptism in Christian piety is simultaneously, as Alexander Schmemann observed, a loss of a distinctive Christian philosophy: there is simply no difference between the values accepted inside the Christian community and those outside of it.[89] Conversely, a high view of baptism engenders a radical view of Christian living in the world, thus realising, in an altogether different way, the very aspirations of charismatic renewal for a form of religion with power.

Again, this suggests that sacraments not only symbolise something but also do something, and the thing they do is convey the very thing they point to.[90] Sacraments, claims Jensen, contain the grace they point to, because 'if sacraments pointed us elsewhere than to where they are themselves happening, it would be up to us to get us there, and faith would again be replaced by works'.[91] As with preaching, sacraments not only mean something but also enact something, and what they enact is critical for the ongoing sustenance of faith. Beasley-Murray and Pawson share this understanding of instrumentality in relationship to baptism.[92]

Far from being alien to renewalist instincts, such a view of sacraments ought to be seen as commensurate with it, for it posits a faith that is enacted, intimate and able to deliver. Through the instrumentality of baptism, an understanding of transference from the kingdom of darkness into the eschatological kingdom of the Son is granted, understood as something that has indeed happened and can be recalled. The bath is the external embodiment of this movement, but it is nonetheless Christ who is doing the baptising.[93] In and through the baptism there is an awareness – one which is absent in any reduction of the gospel along the lines discussed – of the eschatological future breaking into the present. The Spirit's activity in reinforcing this eschatological perspective is critical, as we shall see (which makes it all the more lamentable that charismatic perceptions of the Spirit are so often related only to charismata). For through the Spirit, and in the event of baptism, something more than just a notional understanding of forgiveness is granted. Indeed, through the Spirit and water, the church is enabled to become in the present what in reality it is before God, both eternally and eschatologically.

A similar thing might be claimed for communion, which we alluded to earlier in the discussion of *anamnesis.* In communion, the indicative of faith – the becoming of what we already are through the death and resurrection of Christ – finds space to re-enact. In communion the church offers itself up in the sacrament of Christ's redeeming sacrifice,

> in order that thereby the church itself may become within time what in reality it is before God – the 'fulness' or 'fulfilment' of Christ; and each of the redeemed may 'become' what he has been made by baptism and confirmation, a living member of Christ's Body.[94]

Worship patterns that are influenced by utilitarian concerns or by existential categories, in ways that we have outlined above, may not always realise these dogmatic, liturgical and ontological indices. Indeed, they may mimic the very culture they are seeking to transform, precisely at the point at which worship seeks to be relevant to the culture. Adherence to a sacramental dimension does not *ipso facto* guarantee redress of this situation, of course, because it too can be subject to manipulation. But in the context of revivalistic enthusiasm, it would at least ensure – in the absence of any intentional commitment within the hymnody and rhetoric of the renewal movement – that the salvific contours of Christian theology were highlighted, thereby avoiding the reduction of the gospel to Schleiermacher's 'feeling of dependence'.[95]

A commitment to a sacramental dimension, such as we are advocating here, does not require an abandonment of the liveliness of charismatic-worship, nor an abandonment of its genius in the area of intimacy; one might even argue it requires it as a necessary adjunct. But it does root such worship in recognisably gospel shapes and reinforces, if not introduces, to the worshipper the magnitude of the claims of Christian theology. As Gunton puts it:

> Baptism ... gives social embodiment and expression to that different place in which justification sets the sinner, the place where the Word is heard and the Supper celebrated. To live under the discipline of the Word and the Table *is* to be one whose way of being is altered ...[96]

Baptism is the fulcrum of the theological agenda we are seeking to implement here on behalf of the renewal movement. More than symbolically, baptism brings about a change in being, the new reality of grace among the people of God, which is reinforced by the repeated telling of the gospel and the repeated acceptance of the saving significance of the gospel in the supper. In themselves, they are the power tools for Christian ministry. As such, they allow us to disavow fads, of a spiritual or strategic nature, on the basis that these things can never relay the efficacy of the gospel itself to do its own work, both ecclesiologically and missiologically.[97] Co-option into Christ through baptism and communion is the spiritual core that protects Christian faith from the angst of revivalist religion and, conversely, the potential blandness of contemporary worship.

That such an approach has been termed academic, or indulgent, is an indictment of the quality of the church's faith. Forsyth is pertinent again to our argument here. 'We are charged with being academic', complained Forsyth, 'with offering professional theology when what is needed is practical direction. But has the church really come to treat the soul's whole moral reliance upon Christ's judging and saving death as a piece of professional theology?'[98]

The deployment of the sacrament of the word, baptism and eucharist, are not the church being overly academic – nor overly liturgical, for that matter – but the church being itself: the church attending to what it has done historically to keep alive truly gospel speech. After all, it is Paul who tells us that the Lord's Supper proclaims 'the death of the Lord until he comes'.[99] And by retaining this sacrament of grace, the church challenges the reduction of the gospel to method or experience. It is a summons not only to adhere to but also participate in the facticity of the death and resurrection of Christ, initiated by baptism and sustained by communion, with the notion of remembrance central to both.

The interweaving of this sacramental perspective into the present situation affecting radical evangelicalism could be dismissed as a hopeless marriage of catholic and evangelical doctrines, but, as Stanley Grenz points out, it is only recently that evangelicalism has settled into an uncatholic sectarianism. The forebears of the evangelical awakening 'did not limit their renewal interests but were concerned for the whole church of their day'.[100] Both Wesley and Edwards inherited this catholic vision, he argues; hence, theirs was not the desire to erect a new ecclesiological structure, but rather to re-envision the one church in all its entirety.[101] While it may be the case, aesthetically and liturgically, that catholic and evangelical theology express significantly different spiritualities, these need not be regarded as theologically opposite; rather, the convergence of catholic and evangelical theologies ought to be seen as an attractive option. The urgency of convergence is tied to the cause of theological aesthetics, as well as a wider ecumenism; but most importantly the retrieval of a theology of remembrance, made possible in eucharist and baptism, enables the church to recover and retain its distinctive identity in the world.

Again, such an approach necessitates a suspension of revivalist attempts to resurrect the Constantinian order, or indeed the early church: the attempt to reconstruct a glorious, if somewhat mythical, Christian past. As Walker warns, we must resist the temptation to read revival back into the New Testament record.[102] Instead, the church should be seeking to recover its call as a prophetic, indeed proleptic, sign of the kingdom of God in the world – a concept not entirely alien to early renewal theology; and integral to this is the reawakening of the memory of the church, through the word and the sacraments, to its baptismal identity.

That this recovery should be criticised as a return to the ghetto, or as cultural isolationism, proves how far the church has felt intimidated by the modernist agenda, but also proves how misunderstood the recovery of this identity is. For in recovering its identity, and recovering the gospel, the church enters into the largeness of the purposes of God, embracing the world's predicament with a gospel that can truly save. We must not assume that in this missional purpose the church always has to respond to the world's questions. In fact, unless the inductive principle is qualified by more overtly theological principles it will be guilty of trivialising the gospel.[103] Hence, the church needs the academy, even as academy needs the church, for the separation of church and academy has encouraged the unprecedented development of church praxis outside the bounds set by the theological traditions of the church.[104] We are proposing, in response, an alternative way of conceiving revival, in which revival finds its primary referent in the recovery of the church's distinctive and prophetic place in society. Thus, much of what we call pastoral care and Christian formation, both liturgically and sacramentally, is in fact mission. 'The community, in its corporate life,' claims Richard Hays, 'is called to embody an alternative order that stands as a sign of God's redemptive purposes in the world.'[105] If there is no semblance of sign, corporately and sacramentally, then the church, despite its strident propaganda, has nothing to say.

Part of the prophetic call of the church is to witness to a community in which the old distinctions that demarcate people from one another are eradicated. Specifically, the call of the church is to witness to a faith that refuses to be attenuated into private and penitential piety. Conceiving personhood as an ecclesial, communitarian affair has been, in recent years, a necessary corrective to the overly Augustinian, individualistic bias of western theology.[106] Baptism is not merely an individual faith statement, a private event celebrating personal faith, but an incorporation into the body of Christ: 'For we were all baptised by one Spirit into one body – whether Jews or Greeks, slave or free – and we were all given the one Spirit to drink.'[107] Baptismal language, pneumatologically as well as sacramentally, assumes corporate and familial notions of faith that at the same time bring into judgement the social barriers erected on issues of race, gender, age and wealth.

Such radical reconception of relationship undoubtedly calls into question the Church Growth principle of homogeneity, which, as we have already noted, lies behind a number of evangelistic initiatives in recent years.[108] Neither Jew nor Greek, slave nor free, has within its horizon a vision of a church that embodies in its social diversity and cultural heterogeneity the new society for which Christ died and rose again;[109] homogeneity, on the other hand, though it may facilitate the growth of larger churches, and may make evangelistic sense, is too reminiscent of the cultural world surrounding the church to have any integrity as far as Christian witness is concerned. In fact, homogeneity is itself, as a guiding principle, coterminous with the overall malaise within culture, and in so far as the church adopts it will need, as Miroslav Volf correctly points out, to be healed before it can make any worthwhile contribution to the salvation of Christendom.[110]

The retrieval of baptism is one way, we suggest, of enabling that healing, but central to the retrieval is an insistence upon baptism as an ecclesial affair. This is not as straightforward as it might seem, for the way baptism has been administered, in the Nonconformist setting particularly, has often reinforced individualism. But as Beasley-Murray points out: 'A baptism in which the church is not interested is a curious development of baptism in the church.'[111] Baptism is about entrance into the life of the church; explicating baptism in this way, in the act of preaching, is one way to achieve this.[112] Communion also is vital in underlining the communitarian dimension of Christian faith, not least because the injunction to examine oneself prior to partaking of communion, lest one fails to discern the body of Christ,[113] is in fact an encouragement of this very thing: not introspection concerning private sins, but honesty as to whether one really does accept the commonality of Christian faith with rich and poor alike.[114] If, in the process, a commitment to the principle of heterogeneity does not lead to large churches, revivalists need to ask whether this is, in fact, so disastrous. The principle of heterogeneity – the creation of churches that are genuinely a cross-section of society – is so enshrined as determinative of the new people of God, that without some evidence of its occurrence it is difficult to gauge, despite numerical indices of growth, whether or not the gospel has found a home.[115]

Notes

1   See Pannenberg, *Systematic Theology Volume 3*, 336–69, for a discussion about the ambivalence of the term sacrament.

2   G. Wainwright, *For Our Salvation: Two Approaches to the Work of Christ* (London: SPCK, 1997), 11. In fact, something of an ecumenical convergence has taken place in the twentieth century, 'toward a principle of Sunday assembly in which the scriptures are read and proclaimed and the Lord's meal is celebrated' (14).

3   M.J. Thompson, 'Worship as an Ecclesial Paradigm', *Theology*, 102:1 (1999), 10–19.

4   See Scotland, *Charismatics*, 75.

5   A. Schmemann, *Church, World, Mission: Reflections on Orthodoxy in the West* (Crestwood: St Vladimir's Press, 1979), 60.

6   Percy, *Words, Wonders and Power*, 77–8.

7   See P.J. Lee, *Against The Protestant Gnostics* (Oxford: Oxford University Press, 1989), 103.

8   Irenaeus, *Against Heresies: The Works of Irenaeus: Ante-Nicene Library Volume 2* (Edinburgh: T&T Clark, 1869), 5:2:3: 'When, therefore, the mingled cup and the manufactured bread receives the Word of God, and the Eucharist of the blood and the body of Christ is made, from which things the substance of our flesh is increased and supported, how can they affirm that the flesh is incapable of receiving the gift of God, which is life eternal.' For a fuller treatment of how Irenaeus countered the gnostic heresy and the relevance of his theological vision in the contemporary setting see D. Farrow, *Ascension and Ecclesia: On the Significance of the Doctrine of the Ascension for Ecclesiology and Christian Cosmology* (Edinburgh: T&T Clark, 1999), 66–73.

9   See N. Clark, *An Approach to the Theology of the Sacraments* (London: SCM, 1956), 74–5.

10 Irenaeus, *Against Heresies* Volume 1, 4:17:5.

11 D. Farrow, 'St Irenaeus of Lyons: The Church and the World', *Pro Ecclesia: A Journal of Catholic and Evangelical Theology* 4:3 (1995), 341.

[12] C.E. Gunton, *Christ and Creation* (Carlisle: Paternoster, 1992), 78.

[13] For a discussion of this see A. Thiselton, *Interpreting God and the Postmodern Self: On Meaning, Manipulation and Promise* (Edinburgh: T&T Clark, 1995), 21–5. See also R. Macaulay and J. Barrs, *Being Human: The Nature of Spiritual Experience* (Carlisle: Solway, 1996).

[14] H.U. von Balthasar, *Prayer* (San Francisco: Ignatius Press, 1986 [1955]), 28: 'We Catholics must certainly admire and seek to emulate its [Protestantism's] earnest study of the word of God, but too often it lacks something that could lift it to genuine contemplation and vision, namely, the Word's indwelling, in the order of being, in the eucharist and in the Church at large as the Mystical Body and the vine.'

[15] Farrow, 'St Irenaeus of Lyons', 351–5.

[16] K. Stevenson, *Do This: The Shape, Style and Meaning of the Eucharist* (Norwich: Canterbury Press, 2002), 164.

[17] D. Bonhoeffer, *Life Together* (London: SCM, 1992 [1954]), 96.

[18] Ford, *Self and Salvation*, 137–65.

[19] Stevenson, *Do This*, 164.

[20] Farrow, *Ascension and Ecclesia*, 241–54.

[21] Pannenberg, *Christian Spirituality*, 31–49.

[22] The word cruciformity is coined by M. Gorman, *Cruciformity: Paul's Narrative of Spirituality of the Cross* (Grand Rapids/Cambridge: Eerdmans, 2001).

[23] On the importance of thanksgiving and the remembrance of covenantal history – specifically eucharistic remembrance – as the way of circumventing subjective sentimentality and postmodern epistemology see Pao, *Thanksgiving*, 59–85.

[24] C.E. Gunton, *A Brief Theology of Revelation* (Edinburgh: T&T Clark, 1995), 85. Cf., M. Harper: 'The neglect of the incarnation, and I would say the sacraments, together with the absence of a sound doctrine of creation, inevitably opens the door to gnosticism.' In correspondence with Michael Harper, 16 June 1998.

[25] See Dykstra and Bass, 'A Theological Understanding of Christian Practices' in M. Volf and D. Bass (eds.), *Practicing Theology: Beliefs and Practices in Christian Life* (Grand Rapids: Eerdmans, 2002), 30–31.

[26] T.M. Moore, 'Pastoral Ministry and the Place of the Sacraments' in J.H. Armstrong (ed.), *Reforming Pastoral Ministry* (Wheaton: Crossway, 2001), 206.

[27] For a fuller account of the purpose of ritual as ontological transformation, and the marginalisation of ritual in modern Catholic worship for the sake of relevance see D. Torevell, *Losing the Sacred: Ritual, Modernity and Liturgical Reform* (Edinburgh: T&T Clark, 2000).

[28] Though one must not discount, as Protestant theology tends to do, the important place habituated prayer, sabbath keeping, scripture reading, welcoming, and the like, have in the affirmation and progress of belief. For an exploration of this question: namely, the potential compatibility of Reformed and ascetical theology, see S. Coakley, 'Deepening Practices: A Perspective from Ascetical and Mystical Theology' in Volf and Bass (eds.), *Practicing Theology*, 78–93.

[29] Interestingly, Lovelace regards the recovery of sacraments as unimportant to his own theology of renewal, Lovelace, *Dynamics*, 169–70.

[30] See Pearse and Matthews, *We Must Stop Meeting Like This*, 143–55; Kelly, *Get a Grip*, 227–40; Sweet, *Soulsunami*, 145–59; Peters, *The Evangelist's Notebook*, 26–32.

[31] For a defence of the importance of tradition and memory in Christian self-understanding in the world see R.L. Wilken, *Remembering the Christian Past* (Grand Rapids: Eerdmans, 1995).

[32] Cited in C.E. Braaten, 'The Apocalyptic Imagination' in C.E. Braaten and R.W. Jensen (eds.), *The Last Things: Biblical and Theological Perspectives on Eschatology* (Grand Rapids: Eerdmans, 2002), 26. See also M. Budde and R. Brimlow, *Christianity Incorporated: How Big Business is Buying the Church* (Grand Rapids: Brazos, 2002), 79–82, who highlight the consumerist mentality in recent Church of England marketing campaigns.

[33] For an exploration of the importance of memory for the sustenance of faith, especially in relationship to the Psalms, see W. Brueggemann, 'Suffering Produces Hope', *Biblical Theology Bulletin* 28:3 (1998), 96–7, and 'The Hope of Heaven on Earth', *Biblical Theology Bulletin* 29:3 (1999), 100–101.

[34] See W.J. Abraham, *The Logic of Renewal* (London: SPCK, 2003), 78–92, for a critique of Willow Creek in this regard.

[35] K. Bockmeuhl, 'Secularisation and Secularism: Some Christian Considerations', *Evangelical Review of Theology* 10:1 (1986), 50–1.

[36] K. Bockmeuhl, 'Secularism and Theology' in D.M. Lewis (ed.), *With Heart and Mind and Strength: The Best of Crux 1979–89* Volume 1 (Langley: Credo, 1990), 39–54.

[37] M.J. Manninen, *Living the Christian Story: The Good News in Worship and Daily Life* (Grand Rapids: Eerdmans, 2000), 1–9.

[38] 'What we want is not more Christians but better Christians', wrote Gore, *St Paul's Epistle to the Ephesians* (London: John Murray, 1898), 190. Such an approach reminds us that the gathered church mentality, despite the inclusivity of the parochial system, is a strand of Anglican spirituality, going back to Herbert, Law and Butler. See A. Redfern, *Being Anglican* (London: Darton, Longman & Todd, 2000), 84–95.

[39] John 16:14 NRSV.

[40] Hocken, *Blazing the Trail*, 59, commenting on paragraph 1099 of the Catechism of the Catholic Church.

[41] Walker, *Telling the Story*, 97.

[42] P.T. Forsyth, *Missions in State and Church* (London: Hodder & Stoughton, 1908), 17.

[43] G.D. Fee, *The First Epistle to the Corinthians* (Grand Rapids: Eerdmans, 1987), 558.

[44] See J. Macquarrie, *A Guide to the Sacraments* (London: SCM, 1997), 139–40.

[45] See M. Welker, *What Happens in Holy Communion?* (trans. by J.F. Hoffmeyer; London: SPCK, 2000), 126–33. In describing the various theological positions, Michael Welker offers his own nuanced eucharistic theology where remembrance of

Christ is viewed as an effect of the Holy Spirit and a form of cultural power.

[46] M.H. Sykes, 'The Eucharist as Anamnesis', *The Expository Times* 71 (1960/1961), 117.

[47] G. Dix, *The Shape of the Liturgy* (Westminster: Dacre Press, 1947), 243.

[48] A. Fawcett, *The Cambuslang Revival* (Edinburgh: Banner of Truth, 1971).

[49] Although see T. Morton, *Covenant People* (Basingstoke: Marshall Pickering, 1986), 114–17, and M. Stibbe, *Thinking Clearly About Revival* (London: Monarch, 1998), 120–21.

[50] See L.E. Schmidt, *Holy Fairs: Scottish Communions and American Revivals in the Early Modern Period* (Princeton: Princeton University Press, 1989).

[51] A view perpetuated by William De Arteaga, *Forgotten Power: The Significance of The Lord's Supper in Revival* (Grand Rapids: Zondervan, 2002), 83–5.

[52] W.J. Danaher, 'By Sensible Signs Represented: Jonathan Edward's Sermons on the Lord's Supper', *Pro Ecclesia: A Journal of Catholic and Evangelical Theology* 7:3 (1998), 261–89. See also G.M. Marsden, *Jonathan Edwards* (New Haven and London: Yale University Press, 2003), 352–6.

[53] De Arteaga, *Forgotten Power*, 179–83.

[54] See J.F. White, *The Sacraments in Protestant Practice and Faith* (Nashville: Abingdon, 1999), 81–2.

[55] See L. Ruth, 'A Little Heaven Below: Quarterly Meetings as Seasons of Grace in Early American Methodism' (Unpublished PhD, University of Notre Dame, 1996).

[56] J. Wesley, *The Journal of The Rev. John Wesley, M.A. Volume 2, Nov.1, 1739* (ed. N. Cumock; London: Charles H. Kelly, 1909), 315.

[57] H. Schwartz, *The Knaves, Fools, Madmen and that Subtile Effluvium: A Study of the Opposition to the French Prophets in England 1706–1710* (Gainesville: University of Florida, 1978), 78–81. See also Ward, *The Protestant Evangelical Awakening*, 163–74.

[58] See J. Wesley, Sermon 16: 'The Means of Grace' in *The Sermons of John Wesley Volume 1* (London: Haymer Brothers and Lilly,

1874), 205–14. One notes in all of this the influence of Eastern Orthodoxy upon Wesley. See R.L. Maddox, 'John Wesley and Eastern Orthodoxy: Influences, Convergences and Differences', *Asbury Theological Journal* 45:2 (1990), 29–53.

[59] H. Snyder, *The Radical Wesley and Patterns for Church Renewal* (Downers Grove: Inter-Varsity Press, 1980), 40–44.

[60] D. Frank, *Less Than Conquerors: How Evangelicals Entered the Twentieth Century* (Grand Rapids: Eerdmans, 1986), 49.

[61] A. Kavanagh, *The Shape of Baptism: The Rite of Christian Initiation* (New York: Pueblo, 1978), 160–63.

[62] J.H. Erickson, 'Baptism and the Church's Faith' in Braaten and Jensen (eds.), *Marks of the Body of Christ*, 56.

[63] Kreider, *The Change of Conversion*, 17.

[64] Erickson, 'Baptism and the Church's Faith', 47.

[65] See D. Tomlinson, 'Shepherding: Care or Control?' in L. Osborn and A. Walker (eds.), *Harmful Religion: an Exploration of Religious Abuse* (London: SPCK, 1997), 26–42. See also D. Moore, 'The Shepherding Movement: A Case Study in Charismatic Ecclesiology', *Pneuma* 22:2 (2000), 249–70, who notes the more positive aspects of the shepherding movement.

[66] R. Gill, *A Vision for Growth* (London: SPCK, 1994).

[67] S. Cottrell, S. Croft, J. Finney, F. Lawson, R. Warren (eds.), *Emmaus: The Way of Faith, Stage 1: Contact: Ideas for Meeting People Where They Are* (National Society / Church Publishing House, 1996), 16.

[68] Gumbel, *Telling Others*, 17–18.

[69] See Galloway, 'Cell Church', 34.

[70] See Anon, 'On the Couch', *Idea: The Magazine for Members of the Evangelical Alliance UK* (January / February / March 2000), 24–5.

[71] Ibid., 24.

[72] R.W. Jensen, *Visible Words: The Interpretation and Practice of Christian Sacraments* (Philadelphia: Fortress, 1978), 151.

[73] John 3:5.

[74] D. Pawson, *The Normal Christian Birth* (London: Hodder & Stoughton, 1989), 44–56.

[75] Ibid., 249–57.

76 See G. Dix and H. Chadwick (eds.), *The Treatise on the Apostolic Tradition of St Hippolytus of Rome* (London: Alban Press, 1992), 30–8.

77 Willimon, *Peculiar Speech*, 60.

78 Romans 6:12.

79 Romans 6:1–3, Colossians 1:13–15.

80 G. Beasley-Murray, *Baptism in the New Testament* (London: Macmillan, 1962), 287.

81 Pannenberg notes a tendency among Lutheran theologians to misread Luther in this regard, seeing in Luther's insistence on continual penitence a weakening of baptismal assurance: 'This is a fateful misunderstanding that results in the dissolving of baptism in penitence instead of regarding penitence, after the manner of Luther, as a constant appropriation of the humanity that became concrete once for all in baptism.' Pannenberg, *Systematic Theology Volume 3*, 253.

82 See T.R. Schreiner and A.B. Caneday, *The Race Set Before Us: A Biblical Theology of Perseverance and Assurance* (Leicester: Inter-Varsity Press, 2001), 178–83. Warnings and admonitions are understood here as a means of grace for preserving the faithful.

83 C. Ellis, 'Baptism and the Sacramental Freedom of God' in P. Fiddes (ed.), *Reflections on the Water: Understanding God and the World through the Baptism of Believers* (Macon: Smyth & Helwys, 1996), 23–45.

84 S.K. Fowler, *More Than a Symbol: The British Baptist Recovery of Baptismal Sacramentalism* (Carlisle: Paternoster, 2002).

85 O.S. Brooks, *The Drama of Decision: Baptism in the New Testament* (Peabody: Hendrickson, 1987), 64–5, where he uses the term drama to convey that one's decision to be baptised in the name of Jesus Christ is also a portrayal of the intimate association with Christ.

86 P.S. Fiddes, 'Baptism and Creation' in Fiddes (ed.), *Reflections on the Water*, 57.

87 W. Grudem, *1 Peter* (Grand Rapids/Leicester: Eerdmans/Inter-Varsity Press, 1988), 163–5.

88 C.E. Gunton, *The Christian Faith: An Introduction to Christian Doctrine* (Oxford: Blackwell, 2002), 145, 'Both rites [Lord's

Supper and baptism] are centred on Jesus' death under the judgement of God … To be baptized is to accept that judgement, just as in the Supper, but this time more radically, to be *killed.*'

[89] See A. Schmemann, *Of Water and the Spirit: A Liturgical Study of Baptism* (Crestwood: St Vladimir's Press, 1995³).

[90] Ibid., 57–9. Schmemann notes the separation of 'form' and 'essence' in western sacramentalism, so that the grace of baptism, though it may be regarded as the fruit of Christ's death and resurrection, is not the event itself.

[91] R.W. Jensen, 'The Church and the Sacraments' in C.E. Gunton (ed.), *The Cambridge Companion to Christian Doctrine* (Cambridge: Cambridge University Press, 1997), 213. See also K. Rahner, *The Church and the Sacraments* (Tunbridge Wells: Search Press, 1986), 36, whose sacramental theology is an attempt to recognise the ontological nature of symbol.

[92] Beasley-Murray, *Baptism in the New Testament*, 263–6: 'There is no gift or power available to man in consequence of the redemption of Christ that is not available to him in baptism.' 263. See also Pawson, *The Normal Christian Birth*, 51.

[93] Jensen, 'The Church and the Sacraments', 213: 'It is ecumenical teaching that Christ himself is the agent of baptism; he personally does to the candidate whatever baptism does.'

[94] Dix, *The Shape of Liturgy*, 247.

[95] F.D.E. Schleiermacher, *The Christian Faith* (Edinburgh: T&T Clark, 1928), 5.

[96] Gunton, *The Christian Faith*, 146.

[97] P.A. Newton, 'The Pastor and Church Growth' in Armstrong (ed.), *Reforming Pastoral Ministry*, 263–80.

[98] Forsyth, *The Church and the Sacraments*, 23.

[99] 1 Corinthians 11:26.

[100] S.J. Grenz, *Renewing the Center: Evangelical Theology in a Post-Theological Era* (Grand Rapids: BridgePoint Books, 2000), 346–51.

[101] For an example of such catholicity see P.E. Thompson, 'A New Question in Baptist History: Seeing a Catholic Spirit

Among Early Baptists', *Pro Ecclesia: A Journal of Catholic and Evangelical Theology* 8:1 (1999), 15–72.

[102] Walker, *Telling the Story*, 61–2.

[103] D. McCullough, *The Trivialisation of God: The Dangerous Illusion of a Manageable Deity* (Colorado Springs: NavPress, 1995).

[104] See Braaten, *The Apostolic Imperative*, 183.

[105] R. Hays, 'Ecclesiology and Ethics in 1 Corinthians', *Ex Auditu* 10 (1994), 33. See also N.G. Wright, *New Baptists, New Agenda* (Carlisle: Paternoster, 2000), for the emergence of this perspective in charismatic renewal.

[106] See in particular J.D. Zizioulas, *Being as Communion* (London: Darton, Longman & Todd, 1985), 49–65, where he differentiates between the *hypostasis* of biological and ecclesial existence, the latter constituted by new birth through baptism.

[107] 1 Corinthians 12:13. See also Galatians 3:27.

[108] For a recent exposition of the importance of homogeneity versus the encumbrance of the principle of heterogeneity see G. Kelly, 'New Ways of Being and Doing Church', Spring Harvest, Skegness, 3–4 April 2002.

[109] G.D. Fee, *Gospel and Spirit: Issues in New Testament Hermeneutics* (Peabody: Hendrickson, 1991), 136–7.

[110] Volf, *After Our Likeness*, 18: 'Too often, the latter [Free Churches] merely reflect the cultural worlds around them along with the serious illnesses attaching to those worlds.'

[111] Beasley-Murray, *Baptism*, 282.

[112] Similarly, communion requires dogmatic formulation in preaching. See J. Driscoll, 'Preaching in the Context of the Eucharist: A Patristic Perspective', *Pro Ecclesia: A Journal of Catholic and Evangelical Theology* 11:1 (2002), 24–40.

[113] 1 Corinthians 11:28–29.

[114] See Fee, *The First Epistle to the Corinthians*, 531–68, for an exegesis of these passages along communitarian lines. See also Pannenberg, *Christian Spirituality*, 31–49.

[115] See Zizioulas, *Being as Communion*, 255. See also D. Edwards, 'The Church as a Sacrament of Relationships', *Pacifica* 8 (1995), 196: 'the Eucharist is an event of radical inclusivity and of radical relationality. A Eucharist which discriminates

between races, sexes, ages, professions, and social classes violates its eschatological nature. It fails to be the sacrament of communion.'

Chapter 5

Pneumatological Concerns

The Toronto Blessing and Spirit Baptism

Thus far we have attended to the most familiar marks of the body of Christ within the classical tradition: the practices of preaching the word as well as the sacraments of baptism and communion. It is baptism that initiates membership into the community of Christian faith and creates space for the word and communion to occur. These are the means of grace given to the church by which its internal life and mission are sustained. As such then, the renewal of the church, we are arguing, 'requires not only new ideas about the church, but renewed practices of being the church', which is a theological rather than a structural/strategic approach, and one that transcends the faddish nature of contemporary religion.[1] Moreover, knowledge of God, we have argued, is never unmediated. The practice of theology, through which God is encountered in the various means given to the church, is congruent with the essentially mediated nature of Christian salvation.

Cumulatively, the practices of the church secure and maintain Christian identity in the face of secularisation. They ensure that whatever else charismatic renewal achieves by way of societal impact, it is not at the expense of the church's primary vocation of celebrating, remembering and participating in the faith. Just so, the church remains alert to its christocentric identity. In addition, we have argued that the success of a movement is not to be assessed in the light of its numerical size; to do so is to submit to the dominion of the very idols that Christian faith is seeking to subvert. Rather, it is through faithful witness and worship – in churches that may never attain to the perceived yardstick of numerical success – that those powers are challenged, thereby presenting an alternative way of conceiving revival based on the creation and sustenance of a robust Christian consciousness.

The purpose of this chapter is to explore the relationship between the maintenance of this Christian identity and pneumatology. The absence of a pneumatological dimension would be an odd position for a charismatic pastor-theologian to take, to be sure. Hence, having explained the relationship of preaching and sacraments to such an overtly theological and spiritual agenda, it is here that a distinctively charismatic, pneumatological component of Christian faith and progress needs to be introduced, specifically Spirit baptism, that extends our definition of sacramentality, and dynamically relates to the theological means of grace that we have uncovered so far.

For the new churches, in particular, baptism in the Spirit was for many years the *sine qua non* of church life. The renewal of church structures, including apostolic and prophetic itinerancy, was never contemplated in isolation from the experience of being baptised in the Spirit. In fact, renewal of structures was always regarded as secondary to this critical initiatory rite, given invariably through the laying on of hands. One just cannot understand certain strands of renewal without it.[2] In this chapter we shall be arguing for its inclusion in the sacramental resources of the church, for in many ways, as we shall see, this is how it has been understood: not so much a badge of a particular churchmanship but a sacrament of grace that is vital in the development of Christian self-understanding.

Recent developments in the charismatic movement, namely Toronto, provide the immediate context of our inquiry, as well as a note of urgency; for, paradoxically, Toronto, and indeed the Vineyard movement as a whole, has undermined the classical Pentecostal self-understanding derived from Spirit baptism, and thus eroded the theological and specifically trinitarian categories that, as Hocken has shown, were evident in the very earliest Pentecostal experiences.[3] Of course, as Max Turner has correctly pointed out, charismatics, in general, have never been as insistent as Pentecostals on the notion of subsequence and separability – a phrase that describes the classical Pentecostal position on Spirit baptism, and early Restorationist theology in particular. They have had a more relaxed and flexible attitude towards Spirit experiences, preferring to speak of 'growth experiences'.[4] Toronto conforms especially well to that description; but in pursuing this course, Toronto illustrates a number of things that have already been referred to: the demise of sacramentality in the church, an excessive preoccupation with charismatic manifestations and a continuing captivity to spiritual movements.[5] There is a growing consensus that with the onset of Toronto a vital pneumatological dimension is being lost to the charismatic movement, eventually having repercussions for its overall ideology. At worst, warns John Hosier, 'A testimony to "an indistinct warm feeling" can become accepted as testimony to baptism in the Holy Spirit.'[6]

The blame for this loss is attributable, paradoxically, to the frequency, intensity and peculiarity of Spirit experiences by those involved in Toronto, to the point that the distinctiveness of Spirit baptism as an initiatory rite, bringing both spiritual assurance as well as empowering, has been blurred.[7] With the stress upon the experience of 'resting' and 'soaking', the sacramentality and uniqueness of Spirit baptism appears rather odd; with the focus so much at the level of phenomenology – be it shaking, jerking, laughing or falling over – the soteriological and initiatory purposes associated with classical teaching about Spirit baptism has been almost entirely obscured, if not rendered obsolete.

This is not to suggest that Toronto should be regarded in wholly negative terms. As an example of how Christian faith might successfully be translated into postmodern culture, Toronto has a number of positive aspects.[8] It resonates well with the interiority of postmodern spirituality, and displays a good deal that is authentic. We must beware the danger of ecclesiastical snobbery when it comes to discerning spirits, for there are very few vital movements of the Spirit that are without ambiguity. Negatively, however, Toronto can be viewed as part of a wider pathology of a church that has lost faith with its own articles of doctrine as well as a movement that has lost faith with its own pneumatological convictions about initiation into the Christian faith.[9] Toronto, as many commentators have pointed out, has a decidedly romantic slant: a view of the Spirit's work that is untrammelled by words and dogma.[10]

As Cray rightly points out, there is nothing intrinsically sinister about this situation. As with the epithet 'belonging before believing', 'experience prior to faith' is sympathetic to the postmodern context and may well be the primary way that Christian faith is transmitted in this next generation.[11] Certainly it reflects a commonplace biblicism, in which the Spirit is accorded a far greater place in conversion than is generally acknowledged in evangelical theology. But what Cray underplays, or is at least ambivalent about, is how the Toronto Blessing, in tying Spirit activity so closely to the notion of immediacy and to the cause of revival, has unwittingly weakened the integral place of the Holy Spirit in the *ordo salutis,* and moreover has contributed to the growing immaturity of the movement. 'Denied Baptism in the Spirit, the valid hunger for sensate experience of the supernatural was vulnerable to the offer of sub-biblical experiences ranging from the banal to the bizarre',[12] argues Pawson, concerning the way the Vineyard movement significantly avoided the classical teaching on Spirit baptism, thus detaching charismatic experience from its biblical moorings.

This has been a frequent criticism of Toronto, and explains why a number of evangelicals distanced themselves from the manifestations associated with it.[13] Authentic charismatic-evangelical spirituality requires a pneumatology that reciprocates with christology, but in a movement preoccupied with the peculiarities of Spirit manifestation this mutual dependency is severed, leading to a situation where, to use the Irenaean image of the two hands of God – Christ and the Spirit – the one hand does not know what the other is doing.[14] More pertinently, the loss of the conversion-initiation matrix has allowed an infantile, romantic spirituality to develop, where outside of ever more exotic experiences of the Spirit, nothing else of any spiritual significance is deemed to have occurred; hence, the pressure, within the setting of charismatic worship, to reproduce the atmosphere that allows such experiences to occur. This pressure has beset the charismatic movement throughout. It is a hallmark of revivalistic religion: as Carol Norén notes, 'something has gone wrong if no one "goes forward" at the conclusion of a revival sermon'.[15] But the expectation for ministry in this way has never been more intense than it has been post-Toronto.

Of course, the typical Pentecostal attempt to universalise Spirit baptism as a second work of grace has not always prevented this infantile spirituality either. Spirit baptism has not been followed through to a more mature faith and love, along the lines of the mystical tradition, and has been guilty of the same thing: 'the means of entrance into the land of perpetual holiday'.[16] However, we insist that being baptised in the Spirit, as a distinct phase in the process of conversion-initiation, is vital for ensuring that whatever other growth experiences one might have, they are predicated upon the initial experience of grace and empowering in Spirit baptism. Without this substantive grounding in the initiatory schema of the church, the sort of multiple Spirit manifestations associated with the Toronto Blessing could prove problematic. After all, what is one to deduce when the Spirit ceases to flow in such a way – for such intensity is unlikely to be sustained – and the 'season of refreshing' is over? Because the manifestation of the anointing is tied to such things as continual love for the anointing,[17] unity in the churches,[18] prayer and fasting[19] and impeccable holiness,[20] one can only conclude that an absence of the anointing is a sign of divine displeasure at the failure of the church to sustain these things. Instead of accepting the blessing as a free, sovereign act of God, the new wave of blessing eventually imposes a new burden upon the church to perpetuate it – what we might call the burden of immediacy – because without it grace ceases to operate. It is this that keeps leaders in charismatic renewal vulnerable to ever new 'waves' of the Spirit: 'If religion is to compete in the postmodern world it too must offer eye-catching wares, which is precisely what neo-Pentecostalism does. God has to top last year's eye-catching inventions in this world with something even more eye-catching this year.'[21]

In contrast, a theology of Spirit baptism at conversion, as a distinct and memorable encounter, avoids such legalisms, for it resonates with the grace language of the gospel itself.

Spirit baptism actualises, by way of assurance and seal, the grace of Christ. To be sure, receptivity in classical Pentecostalism, or any view of baptism as a distinct and separate experience, has its own problems too, and has been guilty itself of fostering insecurity among those who claim not to have experienced the gift. But theologically and experientially, we argue, the overall effect of Spirit experiences outside the matrix provided by faith, water baptism, Spirit baptism, as an initiatory and ecclesial process, is symptomatic of the trend we witnessed earlier: namely, an erosion of the dogmatic core of Christian faith and, moreover, a view of sanctification too dependent on continual receiving rather than on the initial grace of Christ.

Spirit baptism as a sacrament: the seal of the Spirit

Transparently, we are viewing Spirit baptism here in somewhat sacramental terms: Spirit baptism as instrumental in the initiation and sustenance of the believer in the grace of God. This is not a usual way of understanding pneumatology, but neither is it without precedent. Immersion in the Spirit, according to Paul, is the sign of the grace of God that precedes even the work of Christ.[22] For Pentecostals and early Restorationists this gift is imparted through the laying on of hands, as an ecclesial and apostolic event, thus appropriating the grace of God effected through the cross of Christ. With this experience comes assurance – the assurance that Romans 8:15–16 describes – whereby the Spirit testifies with our Spirit that we are children of God: the Spirit of adoption whom we have received and in whom we cry 'Abba' Father.

According to this understanding of charismatic activity, it is clear that the Spirit is not to be understood as self-referential (arguably, too much charismatic activity is conceived of in exactly this way, so that Spirit movements are often perceived by outsiders as being too preoccupied with manifestations of the Spirit). Instead, the coming of the Spirit, coupled to the person of Christ, mediates the Father's love.[23] That this should be interpreted via the metaphor of exodus/freedom and not simply intimacy is an important insight offered to us from recent New Testament scholarship, for what is clear is that immersion in the Spirit, concomitant with the gift of faith, is far richer theologically than the manifestations at Toronto, and indeed Pensacola, suggest.[24] It is, in fact, just that gift in the wider trajectory of Christian initiation, including water baptism, which enables the believer to participate in the *perichoresis* of the Father, Son and Holy Spirit. This ought to be the enduring legacy of charismatic renewal – a view of salvation that goes beyond the metaphors of forgiveness and acceptance to the ultimate intention of the work of Christ: persons in relationship.[25]

Such a theology of Spirit baptism, defined as sacrament and related to the doctrine of assurance is not without biblical or historical precedent, as Henry Lederle reminds us. The Puritan concept of baptism in the Spirit as the 'seal of the Spirit' – a view espoused by Thomas Goodwin and taken up more recently by Lloyd-Jones – tallies well with sacramental language.[26] To be sure, Lloyd-Jones, whose influence among Reformed charismatics is understandably considerable, was ambiguous on the issue of Spirit baptism – keen as he was to avoid a two-stage view of Christian experience[27] – yet his theology of assurance was in reality a variation of a two-stage view, concluding from texts such as Ephesians 1:13, Romans 8:15–16 and John 1:26, 1:33 that it was an experience of assurance given to the believer.[28]

In his discussion of Ephesians 1:13 and the terminology of sealing and guarantee, Lincoln notes the possible association of this language with water baptism. However, it seems more likely, he adds, 'that "sealing" in this verse is a reference to the actual reception of the Spirit on the part of the readers – a distinguishable event for the early Christians'.[29] Hence, Spirit baptism is regarded as the eschatological down payment of salvation in the age to come – a view consistent with the already / not yet tension found elsewhere in Paul. Spirit baptism is not a sign of spiritual prowess, nor of raw power, but of anticipation and inauguration.

For a renewal movement showing every sign at this juncture in its history of leaving Spirit experiences undefined, this vital and sacramental understanding of Spirit baptism provides a theological and pastoral grist that is just not in evidence in this more recent wave of charismatic manifestation. Spirit baptism signals, indeed protects, a soteriological and eschatological perspective for the renewal movement, ensuring that theological concerns dominate the understandable interest in phenomena. Moreover, Spirit baptism as a distinct and initiatory experience helps to counter the tendency in revival circles to view the anointing as an elusive, evanescent force, which must be repeatedly welcomed into our midst. Such an understanding of the relationship between the believer and the Holy Spirit is more akin to an Old Testament view, where the Spirit endows persons with charismatic anointing for specific tasks. More helpful, pastorally and theologically, is to recognise the abiding presence of the Spirit in the believer, received at conversion in Spirit baptism, bringing assurance of grace, and from whom the believer draws strength throughout.[30]

The ecclesial setting of the gift of the Spirit relates specifically to the way the Spirit is imparted, namely through the laying on of hands. A reading of Luke–Acts, from the initial Pentecost episode, evinces a paradigm of the laying on of hands, being baptised in the Spirit, followed by speaking in tongues or some other charismatic utterance: in short, spiritual grace that is mediated. Generally, charismatics have not seen the laying on hands in these sacramental terms. An exception to this is Wayne Grudem, who incorporates the laying on of hands into the array of means God gives the church to mediate grace – grace that includes healing, spiritual gifts and baptism in the Spirit.[31] In fact, his biblical treatment of the theme uncovers some interesting textual omissions of the practice. Generally, however, the possibilities for recovering the practice of the laying on of hands, leading to a spirituality that is both incarnational as well as inspirational, has been left underdeveloped. John Gunstone refers to the belief and practice of the laying on of hands in the patristic era, and in so doing seeks to integrate the Pentecostal gift of the Spirit into the sacramental life of the church,[32] but this sacramental view has not been taken up by the movement at large.

The neglect of the practice of the laying on of hands is unfortunate, to say the least. Not only does the omission intensify the increasing belief among charismatics that authentic spiritual experience is only unmediated; it also precludes the agency of the church as the location in which grace is mediated. For faith to be attractive in the postmodern context, this is arguably a good thing. Jürgen Moltmann and others have been urging the church to anticipate the Spirit at work outside the confines of the church.[33] But the weakness of such an approach is that it undermines the ecclesial framework in which Christian faith can only be understood, as well as contributes to an increasingly pantheistic rendition of religious experience which inevitably attaches itself to such an indiscriminating and unmediated view of the Spirit. Spirit baptism, on the other hand, is integral, alongside preaching, water baptism and communion, to the practice of theology in the church and the reinforcement of Christian identity.

Sacraments and the Spirit

Such a view of Spirit baptism as we are expounding here carries with it, of course, all the attendant dangers of two-tier, elitist Christianity: the cultivation of a gnostic dualism. This is a charge that has often been levelled at neo-Pentecostals. The way to avoid it is to intentionally tie Spirit baptism, and charismatic experience in general, to water baptism and communion. This is not to confuse, as some have done, water baptism and Spirit baptism; nor is it to rob Spirit baptism of the essentially new contribution it makes to Christian conversion and ongoing life in the Spirit. What the conjunction of Spirit baptism and sacrament does ensure, however, is the close relationship of pneumatology with the wider catholicity of the church's faith and practice – a catholicity predicated upon the central events of the gospel. Chan gives a good example of how the Eucharist, through the *epiclesis*, can become a place for authentic Spirit infilling, and cites the early Methodists as an example of what can occur when the sacraments take on a decidedly charismatic tone.[34] Not only is the Spirit received afresh in the context of renewed awareness of the body of Christ, the *epiclesis* becomes an invitation to all sorts of charismatic possibilities, such as miracles and healings.

Tying Spirit baptism to the sacraments may be of some concern. Turner, for example, is dismissive of such an approach in that it does not do justice to the powerful experiential reality of Spirit baptism. At one level he is entirely justified. But what we are pressing for here, which necessitates the relatedness of experiential and sacramental categories and practices, is a doctrine of the Spirit that is controlled by and grounded in the doctrine of conversion and initiation – not to be confused with water baptism, but neither to be denuded by mere phenomenology. Moreover, it is a view of Spirit baptism to which further and subsequent experiences of the Spirit, including charismata, can also be related, precisely because the doctrinal and initiatory significance of such experiences has already been established. Fee draws attention to a number of texts such as Galatians 3:5, 1 Thessalonians 4:8 and Philippians 1:19, deriving from them a pneumatology which originates in Spirit baptism but continues in repeated infillings of the Spirit.[35]

Whilst Frederick Bruner might question legitimately, on exegetical grounds, this Pentecostal instinct for 'more' of the Spirit, 'as though the water faith receives from Christ is not entirely satisfying and empowering',[36] it seems consistent with the tenor of biblical spirituality to continue to thirst for ever new experiences of the Spirit. Pentecostal and charismatic spirituality are right at this point and make an important contribution to our overall understanding of the dimensions of biblical spirituality. We insist, however, on the distinctiveness of the initiatory experience of Spirit baptism, for it ensures that it cannot be reduced to a benign concept, or to a vague theological idea. The trouble with Turner's position, as Chan points out, where Spirit baptism is left open ended, is that it 'will not have the capacity for long-term traditioning of the Pentecostal dimension of life'.[37] As charismatics are discovering, a revised theology of Spirit baptism weakens the traditioning process by making the actual experience of the Spirit at conversion optional. More importantly, the absence of a full initiatory experience of the Spirit, understood theologically as well as experientially, means that subsequent charismatic 'waves' or manifestations remain unrelated to the theological indicatives of conversion, of the grace of God in Christ.

To be sure, Toronto was not entirely lacking in this regard. There was indeed a theological motif in the Toronto Blessing related to the theme of intimacy with the Father – a theological motif notable for its depth and potential.[38] But one of the reasons this theme has not emerged as the legacy of Toronto is because it lacked rootage in the initial conversion experience of Spirit baptism. Too quickly the theological rationale of Toronto was eclipsed by many of the long-standing aspirations, as well as phenomenology, of revivalism, and the result has been a diminution of theological categories in favour of a heightened apocalyptic: crudely put, the church was being prepared, according to Arnott for 'probably the greatest harvest in the world ... we could be moving towards the last move of God ... the real power is coming'.[39]

Crucially, it has meant the development of a pneumatology in which experiences of the Spirit, evidenced at the level of phenomenology, become the sole means of legitimising the truth claims of the gospel. The long-term repercussions of this is a renewal movement detached from the central doctrines of salvation in Christ, but also a revivalism that requires ever more outpourings of the Spirit to secure its place in the world. This itself becomes a form of legalism and a source of pastoral insecurity, and not, ironically, the free movement of the Spirit that charismatics so often claim for themselves (the very thing Pentecostalism itself has been accused of, as it has enshrined Spirit baptism into dogma).[40] Indeed, for this reason Wimber excommunicated the Toronto Airport Fellowship from the Vineyard network, accusing them of manipulative practices and cult-like behaviour.[41]

The Spirit and Charismata

It is of some irony that Wimber stood against the exoticism of Toronto, for it is Wimber himself who could be criticised for allowing charismata to develop in isolation from the theological vision of the church. This process can be seen most clearly in the concept of 'Power Evangelism', developed by Wimber, which for a while in the mid-eighties became essential reading for charismatics wanting to engage in evangelism.[42] It became something of a fad, conforming in so many ways to the revivalist mindset: through signs and wonders the gospel might yet enjoy its greatest evangelistic thrust, leading to unprecedented harvest and growth.[43] In fact, Wimber's 'kingdom theology' is heavily imbued with eschatological awareness; generally, it has made a welcome contribution to charismatic theology.[44] But its weakness is that it has further exacerbated the tension between pastoral and evangelistic models of the church.

Typically, in Wimber's schema, the church is portrayed as languishing in its own comfort and security, in contrast to the evangelistic dynamism of 'signs and wonders'.[45] For those who have inhabited the world of charismatic fads, this dichotomy between church (moribund) and latest technique (vital) elicits no surprise. This caricature of mainstream church as a foil to supernatural movements is commonplace, whether we are discussing Toronto, Alpha, Dawn 2000, Strategic Level Prayer Warfare, Cells, or any other iniative.[46] But, as a consequence, the ecclesiological significance of charismata is underplayed,[47] for, contrary to popular rhetoric, the diversity of charismata, under the categories of speech (wisdom and knowledge), deeds (faith, healings and miracles) and utterance (prophecy, tongues), do not pertain to the quick results envisioned by power evangelism but the edification of the body of Christ as an expression of the trinitarian life of God.[48] Just as worship and evangelism have been confused in the cause of seeker sensitivity, so charismata and evangelism have been confused in the cause of Power Evangelism. Not that charismata are without effect in relationship to evangelism; as Fee points out in 1 Corinthians 14:25, the unbeliever who exclaims, in response to prophecy, that

'God is really among you ', is indeed speaking the language of conversion – a text that stands out in charismatic circles as something of an ideal to be attained. [49] Nevertheless, it is not without significance that the one reference to being baptised in the Spirit, in the Pauline corpus, stands at the beginning of a sustained argument concerning the edificatory and revelatory function of spiritual gifts within the Christian community.[50]

Much more needs to be said on this subject, including the correctness of this symbolic approach in relationship to the use of miracle by Jesus himself. Signs and wonders are clearly part of the apostolic ministry conceived by Paul, and require no exegetical or supernaturalist defence; but to assign their use simply to that of evangelistic impact is to lose sight, once again, of the theological, ecclesiological and symbolic richness of their intent. Revelatory charismata pertain to the qualitative witness of the church.[51]

Very few practitioners within the renewal movement have unpacked this ecclesiological and theological dimension of spiritual gifts, preferring to see the charismata of wisdom and revelation, for example, as somewhat recondite. It is obvious why this is the case. Esoteric and inexplicable charismata are exactly the kind of phenomena one would associate with revival and so, by way of circuitous argument, appearance of the inexplicable is evidence that revival is imminent. However, there are exceptions to this understanding. Stibbe notes that the gifts of wisdom and revelation are in fact tied to the teaching ministry of the church.[52] The dominance throughout 1 Corinthians of the theme of wisdom – understood as the message of the gospel itself – makes it clear that to treat the message of wisdom and revelation simply as euphemisms for the supernatural is myopic. Wisdom and revelation derive from the gospel itself, the message of the crucified messiah, which the church rehearses and celebrates through the manifestation of the gift. This does not necessarily imply sermons, but it does imply communication that is essentially gospel speech. Stibbe argues:

> The word of knowledge is an invaluable tool for those called to teach in the Church. It is an invaluable tool for those who are called to speak in an inspirational way of the wide range of blessings which God has given us through Jesus Christ.[53]

Stibbe's contribution to the discussion is to remind us that central to charismata is the message of the gospel itself, strengthening and edifying the believers. His theology of charismata is rooted in the ontology of the church as a theological reality actualised in worship. Here is a belief that the main purpose of Spirit gifts is to underline the centrality of the gospel itself and to trust that the formation of such a charismatic and evangelical community, under the Word and the sacraments, and empowered by the Holy Spirit of God, is the ultimate proclamation of the gospel. Such an ecclesiology is strikingly contemporary because it takes seriously the pneumatic dimension of Christian existence, but, in another sense, is unmistakably old, 'in that it attempts to draw upon the rich resources of the Christian heritage which provide not ready-made answers but rays of illumination for contemporary endeavours'.[54] It was this ecclesial self-confidence that was evident in the very earliest days of the renewal, and led some to criticise the renewal for its exclusivity.

Some might argue that this same self-awareness is still there in the movement, illustrated by episodes like Toronto. But others have argued that Toronto evinces signs of a movement in crisis – if not in its death throes – seeking to recapture a lost vision, and, in the process, intentionally coupling manifestations of the Spirit to their appeal to the culture at large. Arguably, this has always been the case. After all, charismatic renewal is, to some degree, a product of late-sixties' cultural expressionism.[55] But what has been different latterly is the self-conscious exploitation of those connections between church and culture, and from that close correspondence a fresh awareness the evangelistic appeal that a church in revival might have. The motivation is not entirely false, but neither is it without problems. To treat the Spirit merely as the generator of an atmosphere conducive to growth and popularity is to trivialise his purpose. Not only does it underestimate the transcendence of the Spirit; in addition it places the Spirit at the behest of culture, encouraging in the process crude proof-texting as a justification for various charismatic manifestations. Being drunk in the Spirit is not a Christian alternative to inebriation, and should never be crudely regarded as such. Rather it must be understood hermeneutically, as Lincoln has shown, as a counter-cultural imperative: the formation of a community of the Holy Spirit that stands in radical disjunction to the world.[56]

In sum, Toronto has significantly affected charismatic pneumatology, amounting to a radical departure from its classical Pentecostal roots.[57] The Vineyard movement, of which Toronto was initially a member, resonates more with its early Quaker roots: hence, the overriding passive tone of the Toronto blessing, as participants are encouraged to simply be open and vulnerable to the Spirit's presence.[58] This less strident mood of the Toronto Blessing, summarised in the phrase 'resting in the Spirit',[59] is reflective of the changing preferences on the part of the religious consumer, and as such makes Toronto a very good example of postmodern faith. Its essentially non-verbal expression communicates well, not only with evangelicals who are increasingly averse to religious language, but more importantly to those outside the church, whose relativism does not allow for the truth claims of Christianity.[60] The price of this stance, however, has been high. Ironically, by focusing on the manifestation of the Spirit in our midst, Toronto has severed the link between pneumatology, christology and ecclesiology, and further undermined the confidence of the church in its essential rites.

The Spirit and Ethics

Obsession about revival obscures the locative dimension of Christian grace by making grace conditional upon a level of intimacy that is burdensome, for grace cannot always be registered at the level of emotions; nor are the issues always resolved by ever more intense experiences of the Spirit. Such a view can lead to a new form of legalism. However, by virtue of its passive tone, the new wave of Spirit activity has also contributed, to some extent, to a diminished understanding of holiness: conversely, and paradoxically, this same spirituality that creates tension in our approach to God, also relaxes the imperative of Christian faith by suggesting that the main emphasis in the teaching of Christian holiness is simply letting go.[61] The revivalism of Pensacola is an exception to this passive tone. Here the opposite is the case: an imperative of active and decisive repentance. Christian sanctification, however, transcends both the passive tone of Toronto and the militant tone of Pensacola, by making the imperative of Christian ethics dependent upon the experience of grace in Christ, while, simultaneously, being no less forceful in its claims upon the believer to cooperate with the Holy Spirit.[62]

Contrary to the Toronto notion of resting and soaking in the Spirit, holiness is not simply a matter of letting go or resting, but of active appropriation of the power of the indwelling Spirit, who conspires to effect radical and ethical change in the world of the ordinary and the mundane. When the Spirit is consigned merely to the category of the experiential, the therapeutic or the phenomenal, this teleological purpose of the Spirit of conforming believers to the likeness of Christ is obscured, and with it the moral and theological vision of the church. The Spirit is critical in that moral vision, not as the bearer of holiness previously unfamiliar to the believer – the charge Peterson makes against pietistic versions of sanctification where holiness teaching posits an unrealistic and often hyper-spiritual perfectionism – but rather as the one who enables the realisation of that freedom and holiness in Christ.[63] In so far as believers cooperate and come into line with the Spirit – in whose sphere they are already placed – the flesh life is overcome.

Such a view of the Spirit's operations resolves the indicative/imperative dialectic that has been so much the bugbear of New Testament scholarship. Indeed, the resolution of the dialectic, and, in particular, the way the indicative mood ought to precede any moral exhortation lies at the centre of this book. For it should be clear that all Christian imperatives are predicated upon the indicative of grace in Christ, leading to the oft-quoted summary of Pauline ethics: 'Be what you are.' The Spirit, however, as Michael Parsons has shown, is the indispensable link in the resolution of that ethic: 'The Spirit, himself, then, is the link between the indicative and the imperative of Christian reality and existence. He is at once an element of the former and a constituent part of the latter.'[64] Examining a number of Pauline texts, including Galatians 5:25 and 1 Corinthians 6:12–20, Parsons concludes that the promise of the Spirit in Christian living is that God makes possible the life which he demands, justifying the imperative on the basis of the indicative. The pneumatological dimension of Christian existence is central to a theology of grace. The injunction to live by the Spirit in Galatians 5:16 is a reminder of a present reality of new life in Christ; it is not an appeal to a quietist ethic, nor an encouragement to passivity; nor, more importantly, is the exhortation tied to the Wesleyan notion of sanctification,[65] nor to the revivalist's agenda of repeated rededication and salvation. On the contrary, the encouragement to cooperate and participate in the transforming power of the Spirit is made precisely because the realm of the eschatological Spirit is the actual location of Christian existence.[66]

It is important for charismatics to stress the affective element that lies behind this imperative to walk according to the Spirit, for without this 'the righteousness received and declared for will be resisted and the unrighteousness not fully and deeply repented.'[67] The expulsive power of religious affections is what allows for Christian transformation. Nevertheless, one must also be aware how easily this language of the Spirit can yield to hyper-spiritualism, where sanctification becomes a denaturalising process – the destruction of human nature rather than its ennobling.[68] And in the process, it is commonplace to depersonalise the Spirit to the level of force, or power. On the other hand, it is tempting to be too precise theologically in these matters, discounting the many and various testimonies associated with episodes like Toronto, where moral and spiritual transformation is precisely what occurs. Critics are not always best placed to make judgements on these matters. One suspects, however, for the meantime at least, that charismatic activity in many churches will continue to feature in opposition to the pedagogical, ethical and mystagogical apparatus of the church, for 'the "now" and the "new" have no sense of continuity nor church history, no patience with dogma nor ecclesiastical authority'.[69] The Spirit, of course, is no less transcendent than the Father and the Son, but one fears that the Spirit will continue to be regarded, in charismatic circles, as simply the immanent, intimate side of God.[70]

The Spirit and the People of God

Ethical righteousness, related to the proper appropriation of the Spirit's power is, of course, communitarian as well as personal. Indeed, the fruit of the Spirit – the growth in Christian virtue – cannot be understood outside the context of fellowship. Church community is just that provision, or means, in the Christian's experience that promotes the increase in virtues. Holiness, of a kind that is grounded upon the decisive event of sanctification, presupposes the tension that is afforded by the very local and often frustrating idiosyncrasies of full-orbed congregational life. As Fee asserts, unity 'requires heterogeneous people to submit their diversity to the unifying work of the Spirit. Homogenous churches lie totally outside Paul's frame of reference. After all, such churches cannot maintain the unity of the Spirit that either Ephesians 2 and 4 or 1 Corinthians 12 call for'.[71] Arising out of this tension is the challenge to live true to the way of the Spirit in whom we have been immersed, rather than the way of the flesh. The success of the church community in living this way, and not any other way, is precisely what constitutes the witness of God's grace in the world. Unspectacular though it may be, and unpopular though it may be, it is the maintenance of the unity of the Spirit in the bond of peace, reinforced in the fellowship that surrounds the word, the breaking of bread and prayer, that witnesses to Christ's victory in the world over the principalities and powers, and becomes the source of endless missionary possibilities.

We shall look further at how ministry supports this growth in unity. In the celebrated Ephesians 4:11–16, it is this unity of the faith that is the *teleios* of apostolic ministry. Our point here is simply to reiterate that the empowering of the Spirit is critical for the fashioning of such a community that stands in radical contradistinction to the world. The Spirit does indeed operate at the level of phenomenology, and the presence of the Spirit may well act in the postmodern era as a cultural bridge from the church to the world – though Stibbe justifies the strange and exotic phenomena associated with Toronto on this basis alone: namely, that in an 'addictive society' where there is a prevalence of the ecstatic, God accommodates himself to the culture by providing his own intoxicating experiences.[72] But it is essential, nevertheless, for the church to remember that it is the Holy Spirit with whom it is sealed, and that the Spirit's purpose is to fashion a people of God who act and behave as a vanguard and an announcement of the age to come. It is not surprising that this understanding of the church carries its own indicative. The Spirit of wisdom and revelation, and Paul's prayers for such, is concerned with the church's deepening enlightenment concerning this social, corporate and cosmic dimension of the gospel that it has already been delivered into.[73] And from this deepening understanding of the cosmic significance of the relatively insignificant details of what we call church fellowship, the church is strengthened to persevere in this life, while at the same time resisting the false dawns that so often accompany the promise of revival, be it through Power Evangelism or Prayer Warfare, or any other of the various stratagems we have listed thus far. The Spirit effects and sustains a distinct and robust contrast community.

Robert Menzies' understanding of Spirit baptism, and charismata in general, as empowerment for witness ought to be rejected, precisely for this reason.[74] Derived primarily from a Luke–Acts perspective of pneumatology, Menzies links the baptism of the Spirit to the boldness evidenced in Acts to witness to Christ, and generally it is how Pentecostals have viewed the gift.[75] He also reflects, however, a significant number of neo-Pentecostals who, as we have seen, preoccupied with the task of mission, have regarded the coming of the Spirit as the essential component of witness. Such a view should be challenged, if not rejected, precisely because of its reductionism. Empowering for witness is just one feature, as Turner has shown, of the coming of the Spirit of prophecy in Luke–Acts, and to overemphasise its importance is to minimise the place of the Holy Spirit in the whole of Christian life and experience (as well as being guilty, as far as Turner is concerned, of a two-stage pneumatology).[76] Menzies' position is guilty of the same pathology that we have been highlighting throughout, whereby the urgency of mission and evangelism has effectively displaced, indeed almost destroyed, matters of spirituality.[77] In a movement so concerned about its shrinking market and consequently the need to be empowered for mission, the theological richness of language tied to the coming of the Spirit is almost redundant. Ensuring that the message is heard is of far greater importance than the ecclesiological impact of the Spirit.

What this represents is a fundamental mistrust of God's own mission in the world: a mission that is antecedent of our attempts to build the kingdom. Certainly it is possible to be introverted, but the paradox of always seeking to be charismatically effectual is to be introverted precisely in our attempts not to be introverted; in the case of pneumatology, and the whole range of activities that may be described as charismatic, the tendency is to deploy an esoteric in-language of the Spirit, which has the converse effect of alienating outsiders. The revivalist Zinzendorf was guilty of this kind of in-house language, notes Ward, during a time that was known at the Herrnhut community as a 'time of sifting',[78] and all it contributed to, as in our own situation, was the increasing ineffectuality of the Moravian vision. Paradoxically, therefore, it may prove more fruitful for the renewal to channel its charismatic activity into the establishment of robust, Spirit-endowed communities, whose main evangelistic thrust is not centripetal but unashamedly centrifugal: the world coming to the church on its own terms, aware that what is being witnessed to transcends the categories of sociology, for it is a community of the Spirit as transcendent Lord. As Chan points out,

> Acts 1:8 is not just about being empowered to witness as a result of being baptised in the Spirit; it is first and foremost about being witnesses, about lives being transformed. More specifically, it is lives transformed by the power of the resurrection through union with Christ.[79]

Charismatic endowment in Acts, as Turner has shown, is in fact much to do with the maintenance of the church as a community of the Spirit.[80] Undoubtedly, there is an evangelistic task relating not just to the apostles but also to the believers at large. But what we see in Acts is not just the activity of witnessing, but the church, strengthened by the Spirit through charismata and the Spirit of prophecy, focused primarily on becoming a witness by living in the 'fear of the Lord'.[81] By walking in the 'fear of the Lord', as well as the comparable 'encouragement of the Holy Spirit', the church grows in numbers, not in the sense of simple causality, but as an effect of the Spirit's transforming influence on the congregation.

It would be inaccurate to say that numerical growth is incidental to Luke's concerns; but, equally, it would be a mistake to see numerical growth as the driving motivation of Luke's pneumatology. More accurate is to regard the ongoing ministry of the Spirit as related to the strengthening of faith, in order that the church might truly be a witness to the Lordship of Christ:

> Just as the charismatic witness of the apostles and others elicits faith, Spirit-empowered exhortation and teaching informs, extends and strengthens faith. This should not surprise us, for it is entirely in accord with what we might expect of the 'Spirit of prophecy' affording 'wisdom' to the people of God, for example, kindling the sort of understanding of the Gospel that flows into confident faith and/or joyful praise.[82]

Far from charismatic activity being solely concerned with supernatural phenomena – where supernaturalism, as so often in charismatic renewal, takes on the form of apologetic – charismatic endowment is given to provide just that encouragement and confidence in the gospel that we noted above as the *raison d'être* of ecclesial existence. Undoubtedly this includes healings and miracles, prophecies and tongues. Absence of these aspects would be remiss and guilty of theological prejudice in the opposite direction – a direction most commonly associated with cessationism.[83] But failure to appreciate the transforming effect of the Spirit in charismatic revelation of the gospel itself, because of a pneumatology that links the Spirit merely with the irrational or inexplicable, is similarly limited.

Such a rendering of the Spirit's activity as simply self-authenticating phenomena is to misunderstand the purpose of charismata in the church. The charismata of revelatory discernment in Acts 5:1–11, from which Ananias and Sapphira become subject to divine judgement, has as its *teleios*, as Turner points out, the maintenance of the holiness of the community of the Spirit.[84] It is this holiness of the restored and purified Israel that the pair has violated. To treat the Spirit simply as a badge of charismatic churchmanship, therefore giving it that *donum superadditum* over and against the wider church community, is to miss the soteriological function of spiritual gifts in and for the community of faith as a witness of Christ.

We shall refer to other aspects of Toronto in the proceeding chapters. Clearly it has been a defining moment in the charismatic renewal in the UK. Our contention has been, however, that whilst Toronto proffers an authentic emotivism, it has obscured, and in some respects distorted, the important soteriological, ethical and ecclesiological dimensions that associate with a more robust Pentecostal pneumatology – a pneumatology that was evident in the early years of renewal and which now needs to be retrieved.

Notes

[1]   D.S. Yeago, 'The Spirit, The Church and the Scriptures' in Buckley and Yeago (eds.), *Knowing the Triune God*, 93.

[2]   See. T. Virgo, 'Does Anybody Still Believe in Restoration?', *New Frontiers International Magazine* Issue 18 (August-October 2002), 5–9, for confirmation of this point. See also A.O. Sullivan, 'Roger Forster and the Icthus Fellowship: The Development of a Charismatic Missiology', *Pneuma* 16:2 (1994), 249.

[3]   P. Hocken, 'The Meaning and Purpose of "Baptism in the Spirit"', *Pneuma* 7:2 (1985), 125–34. See also T.G. Weinandy, *The Father's Spirit of Sonship* (Edinburgh: T&T Clark, 1995), 104–6, whose trinitarian theology, he argues, derives from his own personal experience of Spirit baptism.

[4]   M. Turner, *The Holy Spirit and Spiritual Gifts: Then and Now* (Carlisle: Paternoster, 1996), 153–68. Similarly, Fee opposes his own Pentecostal tradition on the grounds that the Spirit

is indeed received at conversion, but is understood as powerfully and experientially present, Fee, *Gospel and Spirit*, 105–19.

5 Toronto has its advocates and its detractors. For a sociological, largely negative, critique of the Toronto Blessing, see P.J. Richter, '"God is not a Gentleman!": The Sociology of the Toronto Blessing' in S.E. Porter and P.J. Richter (eds.), *The Toronto Blessing? Or Is It?* (London: Darton, Longman & Todd, 1995), 38–65.

6 J. Hosier, 'It's For You!', *New Frontiers International Magazine* Issue 5 (Winter 1999), 7. See also D. Pawson, *The Fourth Wave* (London: Hodder & Stoughton, 1993), for a fuller articulation of this concern.

7 S. Chan, *Pentecostal Theology and the Christian Spiritual Tradition* (Journal of Pentecostal Theology Supplement Series 21; Sheffield: Sheffield Academic Press, 2000), 23.

8 See G.A. Cray, 'The Toronto Experience in a Consumer Society' in Bartholemew and Moritz (eds.), *Christ and Consumerism*, 152–62.

9 See D. Pawson, *Jesus Baptises in One Holy Spirit: Who? How? When? Why?* (London: Hodder & Stoughton, 1997), 161–7.

10 See Richter, 'God is not a Gentleman!', 30–34. See also M. Percy, *Power and the Church: Ecclesiology in an Age of Transition* (London and Washington: Cassell, 1998), 183–204.

11 Cray, 'The Toronto Experience', 156. See also Chevreau, *Catch the Fire*, 57–69.

12 D. Pawson, 'A Mixed Blessing' in D. Hilborn (ed.), *'Toronto' in Perspective: Papers on the New Charismatic Wave of the Mid 1990's* (Carlisle: Acute, 2001), 84.

13 See S. Sizer, 'A Sub-Christian Movement' in Hilborn (ed.), 'Toronto', 45–61.

14 See T. Smail, A. Walker, N. Wright, 'From "The Toronto Blessing" to Trinitarian Renewal: A Theological Conversation' in T. Smail, A. Walker, N. Wright (eds.), *Charismatic Renewal: The Search for a Theology* (London: SPCK, 1995), 165. Yves Congar's dictum: 'no Christology without pneumatology and no pneumatology without Christology', *Word and the*

Spirit (London: Geoffrey Chapman, 1986), 1, is predicated upon the same concern to not allow Spirit movements to act in isolation from the Word.

15 C.M. Norén, 'The Word of God in Worship: Preaching in Relationship to Liturgy' in C. Jones, G. Wainwright, E. Yarnold and P. Bradshaw (eds.), *The Study of Liturgy* (London: New York, SPCK/Oxford University Press, 1997³), 49.

16 Chan, *Pentecostal Theology*, 75–6: 'Here is where Pentecostalism must be open to the challenge of the mystical tradition. It must recognize that trials and spiritual aridity, even after spiritual defeat and desolation, are part of growth even after one's baptism in the Spirit.'

17 See J. Arnott, 'Valuing the Anointing' in C. Ahn (ed.), *Hosting the Holy Spirit: Inviting the Holy Spirit to Abide with You* (Ventura: Renew, 2000), 22.

18 See T. Tenney, 'Building a Mercy Seat' in Ahn (ed.), *Hosting the Holy Spirit*, 38–9 and also C. Freidzon, *Holy Spirit, I am Hungry for You* (Eastbourne: Kingsway, 1996), 78–82, where unity is seen as a precondition of revival power.

19 See L. Engle, 'Corporate Prayer and Fasting' in Ahn (ed.), *Hosting the Holy Spirit*, 45–8.

20 See S. Scataglini, 'Keeping the Fire Burning' in Ahn (ed.), *Hosting the Holy Spirit*, 148–51; C. Dye, *Hearts on Fire: Walking in Personal Revival* (London: Dovewell, 2002); M.L. Brown, *Whatever Happened to the Power of God* (Shippensburg: Destiny Image, 1991), 109–16 and also Castellanos, *Dream*, 97–103.

21 S. Hunt, M. Hamilton and T. Walter, 'Tongues, Toronto and the Millennium' in S. Hunt, M. Hamilton and T. Walter (eds.), *Charismatic Christianity: Sociological Perspectives* (Basingstoke: Macmillan, 1997), 12. See also M.E. Wilson, *'Revival, True or False: Green Berets for Jesus'*, Reformation and Revival: A Quarterly Journal for Church Leadership 8:2 (1999), 121–37.

22 See Fee, *God's Empowering Presence*, 380–89, 776–84, in which he exegetes the key Spirit texts in the letters of Paul, such as Galatians 3:1–5 and Titus 3:3–8 respectively.

23 T. Smail, *The Giving Gift: The Holy Spirit in Person* (London: Darton, Longman & Todd, 1994²), 30–31. See also T. Smail, *The Forgotten Father: Rediscovering the Heart of the Christian Gospel* (Carlisle: Paternoster, 1996²), 13–19.

24 See N.T. Wright, 'New Exodus, New Inheritance: A Narrative Structure of Romans 3–8' in S.K. Soderlund and N.T. Wright (eds.), *Romans and the People of God* (Grand Rapids/Cambridge: Eerdmans, 1999), 26–35.

25 See Weinandy, *The Father's Spirit of Sonship*, 101–4, whose charismatic theology of adoption by the Spirit into the life of the Trinity is predicated on the thesis that just as the Father begets the Son in the Spirit, so we too are adopted as children of the Father in the Spirit. Such a theology assumes an inherent link between the economic and immanent Trinity.

26 H.I. Lederle, *Treasures Old and New: Interpretations of Spirit-Baptism in the Charismatic Renewal Movement* (Peabody: Hendrickson, 1988), 5–9.

27 J. Brencher, *Martyn Lloyd-Jones (1899–1981) and Twentieth Century Evangelicalism* (Carlisle: Paternoster, 2002), 200–205.

28 See M. Lloyd-Jones, *Joy Unspeakable: Power and Renewal in the Holy Spirit* (Eastbourne: Kingsway, 1984) and also M. Eaton, *Baptism with the Spirit: The Teaching of Martyn Lloyd-Jones* (Leicester: Inter-Varsity Press, 1989).

29 Lincoln, *Ephesians*, 40.

30 See G.M. Burge, *The Anointed Community: The Holy Spirit in the Johannine Tradition* (Grand Rapids: Eerdmans, 1987), 54–6.

31 W. Grudem, *Systematic Theology: An Introduction to Biblical Doctrine* (Leicester: Inter-Varsity Press, 1994), 959–61.

32 J. Gunstone, *Pentecost Comes to the Church: Sacraments and Spiritual Gifts* (London: Darton, Longman & Todd, 1994), 39–41.

33 See J. Moltmann, *The Spirit of Life: A Universal Affirmation* (London: SCM, 1992).

34 Chan, *Pentecostal Theology*, 94–6.

35 Fee, *God's Empowering Presence*, 387–9.

36 F.D. Bruner, *A Theology of the Holy Spirit: The Pentecostal Experience and the New Testament Witness* (Grand Rapids: Eerdmans, 1970), 254–5.

[37] Chan, *Pentecostal Theology*, 92. Chan's position represents something of a *via media* between the Pentecostal two-stage position and the almost binitarian evangelical view of conversion. The way forward, argues Chan, 'for the Pentecostal teaching on subsequence is to locate it within the conversion-initiation complex. But conversion must be seen as a process of development rather than just a crisis experience' (87).

[38] J. Arnott, *The Father's Blessing* (Orlando: Creation House, 1995).

[39] Quoted in Hunt, Hamilton and Walter, 'Tongues', 11.

[40] Fee, *Gospel and Spirit*, 92–4.

[41] See Percy, *Power and the Church*, 102. See also B. Jackson, *The Quest for the Radical Middle: A History of the Vineyard* (Cape Town: Vineyard International Publishing, 1999), 307–23, for a full and wide-ranging discussion of the controversy.

[42] J. Wimber, *Power Evangelism: Signs and Wonders Today* (London: Hodder & Stoughton, 1985).

[43] Jackson, *The Quest*, 99–128. Wimber's association with Wagner at Fuller seminary is of course well known.

[44] See the work of G.E. Ladd, *A New Testament Theology* (Cambridge: Lutterworth, 1985), whose eschatological reading of New Testament theology has underpinned Vineyard theology.

[45] Wimber, *Power Evangelism*, 13–16.

[46] For examples see Chevreau, *Catch the Fire*, 221–2; Gumbel, *Questions of Life*, 221–3; Montgomery, *DAWN 2000*, 78–80; Wagner, *Confronting the Powers*, 6–7.

[47] For a balanced, if at times overly negative, perspective on signs and wonders see J.H. Armstrong, 'In Search of Spiritual Power' in M.S. Horton (ed.), *Power Religion: The Selling Out of the Evangelical Church* (Amersham: Moody Press/Scripture Press, 1992), 61–88.

[48] A. Thiselton, *The First Epistle to the Corinthians* (Grand Rapids/Cambridge: Eerdmans, 2000), 933–6.

[49] Fee, *God's Empowering Presence*, 244–7.

[50] 1 Corinthians 12:13.

51 See N.T. Wright, *Jesus and the Victory of God* (London: SPCK, 1996), 191–6.

52 M. Stibbe, *Know Your Spiritual Gifts* (London: Marshall Pickering, 1997), 18–53.

53 Ibid., 43.

54 I.T. Dietterich, 'A Particular People: Toward a Faithful and Effective Ecclesiology', *Modern Theology* 9:4 (1993), 361–2.

55 See I. Cotton, *The Hallelujah Revolution, The Rise of the New Christians* (London: Little, Brown & Company, 1995).

56 Lincoln, *Ephesians*, 344.

57 Pawson, 'A Mixed Blessing' in Hilborn (ed.), *'Toronto'*, 83–5.

58 See S.M. Burgess and G.B. McGee (eds.), *Dictionary of Pentecostal and Charismatic Movements* (Grand Rapids: Zondervan, 1988), 889.

59 Chevreau, *Catch the Fire*, 62.

60 Richter, 'Charismatic Mysticism', 126–7.

61 This emphasis on passivity resonates well with the holiness teaching of Watchman Nee, *The Normal Christian Life* (Kingsway; Eastbourne, 1961).

62 See J.A. Adewuya, 'The Holy Spirit and Sanctification in Romans 8:1–17', *Journal of Pentecostal Theology* 18 (2001), 71–84.

63 Peterson, *Possessed by God*, 47–9.

64 M. Parsons, 'Being Precedes Act: Indicative and Imperative in Paul's Writing', *The Evangelical Quarterly* 70:2 (1988), 127.

65 Though Ray Dunning claims that Wesley's view of entire sanctification has been misread and misappropriated. See H.R. Dunning, *Reflecting the Divine Image: Christian Ethics in Wesleyan Perspective* (Downers Grove: Inter-Varsity Press, 1998), 36, 43, 60–61. James Bowers, who notes a difference in the way Wesleyan theology approaches the relationship of justification and sanctification to that of Wesleyan-Pentecostal theology, shares the same view. On account of Spirit baptism and the necessity of holiness, the latter has a weak doctrine of justification, whereas Wesleyans saw sanctification as the corollary of a robust doctrine of justification. See J.P. Bowers, 'A Wesleyan-Pentecostal Approach to Christian Formation', *Journal of Pentecostal Theology* 6 (1995), 55–86.

66 See F.D. Macchia, 'Justification and the Spirit: A Pentecostal Reflection on the Doctrine by which the Church Stands or Falls', *Pneuma* 22:1 (2000), 3–21.

67 Land, *Pentecostal Spirituality*, 202. See also J. Edwards, *The Selected Works of Jonathan Edwards Volume 3: The Religious Affections* (Edinburgh: The Banner of Truth, 1961).

68 This was Ronald Knox's main criticism of 'enthusiastic' spirituality. See R. Knox, *Enthusiasm* (Oxford: Clarendon, 1950).

69 Hunt, Hamilton and Walter, 'Tongues', 12.

70 See C.E. Gunton, *The Transcendent Lord: The Spirit and the Church in Calvinist and Cappadocian* (London: Congregational and Memorial Trust, 1988).

71 G.D. Fee, *Paul, The Spirit and the People of God* (Peabody: Hendrickson, 1996), 70. This leads us to question, once again, the direction a great deal of the renewal movement is taking towards the principle of homogeneity. Engagement with youth culture may well permit such an approach – a missiological attempt to accommodate the preferences and dislikes of Generation X – but as an exercise in cultivating holiness it could prove ineffectual. For this and related issues see D. Hilborn and M. Bird (eds.), *God and the Generations* (Carlisle: Paternoster, 2002).

72 M. Stibbe, *Times of Refreshing: A Practical Theology of Revival for Today* (London: Marshall Pickering, 1995), 71. After all, claims Stibbe, 'God always operates in a guise which is appropriate to the culture concerned', thereby making himself relevant to that culture. The Holy Spirit is the Christian alternative to inebriation.

73 See M. Turner, 'Mission and Meaning in Terms of "Unity" in Ephesians' in A. Billington, M. Turner, A. Lane (eds.), *Mission and Meaning: Essays Presented to Peter Cotterell* (Carlisle: Paternoster, 1995), 138–66.

74 R.P. Menzies, *Empowerment for Witness: The Spirit in Luke–Acts* (Sheffield: Sheffield Academic Press, 1996).

75 The dominant understanding of classic Pentecostalism in this area is expressed by David Petts: 'When Pentecostals talk about the baptism in the Holy Spirit, they generally

mean an experience of the Spirit's power, accompanied by speaking in tongues as on the Day of Pentecost. The terminology is derived from Acts 1:5 … The experience is usually closely associated with [many would say "exclusively identified with"] enduement with power for service (Acts 1:8) and is understood to be subsequent to and distinct from regeneration.' D. Petts, 'The Baptism in the Spirit: The Theological Distinctive' in K. Warrington (ed.), *Pentecostal Perspectives* (Carlisle: Paternoster, 1998), 98–119.

[76] Turner, *The Holy Spirit*, 46–56.

[77] By spirituality we mean Christian living, as it pertains to the Holy Spirit of God, not the interiority so often associated with the word. See Fee, *God's Empowering Presence*, 28–32.

[78] See Ward, *Protestant Evangelical Awakening*, 155–8.

[79] Chan, *Pentecostal Theology*, 55.

[80] M. Turner, *Power from on High: The Spirit in Israel's Restoration and Witness in Luke–Acts* (Sheffield: Sheffield Academic Press, 1996), 406–407.

[81] Ibid., 407–408, commenting on Acts 9:31.

[82] Ibid., 408.

[83] See J. Ruthven, *On the Cessation of Charismatic: The Protestant Polemic on Post-Biblical Miracles* (Sheffield: Sheffield Academic Press, 1993).

[84] Turner, *Power from on High*, 406.

Chapter 6

Prayer: Key to Revival?

Fervent Prayer

Revivalistic religion, we have argued, has a distinctive language and spirituality. Central to this is a conviction about the indispensability of intercessory prayer. Virgo's claim that 'if we are going to see a powerful spiritual breakthrough, we will have to develop in intercession',[1] summarises a widely held belief about imminent evangelistic breakthrough and the crucial and indispensable role that prayer has. 'Behind every successful development, every creative plan and every thrust forward,' claims Dye, 'there is and always has been one thing – earnest sustained prayer.'[2] Indeed Hocken reminds us that the evangelical prayer groups for revival scattered around the country, and the Nights of Prayer for World Revival group that formed around Billy Graham's visit to Harringay in 1959, were precursors to the charismatic renewal in the early 1960s.[3] Their particular form of revivalism, contingent upon prayer intercession, has clearly persisted, as illustrated in the well-known song 'We Want to See Jesus Lifted High' (SF2 1105), with its refrain: 'Every prayer a powerful weapon, strongholds come tumbling down and down.' Similarly,

Scott's commitment to an effective prayer strategy, leading to 'a major breakthrough' maybe somewhat nuanced,[4] influenced, as we have already noted, by Wagner's school of Prayer Warfare, but essentially its antecedents are found in the very earliest prayer habits of the charismatic movement. Prayer in revivalist traditions is essentially intercessory, with its own hagiography and not a little historical myth making.[5] The yardstick of evangelical spirituality is the strength of the prayer meeting where God is prevailed upon for souls. 'More than any other tradition,' David Gillett rightly notes, 'evangelicalism has earned the right to be called a spirituality of intercession.'[6]

In sum, revivalistic prayer is fervent, supplicatory and importunate – a mode of prayer that has been reinvigorated over the years by success stories overseas, where corporate prayer has been responsible for the promised breakthrough.[7] Our purpose in this chapter is not particularly to renege on this commitment. As with many other issues in charismatic practice, unless one has imbibed this aspect of evangelical spirituality, it is difficult to understand the very real and authentic passion that stands behind it.[8]

Once more, however, our concern is that prayer can feature in revivalist circles *only* as intercession, thus ignoring the cumulative range of prayer that might feature in other traditions. Apart from the sheer exhaustion that such a commitment to prayer can produce, it has important theological implications. The overemphasis on intercessory prayer has the tendency, in some places, to posit a static God who will only yield up his reward to those who pray long enough and loud enough.[9] In the parlance of evangelical Christianity this type of praying is described as 'besieging heaven' – a perspective of prayer that the psyche of evangelical-charismatic Christianity is heavily imbued with.[10] But in the process God is often portrayed as the *deus ex machina*, who is not only bound by our prayers but also defined by our prayers; thus, ironically, the supernaturalism that is so often associated with revivalism is replaced by a mechanistic faith. This is not the covenantal God who draws us into prayer by his Spirit, nor the one who in freedom can supersede our prayers; this is the God who will act only according to the dictates of faith. 'If we are not praying fervently and regularly for revival', claims Stuart Piggin, 'we should not expect to witness it.'[11]

It should be apparent in such a construct, where there is an anticipation of revival as just around the corner, that prayer is not an end in itself, but simply the means God has given to implore him for the sake of the multitudes outside the faith. The pastoral ramifications of this theology of intercession ought to be apparent, for at once it burdens the congregation with the onus of preparing the groundwork for revival conditions, thus fostering a corporate psychology that can lead in certain cases to paranoia and guilt. Because revivalism is so closely tied to the task of evangelism and church growth, it truncates a proper breadth in praying disciplines. Prayer and fasting are undoubtedly legitimate and laudable ways for congregations seeking to intercede for societal change – throughout the renewal it has recurred as a standard pattern of corporate prayer[12] – but such revivalism has vitiated the overall prayer horizons of the church, especially the mystical and ascetical traditions, as well as foster a neurotic tendency.

To be sure, prayer and evangelism are conjoined in Christian practice in the sense that 'prayer is about our personal experience of God – and evangelism is about telling others of our personal experience of God. The one leads to the other. Moreover, without the one [prayer], the other [evangelism] will always be stunted, artificial and a chore.'[13] Yet, prayer is similarly stunted when it is driven solely by the need to save souls. At this point both evangelism and prayer cease to be organic and integral to the worshipping and praying life of the church and are conceived, instead, as tools for success. Prayer thus becomes a mechanism of evangelistic growth.

Contemplative and ascetical prayer is not opposed to this kind of revivalism, for it too involves intercessory prayer; but the way this is conceived is different. In contemplation the object of prayer is not greater impact for the kingdom, for there is an inherent belief that ultimate responsibility for the kingdom enterprise lies with God himself – after all, only God, as Paul states in 1 Corinthians 3:7, can cause the seed to grow. In contemplative traditions, prayer as an act of communion is valued in and of itself. As such, free of the 'transcendental efficacy' we noted earlier, by which prayer and worship are only a means to a further, ulterior end, the prayer horizons of the church are broadened to include aspects of prayer hitherto inconceivable to the radical evangelical tradition.

By placing evangelistic intercession within the larger mystical and ascetical tradition, where prayer is conceived firstly as adoration, we shall be placing evangelism in its proper theological setting. As Michael Ramsey points out, the contemplative and evangelical traditions are not mutually exclusive. Aaron went into the holy of holies wearing a breastplate with jewels representing the tribes of Israel, and because of that 'adoration turns into "intercession", the bringing of people and needs and sorrows and joys and causes into the stream of divine love'.[14] The rhythmic movement of prayer between adoration and intercession is one of those tensions that require not so much to be resolved as respected. Intercession is the sequel in the logic of unitive prayer. But if revivalists are to avoid the despair and frenetic mood that accompanies so much of contemporary revivalism, then prayer must be conceived as our participation in the Spirit's own work. As Forsyth claims:

> If God's will is to be done on earth as it is in heaven prayer begins with adoration ... before we give even our prayer we must first receive. The Answerer provides the very prayer. What we do here rests on what God has done. What we offer is drawn from us by what he offers. Our self-oblation stands on his; and the spirit of prayer flows from the gift of the Holy Ghost, the great Intercessor.[15]

To understand intercessory prayer in this way, as participation in the already existing *missio Dei,* via adoration, is not an insignificant difference to the way prayer is understood and practised in charismatic traditions. Mission, as Begbie has warned us already in discussing renewal music, 'is not a program or a cause or a project through which we set about making our mark upon history, but a sharing in the mission of the triune God in and to the world'.[16] Thus, prayer is our participation in what God and not we are doing in the world, based on our prior incorporation into the body of Christ: God 'makes room for the response and co-operation of the created world' in the fulfilling of his divine purpose, without compromising his sovereignty.[17]

We shall explore the pneumatological dimensions of this below, particularly as it relates to prayer in tongues; but what this understanding of mission restores is a proper theological and pastoral context, whereby adoration and knowledge of God becomes the source of all evangelistic endeavour and contemporary relevance. Exploring the intricacies of the faith in prayer, seeking communion with the one to whom we are already joined, and participating in the intercession of the Spirit are the heart of contemplative prayer and the primary tasks of the church. As Hansen states, 'Faith wills to know the Beloved. Faith desires to comprehend the Beloved, not to conquer but rejoice in mutual understanding. We rejoice to know God in trinitarian splendour.'[18]

Once accepted, this understanding of prayer could be a source of ecumenical creativity as radical evangelicalism cross fertilises with more liturgical traditions that place at their centre a commitment to the veracity of the revelation, as well as a commitment to celebrating it for its own sake. The rest of this chapter seeks to articulate what this might involve, and in so doing hopes to provide, through practical ascesis, some tentative hints about the future direction of the renewal.

Daily Office

We have been arguing throughout for a more robust theological basis for charismatic revivalism in order to counter the faddish nature of its praxis. It is on this basis that Ramsey encourages us to pay attention first of all to the daily office as a form of corporate prayer.[19] The genius of the office, according to Ramsey, is that in psalm and canticle and lection it 'tells of God's historic revelation and redemption and of the response of the Church down the ages in praise and thanksgiving'.[20] Such a commitment is an antidote to the kind of ahistorical immediacy we noted earlier concerning contemporary worship, and as a pattern – remembrance of God's acts in creation and redemption, exalting the Lordship of Christ, and then intercession – it is well enshrined in the biblical tradition.[21] More importantly, says Ramsey, 'in the daily office we are lifted beyond the contemporary; and let us be sure that we will serve the contemporary scene effectively only if we are sometimes lifted beyond it, praying with the Church across the ages and with the communion of God's saints'.[22]

It is precisely because the office attends to matters of substance rather than relevance, immersing the church in the grammar of faith and revelation, that the church eventually has something powerful and relevant to say; but when the pressure of statistics impinges upon the church, such unhurriedness is not possible. Under this regime, prayer is no longer an encounter but, as Bonhoeffer warned, a means of recruitment to a pietistic spirituality centred on the narrow world of the religious ego.[23] In a culture where spirituality is very much in vogue, there is every chance that this is exactly what prayer could become. Hence, the need for the office to counter the self-conscious worship of the church, providing speech that not only gathers up the whole range of human experience but also does so in a way that is distinctively Christian.

At present, no such office exists, nor daily devotional pattern, to use evangelical terminology. Where corporate prayer exists, it is invariably tied to the revival agenda, thus limiting its potential as a source of church renewal. The daily office, in contrast, requires a certain degree of long-term intention; the office signals a conviction that giving attention to the scriptures and prayer is a worthwhile project in itself, requiring no extra-ecclesial justification. Immersion in the office, and the forming of a baptised imagination, is the first sign of authentic revival. The present crisis in the church is not a matter of structural inefficiency, or spiritual inactivity – although revivalists are never on surer ground than when they lambast the church for its lukewarmness. Nor is apostasy simply a result of spiritual tepidity, to be corrected by increased zeal. This has its own way of contributing to the latent gnosticism of pietistic faith. Rather, spiritual aridity ought to be regarded as a symptom of a more profound problem: the onset of theological amnesia. Though the crisis in the contemporary church may seem, ostensibly, to be about its perceived irrelevance, the crisis ought more properly to be identified as one of loss of the church's theological and baptismal identity as a community situated in Christ, 'occasioned by the distance at which the church lives from the source and sources of its faith and life', namely the scriptures.[24] Hence, the urgency to return to those sources and practices that enable the church to encounter once again the power of those scriptures.

The point of the daily office is to root prayer in those same scriptures, and thereby provide the church with a genuinely spiritual and theological model of renewal, rather than one that is merely organisational. This task, we contend, assumes certain adeptness in understanding the practicalities of church life and the particular tradition one is working in. Plenty of things have been written, for instance, about the reintroduction of the lectionary, but what it requires is a pastor-theologian who understands how this might be implemented, especially where there is a latent hostility to form. This is the complexity, of course, of the situation we are seeking to address, for here is a tradition – namely the charismatic-evangelical tradition – that is avowedly fundamentalist when it comes to scripture, yet refuses to allow its full exposure in the church.[25] The daily office, on the other hand, or something approximating to its devotional import, allows full exposure to scripture as well as prayer that is essentially meditative of the biblical theme.[26]

Enthusiasts may well object to the contrived nature of this ascetical spirituality, but in response will need to be far more intentional themselves if they are to emerge with anything comparable or better by way of devotional patterns. Ascesis is not alien to the radical evangelical tradition;[27] and leaving prayer to chance, based on the assumption that the spiritual immediacy of its worshipping life will carry over into daily prayer routines, is not a sufficient alternative. As Willimon and Hauerwas remind us, 'some things are too important to be left to chance'.[28] Outside of some set discipline of prayer, involving scripture, it is becoming more and more apparent that prayer is unlikely to occur.[29] Charismatic theology and spirituality requires the setting of the wider tradition if it is to successfully propagate itself beyond a first generation.

Praying the Psalms

One of the primary tools for the recovery of ascesis is the praying of the psalms. In Luther's treatment of the seven marks of the church, praying the psalms is one of the signs that 'a holy Christian people of God are present'[30] – and one of the means, we might add, of sustaining the faith response of the church. Psalms are the church's provision of prayer language that is as broad as it is honest. Such qualities can often be overlooked in prayer that is only extempore. Though important as a form of prayer, extempore prayer can often be self-indulgent and over concerned with the immediate aspirations of the church. In contrast, the church historically has understood praying the psalms as acts of obedience, answering the God who has addressed us: 'God's word precedes these words: these prayers don't seek God, they respond to the God who seeks us.'[31]

The renewal movement has not been without an appreciation of such prayer.[32] Many of the early songs in renewal were couched in the language of the psalms,[33] and it has often been noted in renewal circles that the commitment to the apostles' teaching, fellowship, and the breaking of bread, also includes a somewhat enigmatic reference to *the prayers*. In the context of first-century Judaism this would almost certainly include the recitation of the psalms, as

Acts 4 testifies to, where the use of these psalms are not merely messianic proof-texts, but evidences of the basic prayer vocabulary of the earliest Christian communities.

This unique status of the psalms in the church has continued, of course, throughout the history of Christian spirituality as an important component of a wider catholicity. Bonhoeffer attributed special significance to the Psalms in the theological community at Finkenwalde, noting that

> from ancient times in the Church a special significance has been attached to the common use of Psalms. In many churches to this day the Psalter continues the beginning of every service of common worship. The custom has largely been lost and we must find our way back to it again.[34]

But the recovery of psalmody is more than just an ecumenical issue. The provision of psalmody is the necessary corrective to a movement burdened by perpetual spontaneity. After all, notes Forsyth, 'it is very hard for the ordinary minister to come home to the spiritual variety of a large congregation without those great forms which arose out of the deep soul of the Church before it spread into the sectional boughs or individual twigs'.[35] Without anchorage in the prayers of the church, prayer for revival could eventually implode, acting as a source of discontent and not freedom.

This school of disciplined prayer ought to be regarded as no less fervent than revival prayer. Indeed, the spirituality that is generated out of revival settings would benefit by immersion in these primary texts, not least because it is here we learn that revival is not so much a noun as a verb: a legitimate cry from any Christian community for God to 'revive' what has been lost.[36] Concern about the way contemporary revivalism has developed should not obscure this long-standing prayer for God to revive us. Indeed, handled correctly, these particular psalms would be helpful tutors in the art of intercession, countering the hype surrounding 'revival' speak, while simultaneously refusing to accept the status quo. Commenting on Psalm 85 as a prayer for revival, Greenslade notes: 'In the end, when we've "discipled" it, "apostled" it, "named it and claimed" it, amplified it, "Wimber-ised" it, "Peretti-ed" it, territorialized it, inner healed it, "Toronto-ed" it, counselled it, marched around it ... then with relief we turn to God again!'[37] Psalmody focuses revival on primary causes, expressing repentance within, and not apart from, covenantal categories.

Immersion in the language of psalmody would provide a number of other possibilities for the broadening of the church's prayer concerns. First, in the psalms the whole array of human experience is covered, taken seriously, and embraced as legitimate material for the spiritual life. It is by praying the psalms that we become less intimidated, more thankful, full of praise, and wise unto salvation. More specifically, in praying the psalms the renewal is recovering language that embraces, using Luther's hermeneutic, a theology of suffering as well as a theology of glory.[38] Praying the psalms routinely – which is the way commended to us by those traditions most familiar with psalmody – challenges a fundamental weakness of charismatic theology, namely its inability to embrace suffering and pain.

Merlin Carother's *Power in Praise* is perhaps an extreme example of how modern spirituality avoids the problem of pain via positive praise;[39] nevertheless, the theology that underwrites such popular books is still very much in evidence. Charismatic worship is by definition upbeat and strident, with little or no reflection on the place of lament in spiritual development. Alpha confirms that the question of suffering, in terms of basic apologetics, is one of the most fundamental objections to the gospel, not withstanding the pastoral and theological issues raised in believing communities by the experience of pain.[40] Yet renewal spirituality, with its overly triumphalistic tone, is badly placed to deal with the issues of theodicy.[41]

Some attempt has been made certainly, within the movement, to redress the balance but what the psalms suggest, by their repeated use in worship and devotion, is a comprehensive training in the grammar of pain – one that resists sentimentality whilst, at the same time, expressing genuine lament. Praying the psalms invites a changed perspective on the question of pain by embracing it as an integral part of biblical spirituality. Because a large percentage of the psalms are what we might term psalms of lament, or to use Brueggemann's terminology, psalms of disorientation,[42] they permit the expression of grief within the community of faith, while at the same time providing boundaries and context in which grief can take shape.

The Lord's Prayer

The retrieval of Psalms suggests other, more classical ways of conceiving prayer, the object of which is not success in terms of revival, but rootage in terms of identity – the definition of revival we are proposing in this book. The Lord's Prayer is perhaps the most obvious starting place for re-envisioning prayer in the renewal in this way, and, once again, was perceived by Luther to be a mark of the church wherever it was heard and said.[43] It was, after all, an important part of the initiation-nurture mosaic of early Christianity: proficiency in praying the Lord's Prayer was the culmination of the long-term catechetical procedure.[44] Robert Warren reminds us that candidates for baptism were not allowed to know the content of it until well into the second year of their initiation, and even then they were not allowed to write it down because of its politically subversive nature.[45] What it provides for, however, is a rhythm and a language for prayer, which can sustain longevity of faith by virtue of its substantive nature. Its movement from address to intercession, to petition and confession, is thorough and encompassing of the whole range of prayer language. It is, in short, the prayer of the Christian and, as such, needs to be treated reverently as a gift to, as well as a mark of, the church.

In revivalist traditions, where extempore prayer is commonplace, the repetition of the Lord's Prayer is one of those practices so often castigated for its ritualism. Set within the ascetical tradition, however, its practice may be understood differently: one of a set of disciplines that enable faith to survive through the various fluctuations of enthusiasm. It prompts us to see prayer as a gift of language. Like the psalms, the Lord's Prayer provides words to answer God with. Relieved of the burden of spontaneity, as it might be termed, the Lord's Prayer is the means by which spiritual formation takes place through the power of language. Prayer is not a good strategy for 'getting what we want', as in revivalist traditions, but rather a way of 'bending our wants towards what God wants'.[46] Submission to the Lord's Prayer, by repetition and constant reflection, enables the kind of radicalism so prized by the enthusiasts precisely because the power of its language is a constant challenge to have our wills shaped by the divine will. God does not need our prayers. Rather, the act of prayer is the means itself of conforming and shaping the will to the shape of the kingdom of God.

This process of submission is not always apparent in extempore prayer. Fervency in prayer is often considered sufficient proof of its authenticity. This assumption lies behind a great deal that passes off as prayer in the charismatic community. The Lord's Prayer, on the other hand, as it intersects with genuine piety, questions this assumption by filtering those same aspirations and underlying motivations through the scrutiny and rigour of the cross. It is the cruciform shape of Christian spirituality that informs the basic petitions of the prayer. Praying the prayer enables such cruciformity to take place: 'This is the risky, crazy prayer of submission and commission, or if you like the prayer of subversion and conversion. It is the way we sign on, in our turn, for the work of the kingdom.'[47] As such, the Lord's Prayer is a basic identity marker. 'A Christian is none other than someone who has learned to pray the Lord's Prayer.'[48] In praying the Lord's Prayer it is possible that a more profound and radical spirituality might emerge, which, ironically, fulfils the early promise of the charismatic movement as a genuine renewal movement.

A number of things need to be said alongside this basic commitment to praying the Lord's Prayer, which impinges upon matters of spirituality in the charismatic tradition. First, the address 'Our Father' contains a solemnity and respectfulness that stands in marked contrast to the familiarity with the divine found so often in traditions emphasising immanence. Renewalists have been intent on expounding the spiritual intimacy associated with the terminology 'Abba' – famously translated by Jeremias as 'Daddy'[49] – which occurs in the Gospels and in Paul. But the colloquialism, as an attempt at contemporary contextualisation, falls short of the biblical usage, which combines both transcendence and immanence in ways hitherto unexplored within the renewal movement.[50] Praying the Lord's Prayer, beginning with 'Our Father', does not accommodate itself to the culture of immanence, but challenges it by addressing one who is both distant and near, with us and beyond us.[51]

Secondly, the Paternoster reminds us of the non-necessitarian nature of Christian revelation, so crucial if spirituality is not to implode into mere subjectivity. In calling God 'Father', we are describing first Jesus' relationship to God; such is the primary location of all Christian revelation. Christian living is not something we conceive by ourselves, but is derived from the inner-trinitarian life of God. As Paul explains, the primordial cry 'Abba' emanates from the Spirit of adoption, and presupposes incorporation into the body of Christ. Avoidance of the Lord's Prayer, therefore, in preference to a more contemporary, immediate model of praying, is to make the mistake of devaluing this rich churchly language for the sake of relevance.[52]

Conversely, because prayer is to the Father through Christ, and we believe in him through Christ, 'our prayer' says Bonhoeffer, 'can never be an entreaty before God, for we have no need to come before him that way'.[53] Prayer is not shouting into a vacuum, but fellowship that takes place in the *perichoresis* of the Father, Son and Holy Spirit. To conceive prayer as 'prevailing on the gates of heaven' is to introduce an essentially detached deity – one who must be overcome in premeditated prayer if our petitions are to have any chance of success. On the contrary, all Christian prayer, as the Lord's Prayer signals from the very outset, is mediated through the Son. By adhering to the basic shape of Christian prayer found in the Lord's Prayer, charismatics may well engage in petitionary, intercessory prayer, for this is indeed part of its theme. But essential to such petitionary praying is an understanding that the intimacy so often striven for in revivalist settings – the awareness of God's nearness – has already been realised in the way Jesus permits his followers, in the Lord's Prayer, to enter into his fellowship with the Father. The Paternoster is the essential counterpart to the experientialism of revivalist prayer. As Forsyth states: 'He made the all-knowing Fatherhood the true ground of true prayer. We do not ask as beggars but as children. Petition is not mere receptivity, nor is it mere pressure; it is filial receptivity.'[54]

The Lord's Prayer is not the only prayer Jesus taught, but its flexibility and its cadences are so well known that its role as a basic primer in prayer may well yet resurface.[55] For it to do so would require those in the renewal to envisage a shift in the way piety is expressed: a movement from private, subjective devotions to memorable fixed prayer, the value of which intensifies only with use. For such praying to occur would involve something more than a vague assent to this tradition, for praying in this way is part of a wider matrix of initiation into the Christian community, including an underlying commitment to spiritual direction that is just not available at the present time. Various prejudices against the liturgical way would have to be overcome. But unless some progress is made in this direction the renewal shows every sign of espousing a prayerless, contentless spirituality, or, worse still, a spirituality fed by paranoia, as the church seeks to pray the revival into being.

Praying in Tongues

This latter situation is particularly pertinent to the issue to be raised here of praying in tongues, for it is in this context of revivalism, where the church has been anxious to maximise its numbers, that tongues has featured in a somewhat masculine way as a sign of the church in victory. We are referring, of course, to overtly charismatic/Pentecostal communities where tongues are actually practiced. In this setting, as Fee observes, the gift of tongues has been regarded many times as a sign of strength, a proof that God will fulfil his purposes.[56]

From a biblical perspective the irony is fairly apparent, for tongues ought to be regarded, according to the theological doctrines of creation and redemption, as a sign of grace in weakness: the gift of prayer, inspiring the church to intercede even when it no longer knows what to pray for.[57] Tongues fits into the eschatological now and not yet, the respect of which is essential for the future of any charismatic theology, and means that tears ought to be as appropriate to charismatic experience as laughter.[58] Through the gift of tongues, the church signals its identity as the eschatological people of God, but also, through wise appropriation of the gift, it is able to participate in the dislocation of the world from that same eschatological destiny. It is a sign of longing as much as it is a sign of God's possession.

There is some evidence that such reflection concerning the gift of tongues has already taken place. 'It is of particular significance,' writes Cray, 'to some of us who have "laughed in the Spirit" that our experience has resulted in deepened capacity to empathise with the pain of others and make us quicker to tears than to laughter.'[59] Yet, the continued perception that tongues issues forth a particular brand of elitism suggests that tongues is still being used divisively. Speaking in tongues has acted notoriously as a way of isolating the unbeliever from the gathered people of God – a feature that has dogged the charismatic renewal throughout its history. Instead of tongues being a language of prayer, mostly private prayer, helping the church to intercede according to the Spirit's will, it has become a form of public power. In the process, as Robert Gladstone has pointed out, it has failed to identify with the pain of a dislocated world, acting only to judge it instead.[60] The intertextuality of Paul's argument in 1 Corinthians 14 helps to place us in the position of what it would be like to be present in a Christian gathering and not to understand what is going on; all it achieves is an unnecessary isolation and an ecclesiastical pride. The point of tongues ought to move in the opposite direction: a way of participating in the mission of God in the world.[61] Its import is not to attract by virtue of its extraordinary phenomena, but to enable the church to engage the world in its dislocation, and in doing so participate in the trinitarian mission.

As Gunstone comments in his exploration of tongues as a sacrament: 'Initial evidence is not a sign that we "have the Spirit"; rather, it is – or should be – a sign that the Spirit "has us" as participants in the work of the kingdom.'[62] By the Spirit helping us to pray in our weakness, we intercede according to the will of God, all the while anticipating our own redemption as sons of God in the final eschatological vision. The groanings that words cannot express are those first deposits of eschatological glory that move outwards in intercession, but always in recognition that the task of building the kingdom is God's, not ours. Contrary to the way prayer is now frequently conceived in revivalist traditions we are, at best, participants in the kingdom project. The mission of God in the world, Newbigin asserts, is not something that can be prosecuted after the manner of a crusade, for mission is trinitarian. To do the work of God, therefore, is for the church to participate in the Spirit's witness to what the Father is doing, delivering us thereby from the extremes of optimism and pessimism, and delivering us also from an over-heated apocalypticism.[63] Through the exercise of tongues, such participation is made prayerful.

In that sense, it is not inappropriate to view tongues in sacramental terms. Tongues, Chan argues, are 'primordial words that arise spontaneously in response to the invasive coming of the primal Reality to the believers which Pentecostals identify as Spirit baptism'.[64] Glossolalia is primordial language: the sacramental sign of Spirit baptism described in the previous chapter. It is obviously different to the other forms of prayer examined in this chapter, yet has in common with them the notion of response. As well as being the evidential sign that arises in response to immersion in the Spirit of Christ, tongues is the gift of language and means of grace by which the believer, as Killian McDonnell reminds us, sustains intimacy with God.[65] We should admit, unapologetically, the irrationality of such praying, for praying in the Spirit is indeed prayer that bypasses the mind. Nevertheless, it is prayer that is alert to the realities of spiritual adoption in Christ, acting precisely in the same way as the word and the sacraments as God's means of sustaining and edifying faith. As a way of arresting the exhaustive effects of revivalist praying, we commend such theological reflection of tongues to the renewal movement at this critical juncture, for not only does it strengthen the belief that Christian life is indeed located in the grace effected by the Spirit, namely, in Christ, but it also conceives prayer as essentially participation in the Spirit's own intercessions, 'stripped of its dross, its inadequacy made good, and presented as prayer should be. That is praying in the Holy Ghost'.[66]

Where revivalists have emphasised this understanding of prayer, seeing the Spirit as the primary intercessor in the quest for revival, we might concede some ground to the revival mood that has intensified in recent years. Matthew Henry's adage, 'When God intends great mercy for His people the first thing HE does is get them a praying', is often quoted in revival circles, and helps to locate intercessory prayer in the wider matrix of God's grace.[67] Indeed, to regard intercessory prayer in this way would not be dissimilar to the way it was conceived in the very earliest revival traditions. Edwards' Concert of Prayer for world revival was understood precisely in this way: as a response to the unmistakable and surprising evidence of the Spirit at work across two continents.[68] The theological and doctrinal rigour that attended such seasons of prayer, however, has largely disappeared. What is left is prayer approximating, in the case of prayer warfare, to contemporary animism, or, in the extreme cases of revivalistic prayer, to reinvented Baalism. Devoid of a proper rootedness in the Spirit, these are prayers that are anxious and hurried; and until revivalistic spirituality reinterprets prayer through the lens of trinitarian categories, one suspects that prayer for revival will contribute to a general and growing weariness found among evangelical charismatics.

Notes

[1] T. Virgo, *A People Prepared* (Eastbourne: Kingsway, 1996), 106.

[2] C. Dye, *Prayer Explosion* (London: Hodder & Stoughton, 1996), 2.

[3] Hocken, *Streams of Renewal*, 82–5.

[4] Scott, *Sowing Seeds of Revival*, 8.

[5] See A. Brown, *Near Christianity: Sorting Myth From Truth* (London: Hodder & Stoughton, 1996), 68–75.

[6] D.K. Gillett, *Trust and Obey: Explorations in Evangelical Spirituality* (London: Darton, Longman & Todd, 1993), 189. For a classic restatement of revival theology and the importance of 'prevailing prayer' see S. Piggin, *Firestorm of the Lord: The History and Prospects for Revival in the Church and the World* (Carlisle: Paternoster, 2000), 162–75, 179–84.

[7] See P.Y. Cho, *Prayer: Key to Revival* (Berkhamstead: Word, 1985).

[8] For an example of the best traditions of this zeal, see S. Tippit, *The Prayer Factor* (Amersham: Scripture Press, 1988); J. Cymbala, *Fresh Wind, Fresh Fire* (Grand Rapids: Zondervan, 1997); C. Cleverly, *The Prayer of Intimacy* (Eastbourne: Kingsway, 2002).

9   E. Storkey, 'Prayer and the Petitioner', *Bread for the Journey: A Waverley Resource for Pastoral Ministry* Issue 2 (1998), 13. As Elaine Storkey points out, the point of the two parables concerning importunity in prayer (Luke 11:5–13, Luke 18:1–8) is not that God is like an unjust judge, but precisely the opposite. This is not to deny the place for importunate prayer – see P.T. Forsyth, *The Soul of Prayer* (London: Independent Press, 1949 [1917]), 81–92 – yet importunity must always be set in the wider framework of a doctrine of grace, lest it take on a kind of Baalism.

10 Piggin, *Firestorm of the Lord*, 174.

11 Ibid., 162.

12 See A. Wallis, *God's Chosen Fast: A Spiritual and Practical Guide to Fasting* (Eastbourne: Kingsway, 1981), 102–105.

13 J.M. Talbot, *The Blessing* as cited in R. Warren, *An Affair of the Heart, How to Pray More Effectively* (Guildford: Highland, 1994), vii.

14 M. Ramsey, *The Christian Priest Today* (London: SPCK, 1999 [1972]), 15.

15 Forsyth goes on to assert that petition is purified by adoration. As a result of adoration 'we know better what to pray for as we ought'. Forsyth, *The Soul of Prayer*, 35.

16 Begbie, 'Renewal Music', 235.

17 P. Fiddes, *Participating in God: A Pastoral Doctrine of the Trinity* (London: Darton, Longman & Todd, 2000), 141.

18 D. Hansen, *Long Wandering Prayer: An Invitation to Walk With God* (Downers Grove: Inter-Varsity Press, 2001), 41.

19 See A.P. Boers, 'Learning the Ancient Rhythms of Prayer', *Christianity Today*, 8 January 2001, 38–45, on the popularity of the daily office in contemporary spirituality.

20 Ramsey, *The Christian Priest*, 19.

21 P. Bradshaw, *Daily Prayer in the Early Church* (London: SPCK, 1992), 29ff.

22 Ramsey, *The Christian Priest*, 15.

23 See G. Huntermann, *The Other Bonhoeffer: An Evangelical Reassessment of Dietrich Bonhoeffer* (Grand Rapids: Baker Book House, 1989), 99–102, who outlines Bonhoeffer's antipathy to pietistic interiority.

24 Alston and Lazareth, 'Preface', ix.
25 See J.G. Stackhouse, *Evangelical Landscapes: Facing Critical Issues of the Day* (Grand Rapids: Baker Book House, 2002), 47–74, although Willimon refers to the interesting use made of the lectionary in Free Church, specifically Restorationist, churches in W.H. Willimon, 'The Lectionary: Assessing the Gains and the Losses of the Homiletical Revolution', *Theology Today* 58:3 (2001), 131–41.
26 See D.D. Miles, 'Scripture in the Congregation' in Lazareth (ed.), *Reading the Bible,* 150–54.
27 See D.S. Whitney, *Spiritual Disciplines for Christian Life* (Colorado: NavPress, 1991); R. Foster, *Celebration of Discipline* (San Francisco: Harper Row, 1978); D. Willard, *The Spirit of the Disciplines* (San Francisco: Harper, 1988).
28 W.H. Willimon and S. Hauerwas, *Lord Teach Us: The Lord's Prayer and the Christian Life* (Nashville: Abingdon Press, 1996), 18.
29 As David Adam argues: 'If they're left without an office, without prayers they learn or recite, they tend to pray very little.' As cited in Boers, 'Learning the Ancient Rhythms of Prayer', 42.
30 M. Luther, 'In Place of a Preface: Martin Luther on "Seven Marks of the Church' in Braaten and Jensen (eds.), *Marks of the Body,* x–xi.
31 E.H. Peterson, *Answering God: The Psalms as Tools for Prayer* (San Francisco: Harper Row, 1989), 5.
32 See D. Williams, 'Worship Fit for a King', *Equipped: The Vineyard Magazine,* 4:1 (2001), 4–7.
33 D. Fellingham, 'The Focus and Direction of Contemporary Worship' in R. Sheldon (ed.), *In Spirit and Truth: Exploring Directions in Music in Worship Today* (London: Hodder & Stoughton, 1989), 49–68.
34 Bonhoeffer, *Life Together,* 30.
35 Forsyth, *The Soul of Prayer,* 39.
36 Psalm 80 and Psalm 85. See I.R. Stackhouse, 'Revivalism, Faddism and the Gospel' in A. Walker and K. Aune (eds.), *On Revival: A Critical Examination* (Carlisle: Paternoster, 2003), 239, for a development of this point.

37 P. Greenslade, *Songs for all Seasons* (Farnham: CWR, 2003), 141.

38 See L.H. Aden and R.G. Hughes, *Preaching God's Compassion* (Minneapolis: Fortress, 2002), 21–7.

39 See M. Carothers, *Power in Praise* (Eastbourne: Kingsway, 1974).

40 N. Gumbel, *Searching Issues* (Eastbourne: Kingsway, 1994), 9–27.

41 Scotland, *Charismatics*, 192–6.

42 See W. Brueggemann, *The Psalms and the Life of Faith* (Minneapolis: Fortress, 1995). Brueggemann's phrase 'the formfulness of grief' is an attempt to express this pastoral function of Psalmodic liturgy. See also R. Jacobson, 'Burning Our Lamps with Borrowed Oil: The Liturgical Use of the Psalms and the Life of Faith' in S.B. Reid (ed.), *Psalms and Practices: Worship, Virtue and Authority* (Collegeville: The Liturgical Press, 2001), 90–98.

43 Luther, 'In Place of a Preface', x–xi.

44 Warren, *An Affair of the Heart*, 147–60.

45 See M Crosby, *Thy Will Be Done: Praying the Our Father as Subversive Activity* (Maryknoll: Orbis, 1977), 2. The idea that churchly language requires reticence on the part of the addressee is picked up by Bonhoeffer in his notion of the discipline of the arcane. See D. Bonhoeffer, *Letters and Papers from Prison* (London: SCM, 1971 [1953]), 281, 286, 300.

46 Willimon and Hauerwas, *Lord, Teach Us*, 19.

47 N.T. Wright, *The Lord and His Prayer* (London: Triangle, 1996), 32.

48 Willimon and Hauerwas, *Lord, Teach Us*, 18.

49 J. Jeremias, *The Prayers of Jesus* (London: SCM, 1967), 11–65.

50 J. Barr, '"Abba" isn't "Daddy"', *Journal of Theological Studies* 39 (1988), 28–47.

51 See Weinandy, *The Father's Spirit of Sonship*, 123–36, for his criticism of Catherine LaCugna's *God For Us* (London: Harper Collins, 1991). If, in the interests of a theology of God for us, we eliminate the gap between God and us, then, paradoxically, 'we only come to experience and know the phenomenal God of the *oikonomia* and never the noumenal

God who actually exists in his wholly distinct otherness as God', 126.

52 See Norris, *Amazing Grace*, 246–50, where she laments the omission of the Lord's Prayer in modern worship.

53 Bonhoeffer, *The Cost of Discipleship*, 145. Interestingly, Bonhoeffer regarded the Lord's Prayer not merely as the pattern prayer, but 'the way Christians must pray. If they pray this prayer, God will certainly hear them. A disciple's prayer is founded on and circumscribed by it' (148).

54 Forsyth, *The Soul of Prayer*, 63.

55 B.J. Dodd, *Praying Jesus' Way: A Guide for Beginners and Veterans* (Downers Grove: Inter-Varsity Press, 1997).

56 G.D. Fee, *Listening to the Spirit in the Text* (Grand Rapids: Eerdmans, 2000), 118.

57 I am aware that Fee's observations rest on the assumption that Paul is referring in Romans 8:26 to the gift of tongues. For support of this position see F.D. Macchia, 'Sighs too Deep for Words: Towards a Theology of Glossolalia', *Journal of Pentecostal Theology* 1 (1992), 59, 70.

58 See F.D. Macchia, 'The Toronto Blessing: No Laughing Matter', *Journal of Pentecostal Theology* 8 (1996), 3–6.

59 Cray, 'The Toronto Experience', 168.

60 R.J. Gladstone, 'Sign Language in the Assembly: How are Tongues a Sign to the Unbeliever in 1 Cor 14:20–25', *Asian Journal of Pentecostal Theology* 2:2 (1999), 177–93.

61 See J. Shuman, 'Towards a Cultural-Linguistic Account of the Pentecostal Doctrine of the Baptism in the Holy Spirit', *Pneuma* 19:2 (1997), 207–24.

62 Gunstone, *Pentecost Comes to the Church*, 37.

63 See L. Newbigin, *Trinitarian Doctrine for Today's Mission* (Carlisle: Paternoster, 1998 [1963]), 54–5.

64 Chan, *Pentecostal Theology*, 40–72.

65 K. McDonnell, 'The Function of Tongues in Pentecostalism', *One in Christ* 19:4 (1983), 332–54.

66 Forsyth, *The Soul of Prayer*, 63.

67 Quoted in Wallis, *In the Day of Thy Power*, 136.

68 Ward, *The Protestant Evangelical Awakening*, 338.

Chapter 7

The Lost Art of the Cure of Souls

New Apostolic Leadership

A recovery of the various tools of ministry advocated thus far, such as preaching, sacraments and prayer, has repercussions for the way Christian leadership is generally conceived. Collectively, they relate to a model of ministry that might best be described as pastoral, attending to issues of the soul. But this is a model of ministry that has long since been jettisoned as inappropriate for the contemporary church. Indeed, the phrase 'cure of souls' sounds almost antique in the context of modern secular living. Focus instead is given to more managerial forms of leadership, oriented towards growth rather than spirituality, success rather than fidelity. This is hardly surprising. If growth is almost the only criterion for measuring success, then organisational leadership is bound to predominate; if modernity requires that our churches be big, then leadership styles need to be commensurate with that agenda. As Wallace Alston and William Lazareth argue, 'One might well document that the crisis in the church parallels the loss of theological identity by the church and the shift in its understanding of the minister from that of pastor-theologian to that of chief executive officer.'[1]

To say that this managerial model has been lifted straight out of the world of business would be to overstate the case, because there is still a good deal that is recognisably Christian within it. There is no virtue in Christian leadership that does not recognise at some point the importance of vision, strategy and good administration. Nevertheless, managerial leadership is not spiritual leadership as it has been understood within the historic tradition of Christian ministry. Indeed, spiritual leadership of a more pastoral kind has often been set up in opposition as a useful foil by the Church Growth protagonists.[2] In his advocacy of apostolic and prophetic leadership, Wagner is guilty of this very thing: setting up a derisory, lacklustre image of the traditional pastor's role, against which the new apostolic pastor appears as a healthy and welcome alternative. If the traditional pastor is the 'medicine man' of the church, tied up with the religious things of praying, baptising, explaining the Bible, the New Apostolic leader is the tribal chief who envisions the church around the tasks of the kingdom. He is the dynamic, strategic, visionary leader.[3]

To buttress these caricatures, Wagner gives his argument a sociological twist when he comes to describe these two ways of conceiving ministry as the difference between modalities and sodalities: modality is the term used for traditional congregational structures, whereas sodality refers to mission structures or para-church organisations. For modality leaders (local church pastors) people are primary and the task is secondary; for sodality leaders (New Apostolic pastors) the task is primary and the people are secondary. The thrust of Wagner's argument is that church leaders need to be far more visionary, throwing aside the sedentary and all too pedestrian nature of the pastoral office.[4]

To an extent one can sympathise. What is the charismatic renewal, and in particular the Restoration movement in the UK – about which Wagner has surprisingly little knowledge – if not a criticism of the inertia latent within traditional church structures? Apostolic and prophetic ministry, derived from such well-worn texts as Ephesians 4:11–13, is arguably the necessary supplement of itinerant ministry to local based church ministry, and one that challenges the latent parochialism of congregational life by keeping it focused on kingdom objectives. But what is sinister in Wagner's approach, which differs very little, if at all, with the rhetoric of the new churches over the last thirty years in the UK, is the almost complete dismissal of the importance of week to week pastoral ministry, in tasks that Wagner describes as merely religious.

This thesis has argued that it is precisely those religious tasks – what we might call sacramental encounters – that constitute effective ministry in the church. Prayer, teaching the scriptures, baptismal preparation, the laying on of hands, confession and communion are the very means of grace that actually accomplish the ministry and, moreover, have more historical and biblical precedent than the various techniques and strategies in circulation. Without such concrete means, the apostolic and prophetic vision for the church is counterproductive: mere rhetoric without any connection with actualities at the grassroots.

Revivalist churches, many are now realising, have been guilty of this: prophetic at the expense of the pastoral, to the point that many have left the movement lamenting the lack of substance and realism. Even within Anglicanism there has been a shift of emphasis, so that the term 'leader' is increasingly used in Anglican renewal as a substitute for the terms priest, presbyter and even pastor. Steven Croft attributes a good deal of the changing ethos to the impact of Wimber and the introduction of secular management theory, noting that 'one of the several dangers which follow is that prayer and preaching can be little more than servants of the leaders' vision'.[5]

The temptation here would be to set up a 'straw man' of our own, and set pastoral leadership over against visionary, but this would not be a constructive way to proceed. Clearly there is a place for strategic initiative within the church. The history of apostolic and prophetic ministry in the charismatic movement alerts us to the dynamism and strategic nature of such ministries. Moreover, we have to be careful not to romanticise the past by trying to recapture not only pastoral ministry but also a pastoral life. Having conceded as much, however, there is still the issue that if the charismatic-evangelical church is not to be entirely overtaken by the categories of functionality and pragmatism, something by way of a recovery of the classical pastoral ministry needs to occur – a recovery of the lost art of the cure of souls. 'Evidence is growing,' writes Thomas Oden, 'that the time is ripe for a major restudy of classical Christian pastoral care. The average pastor has come to saturation point with fads.'[6]

In the present climate, this sounds a somewhat ambitious project, let alone an ill-conceived one. The potential for being misunderstood is considerable, particularly in a churchmanship that equates the adjective pastoral with the sort of hierarchical one-man ministry abandoned by the renewal. But the risk is a necessary one, given that the charismatic movement is now facing the challenge of a second generation, in which, as we have already argued, there may be a legitimate recalling of some of the lost traditions that were jettisoned at the outset. Our hypothesis is based on this sociological and theological observation: namely, that the necessary iconoclasm of the first generation of any renewal movement ought not prevail into the second generation.[7] The second phase of renewal poses different challenges and requires different tasks, and requires a recovery and acknowledgment of the place of institution, lest its enthusiasm translates into cultish isolationism.

To some that might sound like the death knell of a movement: the ossification of enthusiasm. The recovery of certain traditions, however, may actually be a responsible way forward, in a way that does not compromise but rather supplements the achievements of the first generation. At a time when faddism is very much the hallmark of charismatic ecclesiology, it is our contention that the recovery of more substantial tools of ministry is not only a responsible way forward, but also an urgent one. The retrieval of such practices necessitates the recovery of a more overtly pastoral ministry.

The Recovery of Pastoral Ministry: The Work of Eugene Peterson

There are few guides to help us retrieve the pastoral ministry for renewal churches. Even within mainline denominational churches we have witnessed the diminution of pastoral ministry, or what used to be called pastoral theology, so that Oden's extensive bibliography for his own *Pastoral Theology* lists almost nothing from recent years. As a point of theological method it is a deliberate choice on his part: a decision to 'take the risk of listening attentively and obediently to the wisdom of the tradition'.[8] The idiosyncrasies of his bibliography also highlight, however, a regrettable neglect of the study of the pastoral office in our time. With the exception of Thornton's *Pastoral Theology*, already referred to, and Seward Hiltner's *Preface to Pastoral Theology*[9] there have been almost no attempts, claims Oden, to outline a systematic pastoral theology this century: 'Pastoral theology as a unifying discipline was flourishing a century ago and remained robust until the beginning of this century, yet it has largely faded into such hazy memory that none of its best representatives is still in print.'[10] Within the seminary there has been a discernable shift from the *theology* of ministry towards the *praxis* of ministry, to the extent that the practice of ministry has become the theology of ministry. This development is laudable in so far as it has helped to heal the bifurcation of academy and church, but it has often left pastoral ministry without any underlying theological rationale. Eddie Gibbs says:

> While these initiatives are commendable in many ways, they are in danger of being so competency-based that they fail to provide theological and missiological foundations and critiques to ensure that the growth they seek to enhance is authentic and substantive in terms of kingdom values.[11]

This absence of a theology of ministry is precisely why the evangelical-charismatic church has been prey to the various techniques and strategies emanating from the world of management. Without a common philosophy of ministry, church leadership is tantamount to nothing more than the running of a successful and efficient organisation. Such a reductionist view of ministry is evident, argues David Wells, in the popular ministerial journals such as *Leadership* magazine, where the focus is almost entirely upon the practical concerns of church management.[12]

Within the renewal in the UK, apart from a few popular writings, there is little treatment of the nature of pastoral ministry, or even how to go about what used to be standard ministerial assignments. What there is falls short of a full-blown exploration into the nature of ministry itself; and it is precisely for want of a mature philosophy of ministry that the renewal movement has been vulnerable to faddism, ranging from territorial spirits to the latest Cell Church movement. Each of these initiatives have important insights to glean, no doubt, but the problem with the implementation of such programmed approaches is that they have ended up being the sole definition of what ministry is about.

The Cell Church movement, which has been the latest panacea within the new churches, is, to some degree, guilty of this charge.[13] Apart from the fact that the success of cells ought properly to be seen as a response to growth and not, as many new church leaders mistakenly believe, as a cause of growth, the adoption of cell church principles has also encouraged a highly pragmatic approach to ministry in which only the fit survive. Whilst enthusiastic about the concept overall, Virgo's own discomfort with the managerial/executive approach of the Cell Church movement is due to his appreciation that ministry is more than fulfilling a mandate for church growth, and more than mere activism. Christian ministry has its own internal dynamics and integrity.[14]

One suspects that this concern regarding the functionality of the Cell Church movement is fairly widespread within the new churches, as well as more historic traditions. Despite protestations from Michael Green that 'cell church is not some new fad,'[15] based on the argument that it reflects the housechurch mentality of the earliest Christians – a view that is not without substance – more than one leader has commented privately, however, on the burden of having to implement a Cell Church programme in their local church, simply because it is held up as the next panacea for church growth and revival.[16] This is our main objection: not so much the strategy in question, but the way it is naively tied to an agenda for growth.

It is ironic that it is from North America, where Church Growth has prevailed on a scale unprecedented in the UK church, that signs of a backlash have appeared, most notably with Eugene Peterson who has made the retrieval of pastoral ministry something of a crusade. His convictions about pastoral ministry have been worked out over three decades, in a church that never reached a particularly large membership – a fact that in the North American context could be interpreted as an admission of failure. Peterson, as we shall see, does not think so. The issue of size, for Peterson, is related to a prior commitment to only pastor a congregation where personal knowledge of each and every member is possible. Therefore, a megachurch could not even be countenanced under such a scheme.[17]

Such honouring of the personal and local nature of congregational life, and deliberate distancing from the notion of numerical growth, stands in such sharp contrast to the impersonal and general rhetoric of contemporary church theorists that it is hard to promote Peterson without feeling one is stepping back into a world that has long since been dismissed as amateurish. But that is precisely the point. The heart of ministry, as Peterson defines it, is not frenetic, nor is it consumed by achievement; rather it can best be described as leisurely.

In what must be one of Peterson's most striking images of pastoral ministry, the pastor rises to his feet out of idleness not toil.[18] The image arises from Peterson's consideration of the 'unbusy pastor' – a term that sounds like an oxymoron in the contemporary context. But, for Peterson, unbusy describes exactly the radicality of the pastoral office, where the primary preoccupation is not with making an impact, but with attending to what God is doing. If this sounds esoteric it is more than offset by an earthiness in Peterson's understanding of spirituality, so that the congregational life we are describing here is definitely not an exercise in 'the deeper life'. Peterson has no tolerance for such notions.[19] Attentiveness to God, both in the life of the pastor and in the lives of the congregation, is attentiveness in the very real, and often messy, context of human existence. More importantly, however, the 'unbusy pastor' is a departure, argues Peterson, from the impersonal, functional rhetoric of those obsessed with the notion of successful churches.[20] 'The biblical fact,' argues Peterson, 'is that there are no successful churches. There are, instead, communities of sinners, gathered before God week after week ... the pastor's responsibility is to keep the community attentive to God.'[21]

It is this responsibility – through the vocational apparatus of prayer, attentiveness to scripture and spiritual direction – that is being abandoned, argues Peterson:

> American pastors have abandoned this vocation and have gone whoring after other gods. What they do with their time under the guise of pastoral ministry hasn't the remotest connection with what the church's pastors have done for most of twenty centuries.[22]

It is hard to find a more stinging critique of the contemporary scene than this introduction to Peterson's exploration of the shape of pastoral integrity – for it is integrity that Peterson seeks in terms of the dialectic of ministry and spirituality. Of course, agrees Peterson, pastoral life involves institutional responsibilities, 'but it never occurred to me that I would be defined by those responsibilities'.[23] Pastoral life is vocational. It is about attentiveness to God in prayer, scripture and spiritual direction.

This definition of ministry transcends even the various tools of ministry that comprise classical pastoral ministry. Prior even to the acquisition of specific tools of ministry, the pastoral office witnesses to a way of being: a spirituality, in which the primary vocation is to be with God. That this sounds unrealistic is more a comment on the superficiality of contemporary ministry, preoccupied as it is with growth and success, than it is about the naivety of Peterson's position; the corollary of this preoccupation is a churchmanship that is activist at the expense of contemplative. Thornton agrees:

> Our parishes are full of people who seem to have no vocation to the Christian life of prayer but will do anything for the church – give their money, run the youth club, tidy the churchyard or keep the accounts. Such work is necessary to the parish, but it certainly is not the fruit of faith.[24]

This deficiency within evangelicalism, in the area of spirituality, has, of course, been well rehearsed. But what Peterson alerts us to is that there are other ways of understanding the call to pastoral leadership in the church. Essential to the task of ministry is a foundational spirituality. Once these two – ministry and spirituality – are separated from their necessary dialectical tension, we are left in ministry without a true ascesis. Vocation or calling to a life of prayer is reduced to professional tasks.

The Contemplative Pastor

In respect to the subject of spirituality, and its dialectical relationship to ministry, one notes, alongside Peterson, the widespread appeal of the Catholic writer Henri Nouwen among Protestants in search of ascetical renewal. Since his death numerous biographies have appeared seeking to make sense of his unique spiritual vision.[25] What is clear in Nouwen's work, however, is a relentless attack on the modern distortion of ministry from contemplation to mere activism. Reflecting on Jesus' temptations in the wilderness, Nouwen challenges three contemporary idols in ministry: relevance, sensationalism and power. In response, Nouwen proposes an alternative way of ministry centred on loving Jesus, feeding his sheep and being led. The first is axiomatic of all ministry: the importance of personal contemplation. Instead of the incessant pursuit of relevance, Nouwen advocates the innocuous and seemingly useless pursuit of God himself. He writes:

> If there is any focus that the Christian leader of the future will need, it is the discipline of dwelling in the presence of the One who keeps asking us, 'Do you love me? Do you love me? Do you love me?' It is the discipline of contemplative prayer. Through contemplative prayer we can keep ourselves from being pulled from one urgent issue to another and from becoming strangers to our own and God's heart.[26]

Perhaps this is what makes Nouwen so attractive to evangelicals: his disregard for what might be termed the efficacy of ministry, and a recovery of the primary vocational call of being with Jesus.[27] It represents the replacement of the moral by the mystic, the activist by the contemplative. Apart from this, ministry is shrill.

Elsewhere, in possibly Nouwen's most important and celebrated book, he elaborates on the contemplative nature of life and ministry. *The Return of the Prodigal Son* is the culmination, in many ways, of his theological and spiritual vision. There, he characterises ministry as something of an epiphany of what it means to be the Beloved. This is the absolute centre of what it means to be a Christian – to know that through Jesus, as he comes to us in eucharist and the word 'You are the Beloved'.[28] Ministry is nothing more than living in the reality of this identity oneself. 'To be living reminders of God we must be concerned first of all with our own intimacy with God. Once we have heard, seen, watched, and touched the Word who is life, we cannot do other than be living reminders.'[29] Nouwen insists that in the dialectic of ministry and spirituality, of service and prayer, it must be this way round: the priority of the call *to be* before the call *to do*. According to Nouwen, ministry is simply the revelation to others what one has already seen in contemplation, namely the knowledge through Christ that one is loved; hence, the image of the sculptor:

> The art of sculpture is, first of all, the art of seeing. Michelangelo saw a loving mother carrying her dead son on her lap ... The image of the sculptor offers us a beautiful illustration of the relationship between contemplation and ministry. To contemplate is to see, and to minister is to make visible; the contemplative life is a life with a vision, and the life of ministry is a life in which the vision is revealed to others.[30]

This disciple of 'holy inefficiency', as he has been described, has a great deal to offer to a renewal movement dominated by issues of praxis.[31] Contemplation is the spiritual counterpart to the indicative mood we referred to earlier; it is the appropriate spirituality for a theology where, in Carl Braaten's words, 'Being precedes act.'[32] Ministry is not to be understood as exhortation towards something that previously did not exist, but revelation and reminder of what is a true and present reality through Christ and the Spirit.

Evangelicals may not be comfortable with Nouwen's Roman Catholic rootage. Don Carson dismisses Nouwen's spirituality as not firmly anchored in the biblical tradition: an example of the vagueness inherent in the current interest in spirituality.[33] In fact, Nouwen's spirituality resonates well with the biblical tradition, rooted as it is in a thoroughly Johannine christology. Moreover, his understanding of ministry shares a great deal in common with the evangelical emphasis of heart religion, brought to the fore in charismatic renewal. If a truly evangelical spirituality is to emerge, it will have to recover this priority and learn to be less intimidated by statisticians and sociologists. Undoubtedly, it possesses something akin to Nouwen's spirituality, but in recent years it has been overshadowed by utilitarian concerns.

One suspects, however, that it will take a great deal of courage to insist on the mystical element as the basis of an authentic evangelical ministry. The state of seminary education does not augur well for such a recovery. Spirituality in the context of theological education at the present time is something of an addendum. It certainly does not inform the main disciplines of academic theology.[34] Because of this, it may be left to small-scale and ad hoc developments at the local level to pioneer a different way of conceiving ministry. It is this recovery, we are arguing, that will signal the beginning of authentic renewal. Toronto, surprisingly, was a step in this direction: witness the amount of testimonies of pastors and leaders who claimed to have recovered the 'first love' that Nouwen talks about.[35] Unfortunately, however, this spiritual theme is too entwined in renewal with further agendas, in particular issues of church growth, for it to have any lasting benefit. First love in ministry needs to be exactly that: a celebration and embrace of the love of God in Christ without any extraneous agenda. Until renewalists can learn to appreciate this celebration as a basis of all ministry and ecclesiology, living with the irrelevance of such a posture, the renewal of ministry and spirituality is unlikely to occur.

The ministry of word and prayer

Having established that ministry is first of all a way of being – a way of prayer – it ought to be clear then that the actual tasks of ministry work out of a respect for the continual dialectic of ministry and spirituality. There is no ministry that exists, in a professional sense, which does not arise from contemplation. Ministry is simply the making aware to others what one has already seen, bringing to remembrance what is already a reality.

Remembrance has been a continual theme throughout this book: remembrance as it relates to the act of preaching, baptism, communion, worship, and indeed the baptism of the Spirit. Indeed, as Nihls Dahl points out, 'the first obligation of the apostle vis-à-vis the community – beyond founding it – is to make the faithful remember what they have received and already know – or should know'.[36] This is quite different to current definitions of apostolic ministry, or Christian leadership in general. It is an understanding of ministry, however, deeply anchored in the biblical tradition, where there is an awareness that to remember is not simply to look back at past events, but to bring the past into the present so that it might be entered into and celebrated. Brevard Childs writes:

> The act of remembering serves to actualise the past for a generation removed in time from those former events in order that they themselves can have an intimate encounter with the great acts of redemption ... Although separated in time and space from the sphere of God's revelation in the past, through memory the gulf is spanned, and the exiled people share again in redemptive history.[37]

In that sense it is clear that the retrieval of traditional ministry for evangelicalism is not the recapturing, in sentimental nostalgia, of a lost Christendom. It would be a mistake to regard classical ministry in this way. Instead, the theology of remembrance is to be understood as a return to the source of ministry, the original vision from which the inspiration came. Nouwen explains:

> In this sense all reformers are revisionists, people who remind us of the great vision ... They all have moved backwards, not in sentimental melancholy but in the conviction that from a recaptured vision new life can develop. The French have an imaginative expression: *recular pour mieux sauter,* to step back in order to jump further.[38]

Our thesis is not about abandoning the many positive gains that have accompanied charismatic renewal – though it may be misunderstood that way; rather, our desire is to progress forward in renewal, realising that the radical vision must also retrieve aspects of the tradition as it progresses through subsequent stages: 'The paradox of progress is that it occurs by conserving the great memory, which can revitalise dormant dreams.'[39] The enemy of the church is not without, in the form of territorial spirits, or postmodernity, or indeed secularisation, but within, in the form of a churchmanship that refuses to deploy its doctrinal, theological and sacramental resources for the fight. It is a crisis of faith that can only be remedied, according to Eric Mascall, by a recovery of faith:

> The Church's tradition is a great living inheritance of thought and life, most of whose content has hitherto been undiscerned and most of whose potentialities have hitherto been unactualised. It is by bringing this great living inheritance into impact upon the world in which we live that our task towards that world will be achieved.[40]

What this means in terms of the weekly priorities of ministry is something rather different to that which

Wagner and others conceive. First, it means fidelity to the scriptures as the resource of the believing community and faithful uncovering of the promise contained therein. A theology of remembrance implies something akin to Long's image of the preacher, mentioned earlier, whom the congregation sends out on their behalf to the scriptures, in order that the preacher might bear witness to the gospel. This is more than a commitment to textuality; it is a commitment to vocational integrity: a belief in the ministry of the word and prayer as the presuppositional basis of all Christian ministries.[41] Having vocational integrity means we can resist the temptation to distort the word for the sake of relevance, principles or application. The art of a distinctively Christian ministry is that it delights in the retelling of the story, because there is a belief that the story is subversive of all other stories. No amount of abstraction, principles and growth manuals can convey this subversion; indeed, to abstract is to dilute. The scriptures, Brueggemann reminds us, are prophetic in themselves, and require faithful and diligent attention if their authority is to be fully felt within the church.[42] This is the task of pastoral ministry as it works in the intersection of prayer, pastoral care and preaching.

With contemporary models of ministry so dominated by questions of growth, such a commitment to scripture will require a major revision of the tasks that press upon pastoral ministry – a recovery of a way of life reflecting not the rush associated with the fulfilling of a vision, but of rest derived from the actualities of the Christian revelation.[43] Again, it is Forsyth, in his discussion of ministry, who provides succinct and apposite terms for us to understand this contrast. In *The Ideal Ministry* he arrives at a surprising image of the church as a priestly church: a church whose primary vocation is not to minister to the world, but to offer work to God for the world.[44] The antithesis is typically

Forsythian and we may not want to state the situation as either/or. But Forsyth reminds us that 'when it offers to God the sacrifice of Christ, which it does in every one of its sacred functions – for they are all acceptable in Christ's sacrifice alone – the church is a priestly Church, and it is doing a priestly task for the world'.[45]

We have witnessed this indifference to matters of relevance and popularity before in the prophetic/priestly dialectic in Thornton's work. According to Forsyth, the priestly understanding of the church, and its corollary of a priestly ministry, is a useful test for a church to apply to itself, for it may lead to the surprising conclusion that 'the weakest churches are not the smallest'.[46] Croft agrees: 'we need to question the idea that individuals and communities can sustain continual and meaningful growth: the experience is as likely to lead to overextension, burnout, retreat and exhaustion, as it is to real progress.'[47] The essential task is the substantial one of staying faithful to the contours of Christian revelation.

Integral to such revision is recognition that the Holy Spirit determines and regulates the parameters of ministry. In that sense, ministry is not about doing, but paying attention to what the Holy Spirit is doing; it transcends professional competence, vital though that may be; it also transcends ministry as an exercise in being with people, although good pastoral practice is primarily about drawing alongside as a physical presence; it is an understanding of ministry that is rooted in prayer and that has as its doctrinal basis prevenience:

> God everywhere and always seizing the initiative. He gets things going. He has and continues to have the first word. Prevenience is the condition that God has been working diligently, redemptively, and strategically before I appeared on the scene, before I was aware there was something here for me to do.[48]

That being the case, ministry is far less to do with innovation and initiative than it is to do with listening and attentiveness.

Theoretically, evangelicalism possesses such a rationale for ministry. Certainly the charismatic movement, through an emphasis on the prior work of the Holy Spirit, has been keen to articulate such trust. Often, however, the freedom in ministry implied by this pneumatology has never been allowed fully to develop. In fact, the opposite is often the case. The fact that Jesus said 'I only do what I see the Father doing' has, on many occasions become a pretext for imposing, as well as legitimising, the supernatural – an example of how Spirit movements manipulate the church into the 'surprises of the Spirit'. There is, of course, a fine line between genuine openness to the Spirit and manipulation of spiritual experience; furthermore, we are not unmindful of the fact that motives in ministry are often mixed, even at the best of times. Nevertheless, our concern remains. There is a pressure in revival contexts to achieve and to perform which often negates the leisureliness and spiritual attentiveness of the pastoral vocation. In evangelical circles this is easily disguised as well intentioned activism, but for Peterson it is a betrayal of ministry, which is focused on the more modest task of preserving one's spiritual and vocational integrity, while attending to the routine work of congregational formation.

Spiritual direction

It is worth pausing here to locate the basis of this kind of spiritual and theological understanding of ministry within the history of pastoral theology. In such a history John Patton identifies three phases: the classical, the clinical, and the communal. The classical, he argues, is a model that prevailed from pre-Reformation times through to the impact of modern psychology, dealing with the cure of souls. The impact of modern psychology upon Christian ministry led, however, to what Patton calls the second major phase, the clinical, replaced in recent years by the communal as the limitations of clinical care in the church context became all too apparent.[49] Patton's argument is that the classical tradition, based on the biblical theme of God's remembering, ought to inform both the clinical and the communal. God's remembering of us becomes the basis of our remembering of redemption in Christ and the source of all pastoral care as it seeks to reaffirm Christian identity. This chapter, focusing upon the work of Peterson in particular, represents an unashamed call back to that first phase in the history of pastoral care: the disciplines of prayer, attention to scripture and spiritual direction, as that which defines the work of the pastor. It is based on a conviction that pastoral care has its own integrity, its own disciplines, cumulative traditions and its own theological basis, which is separate and distinct from the contemporary counselling model, though not antithetical to it either.

It is this theological tradition that commends itself to the Christian community as well as those outside seeking help. The community that constitutes the church is not, as David Lyall points out, 'random collections of individuals. They are shaped by historical traditions, creedal statements and confessions, modes of worship, ethical codes'.[50] Therefore, it is entirely appropriate that the kind of pastoral care offered in the church coheres with and derives from these traditions, embracing the sacrament and the word, rather than those offered by psychotherapy.[51] Use ought be made, of course, of the therapeutic model; to not do so would be guilty of an unnecessary retrenchment. Pastoral care, however, works from within the Christian narrative, confident of being able to address the concerns and pains that arise from the peculiarities of a Christian faith community.

Such an approach seeks not to spiritualise pastoral care. Indeed, one of the tasks of classical pastoral care is to relate Christian theology to the whole of life, part of which is to know when to refer to outside, even secular, agencies.[52] Such a procedure should not be seen as inimical to the classical model in a contemporary setting. But *cura animarum*, the cure of souls, does insist on a distinctively Christian mode of diagnosis, which includes confession of sin, the proclamation of grace and the process of sanctification. This is not without complications, of course, for spiritual progress never comes in neat packages. The psalms alone legitimate the expression of the whole gamut of emotions from praise to lament, demonstrating in the process the somewhat erratic and unpredictable nature of spiritual growth. Nevertheless, for ministry not to collapse into mere sentimentality, or mere therapy, *cura animarum* insists on a robust theological framework within which to make sense of such experiences, relating them to ultimate meanings. Stephen Pattison's definition of pastoral care in the classical tradition states this position well: 'Pastoral care is that activity, undertaken especially by representative Christian persons, directed towards the elimination and relief of sin and sorrow and the presentation of all people perfect in Christ.'[53]

This often quoted definition of pastoral care approximates to the theological contours of grace we have outlined throughout. It may be simplified further with reference to Alistair Campbell's definition of pastoral care, which is 'to help people know love, both as something to be received and as something to give'.[54] Such a definition summarises well the pastoral task of witnessing to the work of Christ in a person, respecting that work and providing space for new life to emerge. To support his case Campbell provides ready situations where this love ethic might apply in pastoral care. Pastoral care is not the offering of advice at an intellectual level, nor the eliciting of insight at an emotional level; it is more related to the concept of spirituality, encompassing a vision of authentic humanity and genuine transcendence. As Peterson reminds us regarding the pastoral role of spiritual direction, 'the suggestion to *do* something is nearly always inappropriate, for persons who come for spiritual direction are troubled over some disorder or dissatisfaction in *being*, not *doing*'.[55] What is required, therefore, is a person who is familiar with the language of prayer, and one who, for the sake of the person before them, 'will pay attention to who they are, not a project manager who will order additional busy work'.[56]

Given the professional credibility of the modern counsellor, along with the increasing marginalisation of clerical status, such a vision of pastoral ministry will be hard to achieve; it is precisely because of the perceived irrelevance of pastoral ministry that ministers have sought other forms of legitimation, such as counselling.[57] The cultural climate of postmodernity has put counselling rather than pastoral care in the ascendancy, and the behavioural sciences often are given more credence than the scriptures. Strangely, however, there is a growing conviction concerning the limitations of the therapeutic model for pastoral care in church communities.[58] Peterson's contribution to the recovery of pastoral ministry is one that is being increasingly acknowledged.[59] His understanding of the pastor's task as primarily a theological and spiritual task has had a significant influence on a number of practitioners. In *Jesus the Pastor*, James Frye pays tribute to the way Peterson's understanding of pastoral ministry helped him as a Vineyard pastor to transcend the more functional categories of Church Growth strategies.[60]

Douglas Webster accords Peterson similar importance in his own attempts to combat the more insidious features of Church Growth.[61] What they both describe is a feeling of betrayal in the overuse of managerial language where pastoral vocation has been eclipsed by the concern for statistics. Vivian Thomas is another who has been influenced by Peterson's insistence that managerial and visionary models of ministry fail to account for the personal and often erratic nature of spiritual formation associated with classical pastoral care.[62]

A similar contribution to that of Peterson's toward the recovery of authentic pastoral ministry is provided by Hansen. Hansen takes his cue from Peterson in his distancing from trend driven and task driven ministry. 'Task driven ministry always gives way to time management ministry as opposed to Spirit led ministry.'[63] Pastoral ministry is in essence about following Jesus; more specifically about being a parable of Jesus to those we minister to: 'Being a parable of Jesus shows me how it is possibly true when he says: "He who receives you receives me, and he who receives me receives the one who sent me." '[64] Pastoral ministry thrives on this possibility, that in the hospital visit, or the house call, or in the chance conversation, the pastor actually brings the living Christ to the one we minister to.[65] Far from being those religious things that pastors get bogged down in, this is actually what the ministry is – what we might call sacramental moments, often unplanned, that are predicated on the vocation of a pastor to be a parable of Christ. In fact, according to Oden, the best pastoral care is unplanned. It takes on the nature of serendipity, so that the important thing in the cure of souls is not even the fulfilling of ecclesiastical tasks, but simply being available to the prompting of the Spirit.[66]

Such a view of ministry sounds dangerously un-structured, requiring courage to lay aside preconceived agendas. Indeed, to make it practicable it may be preferable to add a note of planning to such spontaneity.[67] But based on a working belief in the ministry of the Holy Spirit and the random nature of human interaction, Hansen's is a view of ministry that ought to commend itself to leaders in charismatic churches. That it remains unexplored as a metaphor for pastoral ministry indicates however how much leadership within these particular types of churches has been overwhelmed by functional/managerial metaphors.

Future Leadership: A Synthesis

In the context of the charismatic movement, the recovery of pastoral ministry is somewhat problematic. Given the commitment, in certain quarters, to the re-establishment of the five-fold ministry of apostle, prophet, evangelist, pastor-teacher, it may appear, as we have already noted, as a return to the so-called one-man ministry: the exalting of the pastoral office to the detriment of all else. Such confusion is clearly possible, but is not intended. Apostolic and prophetic ministry seems to be one of the constant features of New Testament church polity, and has been one of the most positive contributions of the renewal.[68] It has introduced a welcome dynamism into an otherwise static view of Christian leadership, in particular the notion of team ministry over against the 'solo minister'. But what has often been overlooked in the recovery of itinerant ministry is precisely that ministry which might be described as pastoral and didactic. Caricatured as sedentary and pedestrian, when juxtaposed to the ministry of the apostle and the evangelist, it has received very scant treatment indeed. And so we have an odd, somewhat ironic, situation of a commitment to the five-fold office without appreciating the full range of ministry gifts for the edification of the body of Christ and the equipping of the saints. Recovery of the pastoral and teaching ministry is an essential part of the rediscovery of charismatic forms of leadership.[69]

Writing from within the perspective of the renewal movement, this book is to some extent an attempt to describe that pastoral ministry, as it exists alongside the apostle, prophet and evangelist. More importantly, it is a plea for the actual practice of that ministry. One of the unforeseen effects of the emphasis on equipping the laity, as we shall see, could be the disappearance of actual pastoral ministry as it is administered by the pastor to the congregation. The mutual exclusivity of pastor as shepherd and pastor as equipper is an unfortunate dichotomy and one that need not exist. To equip the church is not to abdicate the responsibilities of ministry, but to share it: to be actually involved in the pastoring of a congregation at the primary level of visiting, counselling and giving spiritual direction.

Coupled to the idealism of the renewal movement, and Wagner's New Apostolic Church perspective in particular, such a response sounds hopelessly outdated and places undue demands upon the pastor; but for Peterson immediacy in pastoral work is prerequisite. One might go further and say that to adequately equip the church one must have a working experience of the gift one wants to impart: hence, the absolute necessity of equippers being also practitioners, in the same way that we might want theologians to be practitioners. For without this, ministry is reduced to pure strategy.[70] Such reductionism is a distinct possibility, if not a reality already, in a churchmanship that has distanced itself from the classical tradition.

The assumption, of course, is that pastoral care will occur through the mutual edification of the members of the church. Whole manuals concerning pastoral care in the church are constructed on this basis – what has been termed by one exponent, the Jethro principle.[71] Two decades of pastoral care through the house group or cell group system has been based on this principle. Again, our purpose is not to renege. Nevertheless, without the focusing of pastoral ministry in the office of a pastoral leader – and one who is personally involved – it is doubtful whether pastoral care ever becomes anything more than the biblical mandate to love one another. Pastoral leadership is a great deal more. Admittedly, notes Oden, 'the lay Christian carpenter, clerk, or janitor also has a clear duty to care for others, but such is not their principle lifelong vocational task. Care of souls is not a side interest in the pastor's life and work; it is the pastor's life'.[72] Moreover, it cannot be just one department in the recent trend of staff specialisation. Pastoral ministry defines what congregational leadership is, so that the dividing of the office into specialisations, where one is visiting, one is preaching, one administrating, is to destroy its integrity. Clearly, there is a call upon the life of every congregation to offer care to one another, and a pastor with an awareness of the task will want to share this ministry; but as to the unique role of the pastor of a church, Peterson contends that

> the pastoral office is scriptural, and historic and essential. It has been abused as everything else has, but it's important to have one person set apart in the community to study God's word and proclaim it, and pray and know in detail everybody's life – the pains and temptations and blessings.[73]

At this point we discover how opposed this view of leadership is to the aspirations of Church Growth, for the logic of the pastoral office, argues Oden, leads to the unsurprising conclusion that no pastor should accept an appointment to a parish in which he or she cannot properly care for the souls in that place; no flock should be so large that it cannot be cared for properly: 'Although we cannot redo history it seems better, where possible, to keep local congregations small enough that a single pastor can look after them.'[74]

In a culture where size often equals success, such a perspective of the local congregation in its relative small-ness seems tantamount to defeatism. Peterson's own experience with a congregation that rarely exceeded three hundred seems rare and odd in a churchgoing subculture preoccupied with growth and mobility. But when the priority in leadership concerns qualitative rather than quantitative issues, the oddity of Peterson's context, or at least the open and unashamed admission of relatively modest numbers, can be appreciated. The issue is one of fidelity rather than success. This is a constant theme in Peterson's writing. The exalting of large, dynamic, problem free churches is nothing less than 'ecclesiastical pornography' in Peterson's opinion, and has done a grave disservice to many pastors who live with a constant sense of having failed.[75] Not that large churches should automatically be treated with suspicion; nor that small is necessarily beautiful. But when size is the only yardstick by which we measure success then we ought to protest. The image approach fails to appreciate, as only a local and long-term pastoral approach can fully appreciate, the daily realities of church life – what Neuhaus describes as the 'Thus and So-ness' of the church.[76]

Again, to those coming from a New Church perspective, in particular those with a Restorationist agenda with its commitment to the recapturing of the heady atmosphere of the New Testament church, such a description of church life could be construed as resignation to the status quo. This criticism is valid. One of the weaknesses of Peterson's approach is that he too readily accepts the existing context as fertile soil for spiritual formation, ignoring the times when radical, indeed schismatic, movements have been a necessity. There are times when an acceptance of the 'Thus and So-ness' of the church is itself a form of accommodation. Nevertheless, for all the raw triumphalism of the charismatic movement, the reality that most pastors have to deal with on a weekly basis is almost exactly as Neuhaus describes it. Without pastoral leadership that can deal with this, vision of whatever kind, and however it is packaged, is mere rhetoric.

Having stated the issues thus, it seems likely that visionary language will continue to furnish the literature and conferences of the renewal movement. The critical issue, therefore, is defining what vision means and determining how vision comes about. The promotional literature about the visionary qualities of various conference speakers could leave many pastors feeling intimidated. Vision from God, we are told, is strategic, global and most definitely large. A cursory glance at the portfolios of any of the main conference speakers would convey that impression. But is this really the case? Exploring the life of Nehemiah, Thomas makes the point that 'vision from God does not come in neat packages. Confusion and emotion are acceptable parts of the human condition'.[77] As the charismatic movement matures, there is a greater awareness that this is in fact the case, but generally the pressure to succeed undoes it.[78] The ambiguity that is part of the reality of church existence is not given its rightful place. The pressure that derives from apostolicity is for large, strategic initiatives.[79] Thomas reminds us, however, that 'it is often the small and unexpected things which have the greatest impact and the huge, and often expensive strategic initiative which dies whimpering on the side'.[80]

Thomas reflects on the nature of Christian leadership in a way that does full justice to the very best of the classical pastoral tradition that we are wanting to uphold here:

'Great leaders engage with the people they serve; they laugh, weep, grow, repent and age with their community.'[81] Peterson calls this 'vocational holiness': that special brand of holiness forged on the anvil of church conflict, difficult parishioners and failed expectations. Little is spoken about it in renewal circles and yet it is universally experienced. It is precisely this type of leadership that is required now at this critical juncture in the charismatic movement, lest it becomes a victim of its own rhetoric. To conclude this chapter and indeed part two, we look again to Neuhaus, who puts the case, succinctly, for spiritual leadership:

> What is needed is not the training of religious technicians but the formation of spiritual leaders. It is important for seminaries to impart skills and competencies; it is more important to ignite conviction and courage to lead. The language of facilitation is cool and low risk. The language of priesthood and prophecy and the pursuit of holiness is impassioned and perilous ... the pursuit of holiness is not the quest for the Holy Grail ... It is rather a question of actualising the gift that is already ours.[82]

Notes

1   Alston and Lazareth, 'Preface', xii. See also K.A. Miller, 'Do You Lead by Thought or Organisation', *Leadership* (Fall, 1998), 130.
2   G. Barna, *The Second Coming of the Church* (Nashville: Word, 1998), 106.
3   P. Wagner, *Churchquake* (Ventura: Regal, 1999), 82–96.
4   Ibid., 96–7.
5   See S. Croft, *Ministry in Three Dimensions: Ordination and Leadership in the Local Church* (London: Darton, Longman & Todd, 1999), 109. See also A.B. Robinson, *Transforming Congregational Culture* (Grand Rapids/Cambridge: Eerdmans, 2003), 32.

[6] T. Oden, *Care of Souls in the Classical Tradition* (Philadelphia: Fortress, 1984), 35. A similar commitment to the cumulated wisdom of the historical pastoral tradition is found in W.A. Clebsch and C.R. Jaekle, *Pastoral Care in Historical Perspective: An Essay with Exhibits* (New York: Jason Aronson, 1975), 2, and W.H. Willimon, *Pastor: The Theology and Practice of Ordained Ministry* (Nashville: Abingdon, 2002), 71: 'There is much to be said for the pastor being educated in the classical forms of Christian ministry.'

[7] Cf., P. Hocken, *The Strategy of the Spirit: Worldwide Renewal and Revival in the Established Church and Modern Movements* (Guildford: Eagle, 1996), 147–8, who envisages the enrichment of revival spirituality of the new churches as it cross-fertilises with historic traditional churches.

[8] T.C. Oden, *Pastoral Theology: The Essentials of Ministry* (San Francisco: Harper & Row, 1983), 7.

[9] S. Hiltner, *Preface to Pastoral Theology* (New York: Abingdon, 1954).

[10] Oden, *Pastoral Theology*, xii.

[11] E. Gibbs, *ChurchNext: Quantum Changes in How We Do Ministry* (Downers Grove: Inter-Varsity Press, 2000), 99.

[12] D.F. Wells, *No Place for Truth, Or Whatever Happened to Evangelical Theology?* (Grand Rapids: Eerdmans, 1993), 113–14.

[13] See Beckham, *The Second Reformation*, 231–41, where he links the terms reformation, spiritual revival and restoration.

[14] Interview with T. Virgo, 23 November 1999.

[15] M. Green, 'Cell Church: Its Strengths and Dangers' in M. Green (ed.), *Church Without Walls: A Global Examination of Cell Church* (Carlisle: Paternoster, 2002), 122.

[16] This is a methodological point. One of the reasons why there is so little self-critique in the charismatic movement, both written and verbal, may be, perhaps, due to the fact that for a leader to question the merits of a particular strategy could be seen as tantamount to disloyalty.

[17] E.H. Peterson, *Subversive Spirituality* (Grand Rapids/ Cambridge: Eerdmans, 1997[2]), 225–7.

[18] E.H. Peterson, *The Contemplative Pastor* (Grand Rapids: Eerdmans, 1989), 24.

19 Peterson, *Subversive Spirituality*, 32–9.
20 Peterson is relentless in his attack on functionality. His lectures on biblical spirituality at Wycliffe Hall/Regent College Summer School, Oxford, 2–6 July 2001 were regularly punctuated by attacks on the way the church has been hijacked by managerial, impersonal language. In personal conversation he noted the way churches were unable to live with the ambiguity and mystery that is integral to gospel communication; 2 July 2001.
21 E.H. Peterson, *Working the Angles: The Shape of Pastoral Integrity* (Grand Rapids: Eerdmans, 1987), 2.
22 Ibid., 1.
23 Peterson, *The Contemplative Pastor*, 58.
24 Thornton, *Pastoral Theology*, 74. Thornton is of particular significance in the development of Peterson's pastoral and spiritual theology, see E.H. Peterson, *Take and Read: Spiritual Reading: An Annotated List* (Grand Rapids: Eerdmans, 1996), 41, 62–3, 105.
25 For an example see D. LaNoue, *The Spiritual Legacy of Henri Nouwen* (New York/London/Continuum, 2001), 49, who notes Nouwen's unusual acceptance among Protestants, particularly after preaching a series of sermons at the Crystal Cathedral for Robert Schuller's televised *Hour of Power* in 1992.
26 Nouwen, *In the Name of Jesus*, 28–9.
27 See Beumer, *Henri Nouwen: A Restless Seeking for God* (New York: Crossroad Publishing Company, 1997), 143.
28 H. Nouwen, *The Return of the Prodigal Son: A Story of Homecoming* (London: Darton, Longman & Todd, 1994), 37–44.
29 H. Nouwen, 'The Living Reminder' in *Making All Things New and Other Classics* (London: Fount, 2000), 250.
30 H. Nouwen, *Clowning in Rome: Reflections on Solitude, Celibacy, Prayer and Contemplation* (New York: Doubleday, 1979), 87–8.
31 P. Yancey, 'The Holy Inefficiency of Henri Nouwen', *Christianity Today* (9 December 1996), 80.
32 C.E. Braaten, *Eschatology and Ethics* (Minneapolis: Augsburg, 1974), 121.

33 D.A. Carson, *The Gagging of God: Christianity Confronts Pluralism* (Leicester: Apollos, 1996), 567, n. 35.
34 Peterson, *Subversive Spirituality*, 58–9.
35 See Chevreau, *Catch the Fire*, 145–204.
36 N. Dahl, 'Anamnesis: Mémoire et Commemoration dans le Christianisme Primitif', *Studia Theologica* 1 (1947), 75.
37 B.S. Childs, *Memory and Tradition in Israel* (London: SCM, 1962), 55, 60.
38 Nouwen, 'The Living Reminder', 269.
39 Ibid., 269.
40 See E.L. Mascall, *Theology and the Future* (London: Darton, Longman & Todd, 1968), 15–39. See also Mascall, *Theology and the Gospel of Christ*, 15–30.
41 Peterson, *Working the Angles*, 10–12.
42 W. Brueggemann, *Finally Comes the Poet: Daring Speech For Proclamation* (Minneapolis, Fortress, 1996).
43 Significantly, Tim Stafford notes a degree of disillusionment in the thinking of church growth strategist George Barna. See T. Stafford, 'The Third Coming of George Barna', *Christianity Today* (5 August 2002), 33–8.
44 P.T. Forsyth, 'The Ideal Ministry' in *Revelation Old and New: Sermons and Addresses* (ed. J. Huxtable ; London: Independent Press, 1962 [1906]), 93–114.
45 Ibid., 98.
46 Ibid., 98.
47 See S. Croft, 'The Art of Seeing Clearly: Developing Vision in Organisations', *Borderlands: A Journal of Theology and Education* 1 (2002), 13.
48 Peterson, *The Contemplative Pastor*, 60.
49 J. Patton, *Pastoral Care in Context: An Introduction to Pastoral Care* (Louisville: Westminster/John Knox, 1993), 4, 28–31.
50 D. Lyall, *Integrity of Pastoral Care* (London: SPCK, 2001).
51 See W. Kilpatrick, *Psychological Seduction* (London: Arthur James, 1983).
52 On the relationship between counselling and pastoral theology, and the moral issues raised by reliance on the therapeutic see G. Lynch, 'The Relationship between Pastoral Counseling and Pastoral Theology' in J. Woodward and

S. Pattison (eds.), *The Blackwell Reader in Pastoral And Practical Theology* (Oxford: Blackwell, 2000).

53 S. Pattison, *A Critique of Pastoral Care* (London: SCM, 1988), 13.

54 A. Campbell, *Paid to Care: The Limits of Professionalism in Pastoral Care* (London: SPCK, 1985), 1.

55 Peterson, *Working the Angles,* 127. See also J. Firet, *Dynamics in Pastoring* (Grand Rapids: Eerdmans, 1986).

56 Ibid., 127.

57 See F. Greeves, *Theology and the Cure of Souls: An Introduction to Pastoral Theology* (London: Epworth, 1960), 18–31. For an elucidation of this point see C. Moody, *Eccentric Ministry: Pastoral Care and Leadership in the Parish* (London: Darton, Longman & Todd, 1992), 7–15.

58 See L. Crabb, *Hope When You're Hurting* (Eastbourne: Kingsway, 1997), 168–89 who questions the individualism and narcissism encouraged by the counselling movement, of which he was a pioneer. See also J.H. Olthius, *The Beautiful Risk: A New Psychology of Loving and Being Loved* (Grand Rapids: Zondervan, 2001).

59 See P. Goodliff, *Care in a Confused Climate: Pastoral Care and Postmodern Culture* (London: Darton, Longman & Todd, 1998), 14, 21, 197–9.

60 J. W. Frye, *Jesus the Pastor* (Grand Rapids: Zondervan, 2000), 40–2: 'My reaction is caused by Peterson's steady, drumbeat reminder that authentic pastoral work is not grounded in current trends or social sciences, but in ancient truths and scriptural personalities. Peterson painstakingly sinks a shaft into the deep strata of biblical revelation and mines precious metal from which to forge a resilient vision of the pastoral calling.'

61 D.D. Webster, *Finding Spiritual Direction: The Challenges and Joys of Christian Growth* (Downers Grove: Inter-Varsity Press, 1991), 42–3.

62 V. Thomas, *Future Leader: Spirituality, Mentors, Context and Style for Leaders of the Future* (Carlisle: Paternoster, 1999), 136–8.

[63] Hansen, *The Art of Pastoring*, 20. Hansen takes this terminology of parable from Eberhard Jüngel, *God as the Mystery of the World* (Grand Rapids: Eerdmans, 1983), who describes Jesus as the supreme parable of God. It allows Hansen to say that 'when Christ is heard and received through Word and sacrament, God comes to us. This is the foundation of Christian faith, and it must also be the foundation of the pastoral ministry' (23).

[64] Ibid., 24.

[65] D. Hansen, 'The Art and Heart of Pastoring', Pastors Conference, King's Centre, High Wycombe, 23–24 June 1998.

[66] Oden, *Pastoral Theology*, 181.

[67] See N.J. Gorush, *Pastoral Visitation* (Minneapolis: Fortress, 1999), 8.

[68] Fee, *Gospel and Spirit*, 120–43.

[69] See Sullivan, 'Roger Forster and the Icthus Christian Fellowship', 256. Forster openly disavows pastoral leadership of the church in favour of the evangelist.

[70] Note the testimony of Derek Fraser, hospital chaplain to Addenbrooks, Cambridge, who attributes his own move from Baptist church ministry to hospital chaplaincy to 'the changes impacting church ministry with an emphasis on keeping the show on the road, tolerating anything that was suggested and a significant diminution of pastoral care. I reflected that the ministry I was trained for in the 1970s was very different to the 1990s with trends to success, growth, and an increasing disregard to vocation accompanied with an accelerating sense of violence towards clergy.' D. Fraser, 'Chaplaincy Reflections' in *Ministry Today: The Journal of the Richard Baxter Institute for Ministry* Issue 17 (October 1999), 3.

[71] See P.Y. Cho, *Successful Home Cell Groups* (South Plainfield: Bridge, 1981), 21–4.

[72] Oden, *Pastoral Theology*, 191.

[73] In correspondence with Eugene Peterson, 12 August 1999.

[74] Oden, *Pastoral Theology*, 196.

[75] E.H. Peterson, *Under the Unpredictable Plant: An Exploration in Vocational Holiness* (Grand Rapids/Leominster: Eerdmans/Gracewing, 1992), 22.

76   Neuhaus, *Freedom for Ministry*, 1–18.
77   Thomas, *Future Leader*, 24.
78   See I.R. Stackhouse, 'Dealing with the Success Idol' in *Ministry Today: The Journal of the Richard Baxter Institute for Ministry* Issue 20 (September 2000), 14–18.
79   See Breen, *The Apostle's Notebook* (Eastbourne: Kingsway, 2002), 15–27. Although Breen is also sensitive to the importance of settled as well as pioneering congregations.
80   Thomas, *Future Leader*, 23.
81   Ibid., 26. See also C. Barnes, 'The Most Important Thing You Do', *Leadership Magazine* (Spring, 1999), 50–5, on the need to recover the pastoral prayer; and Norris, 'Amazing Grace-filled Gossip', 58, on the urgency of reintroducing prayers of confession.
82   Neuhaus, *Freedom for Ministry*, 219.

PART 3

CONCLUSION

Chapter 8

The Church Apostolic

Equipping the Saints: Ephesians 4

The charismatic movement in the UK, we have argued, is at a critical place in the overall trajectory of renewal. For all its notoriety, the Toronto episode has not totally removed the growing conviction that a period of self-critique is necessary. Faddism, as we have described it, is still prevalent and continues to stultify serious theological and cultural reflection about the nature of challenges ahead. The attraction of a fad is that it offers hope to a demoralised movement, promising growth instead of atrophy, but what transpires instead is a growing unrealism – what we might call spiritual utopianism – that is unhelpful to the real cause of mission and renewal. Whilst we would not be so cynical as to deny the positive impact that some strategies can have, our main complaint relates to the na ve optimism it can engender as well as the theological reductionism it often requires. Our final illustration of this is the lay ministry strategy of 'equipping the saints' – as it is referred to in popular parlance. Examination of this particular methodology will allow us a further insight into the increasingly functional nature of charismatic renewal,

but, more importantly, provide us a point of entry into the
wider issue of charismatic-evangelical ecclesiology.

As a phrase, 'equipping the saints' is something of a
euphemism for a particularly anti-clerical, democratic
ecclesiology.[1] It has been invoked regularly in the renewal
movement as a slogan that covers a number of themes: the
importance of every member ministry, the realisation of that
ministry in the church and the workplace, and the focusing
of church leadership on the effective mobilisation of that
ministry. This last theme has revolutionary implications for
ministerial authority in the church, for it can be seen at once
that the task of leadership is not to do ministry, but rather,
according to Ephesians 4:11 – something of a celebrated text
in renewal circles – to equip others to do ministry.[2] More
specifically, returning to the theme of church growth, the
effective deployment and mobilisation of lay ministry is
regarded by many as the guarantor of multiplication. Dye,
once again, summarises a widely held view: 'I guarantee
that you will see people flourish as you release them in
ministry. The work of God will multiply and the church
of Christ will grow.'[3]

That the church should realise its full potentiality as
the body of Christ in the world is something of a truism,
and something about which there is consensus amongst
Protestants and Catholics. Furthermore, the renewal
movement has been audacious in the way it has challenged
hierarchical models of church[4] – though paradoxically, in
certain circles, it has buttressed male, authoritative patterns
of leadership. Nevertheless, the belief that releasing people
into ministry is a guarantor for growth not only contributes
to the prevalence of mechanistic approaches to ministry,
but also, as a consequence, has the potential of reducing
ecclesiology to mere pragmatics.[5] Whilst it is legitimate
and practicable for the church to organise the various
abilities of church members, a definition of equipping

that relates merely to the functions of the church, and its growth thereby, is not commensurate with the biblical word *katartismon* as it appears in Ephesians 4:12, where the emphasis is more upon tackling issues of church disunity, doctrinal deficiency and moral laxity.[6] Equipping the saints is not a pretext for spiritual gift inventory forms, but rather a vision for a robust Christian community where spiritual formation is considered the basis of all mission. It is this we must now prove, from the text under consideration.

First, the emphasis on growth in the pericope: 'speaking the truth in love, we must grow up in every way into him who is the head, into Christ',[7] is not quantitative but qualitative:

> The church is in Christ and has to grow up toward him. This underlines that the Church's growth is not being thought of in terms of quantity, a numerical expansion of its membership, but in terms of quality, an increasing approximation of believers to Christ.[8]

Consequently, equipping the saints, as a somewhat technical euphemism, is not so much about effective deployment for growth – although it will include this – as it is about strengthening the church as an authentic christocentric community. The apostolicity of the church is measured by christological criteria, namely, Christian maturity that is unto Christ.[9] The intent of ministry in the passage, whether through word ministries of apostles, prophets, evangelists, pastors and teachers, or whether, indeed, through the saints themselves, as they are equipped to build up the body of Christ (which is how v. 12 would read if it were left unpunctuated), is specifically confessional as well as communitarian: 'until we all reach unity in the faith and in the knowledge of the Son of God'.[10] Ministry is concerned with the *homologia* and *koinonia* of the church, its confession and its communion, the intent of which is to ensure that the church is not 'tossed back and forth' by 'every wind of teaching' – precisely those fads that have beset the church, purporting to be panaceas, but which undermine the security of the believer in Christ, as well as distract from the very mundane and practical tasks of congregational life.

The irony of the present situation in charismatic renewal ought to be apparent. By being preoccupied with every latest fad that has arrived on the Christian market, and devoid of any defined philosophy of ministry, charismatic-evangelicalism has found itself captive to the very thing that Ephesians 4 ministry is designed to prevent. Redress of this situation, therefore, is to restore back to those ministries their essentially doctrinal and spiritual role. As Guder rightly discerns, concerning apostles, prophets, evangelists, pastors and teachers:

> Their common and most important characteristic is that they are ministers of the word ... Their office is not the most important thing about them, but rather their calling and gifting to serve the community as students and expositors of the Word.[11]

Such a view does not require concepts of ordination; nor does it require effective management of the church, though, as we have already argued, facilitating the ministry of others in the church is valid work. The restoration of classical pastoral care and ministry, even for Oden, does not exclude this vital democratisation of ministry, for 'it is pride and an overweening need to control that causes the pastor to attempt to do the work of the entire congregation'.[12] Moreover, in the passage under consideration, the participatory and functional aspects of ministry are preserved in the notion of each part doing its work.[13]

Nevertheless, the reason the ascended Christ gives gifts to the church is in order to bring the saints to completion: namely, to build up the body of Christ unto maturity, so that the Christian community is theologically as well as experientially able to grow unto Christ, while remaining impervious to theological flux. Ephesians 4 ministry, so-called, is centred on an essentially ecclesial and confessional task.[14] The evangelist, and indeed the apostle and the prophet, 'must constantly evangelise the community so that it can be about its work, its evangelising witness. The community should experience the constant challenge of the gospel to our reductions and conformities.'[15]

Central to the task of re-evangelising the church is the redress of a number of theological concerns, not least of which is the way that the doctrine of sin has been trivialised, leaving an attenuated gospel that inspires little awe or wonder.[16] Furthermore, the proclivity of popular preaching to overrealise its eschatological horizon, thereby leaving little place for failure or doubt, should also be subject to scrutiny. It is the task of ministry to address this state of affairs simply because there is little point seeking to evangelise the world when the church itself remains diffident about the radicality of its own gospel, or is unable to cope with the paradoxes of its faith commitment. As long as the church is vulnerable to the cultural *Zeitgeist*, as reflected in its dalliance with a therapeutic re-reading of the gospel, or with such movements as the 'health and wealth gospel', then it has an apostolic mission to embrace which – beyond the obvious apostolic imperative to found new churches – is centred on living by faith in the eschatological now and not yet.[17] Thus, when Tomlinson warned the charismatic movement, in the forward to Dan McConnell's book on 'health and wealth' theology, to take seriously the charge of heresy levelled against Kenneth Hagin's teaching, he was perhaps, inadvertently, fulfilling an apostolic role, even though his convictions about the Restorationist model of leadership had long since changed.[18] His call to the charismatic movement to stay within the theological boundaries of historic orthodox Christianity is exactly what apostolic ministry should be concerned with.

The burden of Ephesians 4:11–16 is 'unto maturity'. While Paul does not use the language of discipleship, nor catechesis for that matter, the belief in a church that takes seriously the initiation of fledgling converts, as well as the ongoing nurture of believers, is clearly there. That the church could be called back to this task at the present time is significant because the present culture evinces many of the hallmarks that made catechism in the early church such a vital process. The churchly intent of such procedures ought not to be baulked at. Jensen reminds us:

> Instead of perverting her essential rites, the church must catechise. She must rehearse her would-be members in the liturgies, take them through step by step, showing them how the bits hang together, and teaching them how to say, sing or dance them.[19]

Perhaps that is why courses such as Alpha ought to be regarded as a sign of hope. As long as they are not regarded as the final product, but merely the beginning of the retrieval – what some are calling an incubation period – they ought to be encouraged. 'One way to breathe new life into a dying church,' Abraham reminds us, 'is to expose it to the freshness of new converts who through the ministry of the church are finding new life in Christ.'[20] And to this extent, anxiety about the numerical decline of the church, to which we have attributed the disturbing trend towards faddism, has been of proper pastoral concern. As Kavanagh states:

No liturgical structure in the Church has more to do with the sustained renewal of Church life than its initiatory structure. Here, its new members are reformed according to the criteria of the gospel. The fresh appropriation in them of gospel faith as a way of thought and life on all levels renews not only them but the Church which initiates them into itself.[21]

A Charismatic Ecclesiology: The Church as Sacrament

Our concern throughout this critique of contemporary revivalism is with the way church growth, by indiscriminate means, has become a guiding motif of the charismatic movement, to the detriment of an incipient ecclesiology that was evident in the early years of renewal. Our re-reading of Ephesians 4 seeks to retrieve the promise of such an ecclesiology by demonstrating that the completion of the saints unto spiritual maturity, onto a realisation of the unity inherent in the faith and the knowledge of the Son of God, is the only guarantor of its mission in the world. As Lincoln notes:

The focus of the passage is on the Church's inner growth rather than on its mission, but the quality of its corporate life has everything to do with the Church's fulfilling its role in the world. The writer's belief is that Christ's ascension far above all the heavens was in order that he might fill the whole cosmos with his sovereign rule and that his work in his Church is part of the carrying out of that rule (v. 10, 11). Christ has been exalted to fill the whole cosmos, but at present only the Church *is* his fullness. So where the Church is increasingly appropriating what it is and attaining to the measure of the stature of the fullness of Christ (v. 13), it is allowing Christ to take more and more possession over the world over which he is Lord.[22]

By growing in its own internal life, the church fulfils its role in the world, paradigmatically announcing the rule of Christ to the whole cosmos.

In this vision of the church, christology is not displaced by ecclesiology, for it is Christ who remains Lord of the church and who, in his ascension, gives grace to the church through ministers of the word. Nevertheless, the church is imaged as the body of Christ, becoming what it already is in Christ, thus acting as an eschatological sign to the rest of the cosmos and its powers of God's purpose for his world.

Power language, as New Testament scholars are increasingly pointing out, is prevalent in Paul's cosmology:[23] namely, the plundering by Satan of corporate identities and structures, to which the church enacts a counter strategy. But the nature and method of that counter strategy is what divides opinion. Our argument is that the subversion of the principalities and powers takes place not through an equivalent display of power, but rather through the church modelling a counter-consciousness, developed by criteria wholly other to those employed in the world. Appropriation of the unity the church already possesses in Christ, growing up unto Christ in whom the church already locates its existence, is the way it succeeds: growth is organic rather than by accretion, nutrition as opposed to addition. For the church to employ criteria of business and commerce, where growth is measured in terms of numbers, is a perilous alternative for, as Dawn points out,

> Both the concern for 'church growth' and the concern for survival (which sometimes are the same thing) lead to many of the tactics of fallen powers, such as competition, the overwhelming pressure on church leaders to be successful, reduction of the gospel for the sake of marketing, and so forth.[24]

When that occurs, the church is reduced to mere statistics: an association of people united for the common purpose of evangelism and the needs of individual Christians.[25] Concentrating on the pragmatic and the practical in this way is a direct consequence of the modern rejection of transcendental notions of sociality. Hence, instead of employing scripture texts to legitimate and perpetuate such a situation, a charismatic-evangelical rendering of Ephesians 4:11–16 ought more properly to highlight the spiritual and theological reality of the church, which is not contingent upon, but theologically prior to the stratagems of individual Christians, thus giving them their identity, 'for to be a Christian,' Chan reminds us, 'is to be identified as one who is baptised or grafted into a pre-existing reality, the Body of Christ'.[26]

This overtly ontological understanding of the church is not unnatural to charismatic ecclesiology. The early rhetoric of the charismatic movement fostered a conviction that the restoration of all things was crucially about the restoration of a high view of the church as the body of Christ: the administration of God's grace in the world and existing for no higher purpose than the glory and praise of God himself.[27] We have argued, however, that anxiety concerning what this amounts to numerically has caused it to become discontent, paying too much attention to the Lyle Schaller school of organisational theory than to scripture.[28]

Schaller's contribution to church leadership and church growth has been to focus church leaders upon the organisational blockages to growth. Equipping the saints, in charismatic renewal, has similarly focused on the most effective deployment of resources as a precursor to growth. The church, like any other organisation, should understand the more dysfunctional aspects of its internal organisation, thus increasing its potentiality. Kept at this modest level, Schaller has a great deal to offer in terms of practical wisdom. Such pragmatism, however, can never be enough for the church, for, as Clare Watkins points out, 'the central theological fact about the people to be managed in the Church is that they are saved sinners',[29] which no church management theory can account for. The only proper inducement that can be called upon, Watkins correctly discerns, is that of the call to follow Jesus in the community of grace.

Revival and revivalism within the charismatic movement, to be consistent with its theological roots, ought to focus, we contend, more upon this ecclesial dimension than upon any societal impact it might or might otherwise have. It would represent a retrieval of an ecclesiology that accords well with the concept of the church as it developed among Catholic theologians, prior even to the renewal itself, with the emphasis upon the church as the body of Christ.[30] Here, free of the burdens that hamper a broad ecclesiology, prominent theologians such as Yves Congar and Karl Rahner were already developing the concept of the church as the charismatic body of Christ. According to Smail, the richness of such an ecclesiology was inadvertently lost to the renewal movement when the Fountain Trust was disbanded.[31]

The development of a truly charismatic ecclesiology, centred on the *koinonia* of the church, as well as its confession, is the theological horizon of the passage before us, which to treat as a piece of Church Growth rhetoric is to seriously abuse its intent and import. '*Koinonia* has nothing to do with size or locality,' insists George Tavard, 'for it rests entirely on the degree to which the faithful are intimately united to their Lord and to one another.'[32] The current use made of Ephesians 4, as a pretext for growth, illustrates well the wider pathology of the renewal movement; equipping the saints, as it is understood in contemporary models of ministry, is symptomatic of a wider malaise in the church, seeking to be culturally relevant and technically efficient but often at the expense of its own ecclesial practices, identity and communion.[33] Because it is so closely tied to the Church Growth agenda, the theological resources that apostles and prophets represent have been overshadowed by utilitarian concerns. By reclaiming these resources through the hermeneutic of the body of Christ, we can see that the *teleios* of church ministry is not merely functional – although it is never less than that – but spiritual: the creation of a social reality called the church as the expression of God ruling in the world.

That the social reality is a community that takes the tradition seriously is unquestionable, because first and foremost it is a community of the Word. In this sense we cannot escape the definition 'sect', if the Word is to be taken seriously.[34] Yet, as Lewis Mudge points out, the church is not just sect, for

> we are discovering that the content of this tradition demands that we see ourselves not as persons saved out of a fallen world, but rather as persons called to be that very world reconstituted as the social space, and therefore as the worldly reality of God's rule.[35]

The Barthian dialectic of faith and religion has not allowed for a proper exploration of what this sociology of the Word of God might look like; it has tended to be indifferent about the actual sociology of the church. For a true understanding of the church, he argued, we must look only to revelation, the Word: 'under no pretext or title should alien principles of explanation in the form of metaphysical, anthropological, epistemological or religio-philosophical presuppositions be intruded upon it.'[36] There is an alternative, however, to the anti-cultural tendency of

Barth, whilst avoiding the accomodationist option, and that is to see the church in sacramental terms: the spiritual community of faith located in history and empirical fact.

This is an attractive option because its earthiness counters not only the anti-cultural dialectic of Barth, but also the statistical idealism of contemporary assessments of the church: for it is with the church as it is that we have to deal.[37] Yet, at the same time, we can conceive such a church, rooted in social reality, in transcendental terms. To recognise the church as it really is, according to Watkins, 'is essentially a view of the actual, here and now Church as a mystery, a sacrament.' A sacramental ecclesiology 'may employ insights from the managerial sciences, but always within a critical context which allows for theology to be theology, and deal with the sacramental structure of the church in its own distinct way.'[38] Consequently, the church possesses that ability in the Spirit, as the body of Christ, to embrace as well as transcend the categories of sociology.[39] Its sheer earthiness is precisely what qualifies it also to be seen as the communion of saints.

Furthermore, since the church seeks to enshrine in its members the particular way of living called forth in the gospel – in which the first is the last and the greatest is the servant of all – it has the ability to act as more than simply a counter culture. Rather, it possesses that ability, using Niebuhr's terminology, to transform culture,[40] by incarnating in advance the specifics of what it means to be the people of God, a new society as God intended. The church as an alternative polity does not mean retreat from society; rather, it means the serving of society 'on the church's own terms, keeping faithful to its own distinctive way of life'.[41] As Bonhoeffer argues, the church is the world as it is meant to be in Christ, the space where it is structured according to its true centre, testifying 'to the foundation of all reality in Jesus Christ'.[42]

Again, it is important to stress that no ghetto is implied by such an ecclesiology. Even though the church requires, for Bonhoeffer, a commitment to meditating on scripture, hymns and confessions – for there will be no true sociology of the Word unless at its centre are people who celebrate the biblical tradition – this does not involve separation. That would simply amount to the creation of space for faith, argues Mudge, leading to the domestication of the Word in the realm of the private. Charismatic spirituality has often been criticised for exactly that.[43] What Bonhoeffer envisages, however, according to Mudge, is a space of faith, 'which is existing society seen as, restructured as, reconstituted by the power of the grace as, the realm of God ruling'.[44] As Bonhoeffer states: 'And so, too, the church of Jesus Christ is the place, in other words the space in the world, at which the reign of Jesus Christ over the whole world is evidenced and proclaimed.'[45] This is a vision not wholly unfamiliar to renewal ecclesiology, to which Ephesians 4 contributes. The church is not simply a counter-culture, nor, most definitely, anti-culture, but a new society acting as the eschatological vanguard of the kingdom of God, wherein God will be all in all.

That charismatic ecclesiology, in pursuit of such an eschatological prospect, has tended towards a hierarchical view of church government, coupled to a latent triumphalism, has something to do with the fact that Restorationist theology, as indeed a good deal of evangelical Puritan theology, is post-millennial.[46] And it is this that has given the renewal a decidedly militant, aggressive slant. However it may have emerged, the militancy it has engendered in certain settings looks not unlike the stratagems employed by the world to achieve its ends, thus rendering it bogus as a way of constituting the people of God. The attempt, conversely, within this overall eschatological vision, to attract the world by the means of relevancy is similarly flawed, for it is all too conspicuous in its falsity. But where the renewal resists the pressure to assert itself, retaining its own theological and spiritual integrity, it may be closer, as Lindbeck argued, to achieving this goal of being a transformative society.[47] Paradoxically, as the church forgets about the effectiveness of its actions, concentrating instead on fidelity to the Jesus narrative, it may prove to be more effectual in the long term. The church in renewal will be most effective to the degree it separates itself from the prevailing idolatries of the culture – whether goods, status, identity, nation, success or righteousness – thus being a 'lantern of righteousness' to that culture. 'The new life is simultaneously less involved and more involved in culture.'[48]

Following through the trajectory of thought in Ephesians 4, this is precisely what we see in the ensuing Pauline ethic to be the people of God in chapters 5 and 6. As stated earlier, this is not a straightforward indicative/imperative juxtaposition. Rather, it is a description of the kind of moral community that arises from such a radical confrontation of the world and its culture through the message of the cross. Such a community is sustained, as we claimed earlier, by constant re-appropriation of gospel realities, mediated through the judgement of the cross (the cross in this sense being an interpretative lens upon the world, as well as a soteriological fact). From this new way of seeing, the church can provide not only an alternative to, but also a confrontation of, the culture, transforming it by the Spirit; for as the church attends to the shape of its own story in the midst of a fallen world, the surrounding culture will thereby be transformed by that light, for 'everything exposed by the light becomes visible, for it is light that makes everything visible.'[49]

This is no text to legitimate the creation of exclusive communities, but rather the fostering of a community of character,[50] which in and of itself has the resourses to transform culture as it deepens in its understanding of the radicality of what it means to live out the cross-shaped life.[51] Bonhoeffer claims:

> The space of the church is not there in order to try to deprive the world of a piece of its territory, but precisely in order to prove to the world that it is still the world which is loved by God and reconciled with him.[52]

Ephesians 4 ministries ought properly to be about this task: not the efficient management of church structures, nor the stimulation of a moribund revivalism, but the perfection of the saints, and the building up of the body of Christ, so that out of all the competing individualisms of infants we have one new man in Christ, rightly related to his headship, and demonstrating to the world, and for the world, the wisdom of God. In this respect baptism, as Brian Haymer points out, is not a rite of sectarian exclusivity, for Christians are called to serve in the present age. Baptism is initiation into the church where our humanity is radically reconceived through the person and work of Christ.[53] The church is called out of the world, for the world.

Whence Revival?

Such an ecclesiological emphasis is a very different agenda for the renewal movement to that espoused by contemporary revivalists (though not one unsympathetic to the more robust theological vision of its early pioneers). Its posture vis-à-vis the world is not the one of militancy or domination, found so often in revivalism, but one of humility as the church attends to its own intramural life and the social implications of its own texts. We can infer from the Gospels, and indeed from the Pauline corpus, how this may have occurred for the earliest Christians, for, as recent enquiries into the historical Jesus have shown, joining the Jesus community 'must have meant experiencing an upheaval in one's symbolic world, especially where issues of ultimate and penultimate power were concerned'.[54] The messianic glory anticipated by the disciples through the ministry of Jesus comes not in the way expected, but through the suffering servant. Thus, to embrace this way is to be prised away from the language of violence associated with the clamouring for power, and to enter, as Luther was to expound, a theology of the cross. Baptism is critical to this vision as a rupture of the status quo, signifying death to the world of success, power and competition, and immersion into a new *phronesis*, a new way of thinking, concerning the issue of authority.

This is clearly the consistent witness of the New Testament as it reflects on the issue of power and the authority of God's people in the world: the church is most faithful to its vocation to be the people of God as it embraces the beatitudinal life of compassion and mercy rather than the way of success. The paradox of faith is that the church is most effectual when it ceases trying to be effectual and concentrates on the substantive and simultaneously subversive confession that arises from its own cherished texts, the revolutionary and prophetic nature of which are often overlooked by sheer familiarity. Instead of the renewal being obsessed with the need to justify its place in the world by submitting to the world's criterion of success, it must allow itself to be disoriented by the revolutionary impact of its own scriptures.[55] In sum, we envisage a confessional rendering of faith: the perfection of the saints through the configurations of scriptural language that is simultaneously confrontive of the world by virtue of it being reconstrued through the hermeneutic of the cross.[56]

In this sense, as Reinhard Hutter claims, all believers are basically, or should be, theologians, because 'theology is a practice of judgment inhering in the praxis of faith – a practice all believers perform'.[57] Following Lindbeck, Hutter argues for the renewal of theology as a distinct church practice on the basis of an increasing awareness of catholicity among Protestant churches. Its existence as a witnessing community to the Lordship of Christ demands such thoroughgoing initiation in the faith. And as the Christian community submits to the Lordship of Christ, reflecting in its inner life the obverse to the world's definition of power, it announces in advance the situation that will exist in the *eschaton* when every knee will bow to the name of Jesus. 'This future situation will be a confessional event, even a language event. "Every tongue" will then "confess", *homologein*, that the world's scheme of identities and values has been rearranged in accordance with a new power geometry.'[58] As the church does its thinking now in alignment with this new orientation, it becomes in its own organic life a medium through which the gospel finds expression. This is the body of Christ, in the midst of the world, not only anticipating through its life the eschatological promise to come, but also creating in time and space a location where this kingdom rule might begin to infiltrate the world.[59]

All of this is to suggest that the aspiration of revivalism, while not entirely misplaced, is somewhat secondary to this vocation of the church – if by revivalism we mean the once for all invasion of the Holy Spirit resulting in the unprecedented evangelistic success. A perspective on the church as subversive community, infiltrating culture by virtue of its robust and vibrant identity, does not require such a cataclysm – a view increasingly supported among charismatics.[60] Instead, the church promises *an inauguration* of God's rule in the world, showing the world its potentiality, as it too is judged and re-imaged by the baptismal summons of death and resurrection.

This is a churchmanship, therefore, which can conceive of the possibility that revival could mean shrinkage as much as it could mean growth. It is implicit in many popular renderings that revival is tantamount to growth. Constantinianism, in this sense, was the apotheosis of a movement – something which revivalism is trying to recapture. But the epistemological basis upon which Constantinianism was based, and any modern version of it, has disappeared. This much we can concede to post-modernity. It may be that the future is with small bands of disciples, who through the intent of their commitment act as a sign of hope in the midst of cultural decadence and decline.[61]

In that sense, as Warner argues, the renewal has to re-imagine its cultural context as analogous not so much to Nehemiah, which has long been a favourite narrative of charismatic renewal,[62] but to Jeremiah.[63] In this latter narrative, the cultural context of religious decline – what some, evidently, are calling exile – does not permit fantasy or escapism, but brutal realism.[64] It is a time, as Jeremiah encouraged the exiles, to create authentic Christian communities, in actual locations with actual people. This may seem rather defeatist even, a form of social pessimism when compared to the triumphalist rhetoric of revival Christianity. Certainly, it proffers a very different definition of revival.[65] But the stripping away of such rhetoric would not only protect the church from disillusionment consequent upon unrealistic expectations, but also render a faith that is truly engaging with a world caught in the pain of its own dislocatedness.[66]

How this looks in terms of the institution is still a moot point. Renewalist rhetoric has tended to be far too ideological to act as a helpful way forward, for it fails to account for the everyday situatedness of the pastoral context. Moreover, it has been divisive, lacking any proper ecumenism. On the other hand, renewal from within the church – the *ecclesia* within the *ecclesia* model – is not without its problems either, involving various theological compromises. More recent voices have advocated a thoroughgoing restructuring of the church, such as Liquid Church,[67] Cell Church,[68] church from scratch[69] and Youth Church.[70] But we have argued that such an innovative approach does not get to the heart of the problem, for at root the problem is not structural, nor cultural, but a crisis of faith and a loss of gospel speech. To attend to only the structural apparatus of the church or to attempt to re-imagine it in contemporary colours is to misunderstand the nature of the problem. The nature of the crisis is theological amnesia concerning the dogmatic core of historic and evangelical Christianity, to which the answer, we have argued, is the recovery of the classical practices of the church as a way of reconnecting with the gospel.

Providing these basic practices of the church are present, the logic of our approach ought to permit any number of structural and cultural variations. Indeed, in describing the concept of Liquid Church, Ward is sensitive to this argument and seeks to contextualise in the light of what Christian tradition has understood to be marks of the church: word, sacrament and prayer.[71] This is a welcome note and allows us to see that one can challenge the prevailing ecclesiastical structures, yet remain committed to a classical version of Christian practice. Despite our reservations about Cell Church – particularly the way small group spirituality is held out as a panacea for growth – this movement has sought similarly to reflect a commitment to the basic core practices of the church.

We insist, however, that whatever ecclesiastical shape should emerge, the incipient idealism that was so much a part of the charismatic renewal will have to be jettisoned. Mess, as a feature of Christian community, is a pastoral reality, for one is dealing with sinners and not simply with vision statements.[72] The acceptance of the pastoral reality is not latitudinarianism, nor does it prevent the cultivation of the ascesis within the church. Indeed, it is the development of an ascetical and dogmatic core in the church, we are arguing, that is the future hope for the renewal movement. It is this that preserves the gospel and creates a space of faith where, albeit in small and apparently unimpressive ways, a truly Christian ethic, understood as a way of knowing, can be witnessed. Meanwhile, however, as Peterson attests to, the wheat and the tares of the congregation need to grow together, lest in our impatience we mistake our own efforts of organisation as the work of God.[73]

Such a perspective challenges the opportunism and triumphalism of a church in renewal that often has seen its primary vocation as self-aggrandisement.[74] Within the eschatological tension of the Christian revelation such a theological as opposed to functional ecclesiology takes seriously the pastoral vocation as primarily to do with the *cura animarum*. Precisely because life is lived in the now/not yet, pastoral and spiritual direction is essential for sustaining faith and preserving what Peterson describes as 'redeemed apocalypticism'. 'This is an urgent time,' Peterson agrees, 'and the task of the Christian is how to maintain that urgency without getting panicked, to stay on our toes without caving into the culture.'[75]

Revivalism in the charismatic renewal has been an example, we have argued, of precisely that: panic and insecurity as it enters a second generation, with little sign of it fulfilling its grand vision. In the process, it has adopted the mindset of modernity, and indeed postmodernity, in its quest to uncover the key to the promised harvest, and has thereby forsaken the very tools of ministry that would keep it urgent, without being intimidated. It is tantamount, as Cullmann lamented concerning his own generation, to a crisis of faith: reluctance on the part of the church to think theologically and doctrinally about the pressing issues of the day.[76] Cullmann is no isolationist, nor immobilist, but he declares, 'it is not the Holy Spirit who is at work, but spirits of quite another kind, when without discernment of spirits we abolish radically and without reverence all that has been handed down to us'.[77] The abandonment of all that has been handed down – preaching, sacraments, prayer and charismata – has meant, ironically, the abandonment of the very things that would keep the renewal related to the power of the gospel itself, rather than the supposed energy and activity generated by any and every latest fad.

Without some relationship to these means of grace, and without a more robust ecclesiology that is based on more than just statistics, the charismatic renewal will continue to be vulnerable to latest trends. Given the incipient ecumenism of its early years, would be unfortunate. What this book attempts, in response, is an elaboration of that early ecumenical vision, showing how the cross-fertilisation of evangelical, charismatic and catholic spiritual traditions – what many are now calling 'Deep Church' – could harness the present renewal movement to a more lasting future. It may not be the future that early revivalists envisaged for themselves, but then every movement is tempered by experience. And what the experience of charismatic renewal is now confirming is that without serious theological critique of some of its most cherished aspirations, it could very quickly move to the periphery of serious and relevant Christian activity. The search for cultural recognition in terms of numerical success could finally prove to be its ultimate undoing, leaving many believers disaffected from not only the charismatic movement but from the Christian faith altogether.

278 The Gospel-Driven Church

Forsyth has been one of our main conversation partners throughout this book. His essentially pastoral theology has provided us with a hermeneutical grid with which to critique aspects of the revivalist mentality that have been so prevalent in charismatic renewal. It seems apt, therefore, in addressing this particular sickness of hurriedness in the evangelical soul, to allow Forsyth the last word:

> There is a form of the thirst for souls, of religious eagerness, of evangelical haste and pious impatience which is far too voluble and active to be impressive. It is more youthful than faithful, more ardent than sagacious, more energetic than inspired. It would express everything and at once in word or deed … His institutions were not devised in the interests of the world's speedy evangelisation. He could wait for the souls He redeemed as well as for the God he revealed. The waiting energy of the Church is just as faithful as its forward movements, and at certain times more needful. Faith has ever a holy indifference and a masterly negligence which rest on the infinitude of divine care and the completeness of Christ's work.[78]

Notes

[1] See P. Stevens, *The Abolition of the Laity: Vocation, Work and Ministry in a Biblical Perspective* (Carlisle: Paternoster, 1999).
[2] See Greenslade, *Leadership*, 121–72, for a delineation of emerging structures of leadership within the house church movement. Cf., Breen, *The Apostle's Notebook*, 146–71.
[3] Dye, *It's Time to Grow*, 97.
[4] See also Beckham, *The Second Reformation*, 48–9. Part of Beckham's critique of traditional models of ministry is a legitimate one: namely, that hierarchical models can encourage a consumerist mentality and a burden to develop bigger and better church premises.

⁵ See M. Green, *Freed to Serve: Training and Equipping for Ministry* (London: Hodder & Stoughton, 1983), 26.

⁶ See Greenslade, *Leadership*, 168–70.

⁷ Ephesians 4:15 NRSV.

⁸ Lincoln, *Ephesians*, 261.

⁹ The distinction in the passage between the prepositions *en Christ* (in Christ) and *eis Christ* (unto Christ) – verse 15 – have a number of possibilities for an overtly charismatic view of sanctification, in that it sees Christian living as dynamically related to the ongoing appropriation of Christ, all the while rooted in assurance that one is already in Christ. See Ford, *Self and Salvation*, 113–14. More pertinently, the preposition unto Christ is unmistakably ecclesial, in the same way as *eis Christ* in Philemon 6 is a challenge to one who is in Christ to live in the unity, completeness and mutual participation of the body of Christ, Wright, *The Climax of the Covenant*, 53–5.

¹⁰ Ephesians 4:13.

¹¹ Guder, *The Continuing Conversion of the Church*, 161.

¹² Oden, *Pastoral Theology*, 156.

¹³ Greenslade, *Leadership*, 168–72.

¹⁴ An alternative reading of Ephesians 4:12 relates all the tasks of equipping, the work of ministry, and the building up of the body of Christ, solely to word ministries. It is legitimate to interpret the verse in such a way – see Lincoln, *Ephesians*, 253–5 – and would undoubtedly prevent the denigration of the doctrinal and doxological intent of the passage. Cf., P.T. O'Brien, *Ephesians*, Apollos: Leicester, 301–305, who discusses the various alternative readings of the text.

¹⁵ Guder, *The Continuing Conversion*, 163.

¹⁶ D.D. Webster, 'Evangelising the Church' in T.R. Phillips and D.L. Okholm (eds.), *Christian Apologetics in the Postmodern World* (Downers Grove: Inter-Varsity Press, 1995), 194–208.

¹⁷ Apostolicity, as it has emerged in the Restoration movement, has a healthy regard for this task. See Morton, *Covenant People*, 104–105 and T. Virgo, *No Well-Worn Paths: Restoring the Church to Christ's Original Intention* (Eastbourne: Kingsway, 2001), 288–300, who sees apostolic ministry as primarily

concerned with keeping alive the doctrines of grace in the ongoing fight against legalism.

18 See D. McConnell, *The Promise of Health and Wealth: A Historical and Biblical Analysis of the Modern Faith Movement* (London: Hodder & Stoughton, 1990), ix–xiii.

19 R.W. Jensen, 'Catechesis for Our Time' in Braaten and Jensen (eds.), *Marks of the Body*, 144. Without such a commitment there could well be growth, argues Jensen, 'but not of the church', 145. 9. See also B.P. Webb-Mitchell, *Christly Gestures: Learning to Be Members of the Body of Christ* (Grand Rapids/ Cambridge: Eerdmans, 2003), 164.

20 W. Abraham, 'On Making Disciples of the Lord Jesus' in Braaten and Jensen (eds.), *Marks of the Body*, 164–5.

21 Kavanagh, *The Shape of Baptism*, 166.

22 Lincoln, *Ephesians*, 268.

23 The literature on this is extensive. For a useful introduction see W. Wink, *Naming the Powers, The Language of Power in the New Testament* (Philadelphia: Fortress, 1984).

24 M.J. Dawn, *Powers, Weakness and the Tabernacling of God* (Grand Rapids: Eerdmans, 2001), 75.

25 See D.W. Hardy, 'Created and Redeemed Sociality' in C.E. Gunton and D.W. Hardy (eds.), *On Being the Church: Essays on the Christian Community* (Edinburgh: T&T Clark, 1989), 28–31.

26 Chan, *Pentecostal Theology*, 98.

27 See Harper, *None Can Guess*, 147–55; T. Smail, *Reflected Glory: The Spirit in Christ and Christians* (London: Hodder & Stoughton, 1975), 21–3; T. Virgo, *Restoration in the Church* (Eastbourne: Kingsway, 1985), 12–20.

28 See D.V.A. Olson, 'Learning from Lyle Schaller: Social Aspects of Congregations', *The Christian Century* (27 January 1993), 82.

29 C. Watkins, 'The Church as a "Special" Case: Comments from Ecclesiology Concerning the Management of the Church', *Modern Theology* 9:4 (1993), 380.

30 A.J. Dulles, 'The Church as Communion' in B. Nassif (ed.), *New Perspectives on Historical Theology: Essays in Memory of*

John Meyendorff (Grand Rapids/Cambridge: Eerdmans, 1995), 125–39.

31   In conversation with T. Smail, 11 September 2001.

32   G.H. Tavard, 'Considerations on an Ecclesiology of *Koinonia*', *One in Christ*, 31:1 (1995), 43.

33   See S. Hauerwas and W.H. Willimon, *Resident Aliens: Life in the Christian Colony* (Nashville: Abingdon, 1989), 19–24.

34   We agree with Walker when he claims that the immediate future of Christianity in the UK lies in the model of sect: not sect as deviant, nor sect as isolated and unrelated, but sect as an unpolluted form of Christianity. See A. Walker, 'Sectarian Reactions: Pluralism and the Privatization of Religion' in H. Wilmer (ed.), *20/20 Visions: The Futures of Christianity in Britain* (London: SPCK, 1992), 46–64.

35   L.S. Mudge, *Rethinking the Beloved Community: Ecclesiology, Hermeneutics, Social Theory* (New York: University Press of America, 2001), 39.

36   K. Barth, *Church Dogmatics* Volume 4:3 (trans. G.W. Bromiley; Edinburgh: T&T Clark, 1962 [1959]), 72.4.

37   See D. Bonhoeffer, *Sanctorum Communio: A Dogmatic Inquiry into the Sociology of the Church* (trans. R.G. Smith; London, Collins, 1963 [1927]), 144–50.

38   Watkins, 'The Church as a Special Case', 376–7. See also K.J. Vanhoozer, 'Evangelicalism and the Church: The Company of the Gospel' in C. Bartholemew, R. Parry and A. West (eds.), *The Futures of Evangelicalism* (Leicester: Inter-Varsity Press, 2003), 40–99, who argues for a richer, more catholic, ecclesiology in evangelical thinking.

39   For a similar appeal to social empiricism, social gestures in particular, as 'signals of transcendence' and as a way of resolving the antipathy of the Barthian and Bultmannian approaches to theology, see P.L. Berger, *A Rumour of Angels: Modern Society and the Rediscovery of the Supernatural* (London: Penguin, 1973), 33–42.

40   H.R. Niebuhr, *Christ and Culture* (New York: Harper, 1951).

41   See C. Scriven, *The Transformation of Culture: Christian Social Ethics after H. Richard Niebuhr* (Scottdale: Herald, 1988), 135.

[42] D. Bonhoeffer, *Ethics* (London: SCM, 1960 [1949]), 67–9.

[43] See K. Leech, *Soul Friend: Spiritual Direction in the Modern World* (London: Darton, Longman & Todd, 1994), 17–19.

[44] Mudge, *Rethinking the Beloved Community*, 37–8.

[45] Bonhoeffer, *Ethics*, 68.

[46] See I.H. Murray, *The Puritan Hope* (Edinburgh: Banner of Truth, 1971).

[47] Lindbeck, *The Nature of Doctrine*, 132. Appeal to Lindbeck's post-liberalism is not without its problems for evangelical theology. For a discussion of the issues see A. E. McGrath, 'An Evangelical Assessment of Postliberalism' in T.R. Phillips and D.L. Okholm (eds.), *The Nature of Confession: Evangelicals and Postliberals in Conversation* (Downers Grove: Inter-Varsity Press, 1996), 23–44.

[48] Borg, *Jesus*, 194.

[49] Ephesians 5:13–14.

[50] See S. Hauerwas, *A Community of Character* (London: University of Notre Dame Press, 1981).

[51] Sweet is not far from this position when he critiques the counter-cultural response to culture in contrast to a preferred incarnational response. Under this heading the church 'takes into account the coordinates of its time but creates a new spirit of the time … It is in touch with the culture, but not in tune with it.' L. Sweet, *Aqua Church: Essential Leadership Arts for Piloting Your Church in Today's Fluid Culture* (Loveland: Group, 1999), 78–81.

[52] Bonhoeffer, *Ethics*, 68.

[53] B. Haymer, 'Baptism as a Political Act' in Fiddes (ed.), *Reflections on the Water*, 78–82.

[54] Mudge, *Rethinking the Beloved Community*, 153.

[55] See also Hauerwas, *Christian Existence*, 149–67, for his reflections on the role of the pastor as prophet – a role usually considered improbable because of the domestication of the pastoral role.

[56] Borg simplifies this, in the language of first century Palestine, to a straight choice between the 'politics of holiness' versus 'the politics of compassion': the embracing of the marginalised as opposed to buttressing the religious and cultural status quo.

M.J. Borg, *Conflict, Holiness and Politics in the Teaching of Jesus* (Lampeter: The Edwin Mellen Press, 1984). Similarly Wright conceives following the historical Jesus as the eschewal of nationalism – whereby Israel had succumbed to the idolatry of the world – and the embracing of suffering for the sake of the world. N.T. Wright, *Jesus and the Victory of God* (London: SPCK, 1996).

57   R. Hutter, *Suffering Divine Things: Theology as Church Practice* (Grand Rapids: Eerdmans, 1997), 50.

58   Mudge, *Rethinking the Beloved Community*, 155.

59   See G. Wainwright, 'The Church as a Worshipping Community', *Pro Ecclesia: A Journal of Catholic and Evangelical Theology* 11:1 (1999), 56–67.

60   See T. Hunter, New Wine Leaders Conference, Swanwick, 5 June 2001.

61   J. Barzun, *From Dawn to Decadence: 1500 to the Present: 500 Years of Western Cultural Life* (London: Harper Collins, 2000), 801. See also D. Walsh, *After Ideology: Discovering the Spiritual Foundations of Freedom* (San Francisco: Harper, 1987), 241–57 and A. Macintyre, *After Virtue: A Study in Moral Theory* (London: Duckworth, 1985), 262–3: 'We are waiting not for Godot but for another – doubtless very different – St. Benedict.'

62   For an example of the enduring power of this Restorationist narrative see Noble, *The Shaking*, 106–16.

63   R. Warner, 'Ecstatic Spirituality and Entrepreneurial Revivalism: Reflections on the Toronto Blessing' in Walker and Aune (eds.), *On Revival*, 235.

64   See T. Smail, 'The Ethics of Exile and the Rhythm of Resurrection' in Walker and Aune (eds.), *On Revival*, 57–68, and also Stackhouse, 'Revivalism, Faddism and the Gospel', 249–50, in the same book. See also B.B. Taylor, 'Preaching the Terrors' in E. Clarke (ed.), *Exilic Preaching: Testimony for Christian Exiles in an Increasingly Hostile Culture* (Harrisburg: Trinity Press International, 1998), 83–90.

65   See M. Harper, 'Is it Revival or Survival?', *Renewal* (May 1998), 12–14, in which he challenges the renewal to take stock of the output of prophecies as well as the unrealism of its revivalism.

[66] 'What we make of pain [and pain-bearers] is perhaps the most telling factor for the question of life and the nature of our faith.' W. Brueggemann, 'A Shape for Old Testament Theology, I: Structure Legitimation', *Catholic Biblical Quarterly* 47:3 (1985), 44.

[67] See S. Hall, A. Robbins and P. Ward in Debate, 'Liquid Ministry', *Renewal and Christianity* (July 2001), 14–17.

[68] P. Potter, *Cell Church: Getting to Grips with Cell Church Values* (Oxford: Bible Reading Fellowship, 2001), 18–19.

[69] R. Warner, 'Church from Scratch', *Renewal* (March 1999), 45.

[70] D. Roberts and J. Buckeridge, 'The New Jesus People?', *Alpha* (February 1991), 18–23.

[71] See P. Ward, *Liquid Church* (Carlisle: Paternoster, 2002), 49–71.

[72] Peterson, *Under the Unpredictable Plant*, 22–8.

[73] Ibid., 26. See also Bonhoeffer, *Life Together*, 18, who similarly warned against the idealisation of the church and the failure to reckon on its empirical reality: 'Just as the Christian should not be constantly feeling his spiritual pulse', warns Bonhoeffer, 'so, too, the Christian community has not been given to us by God for us to be constantly taking its temperature.'

[74] J.R. Middleton and B.J. Walsh, *Truth is Stranger Than It Used To Be: Biblical Faith in a Postmodern Age* (London: SPCK, 1995), 150–2.

[75] Peterson, *Subversive Spirituality*, 242.

[76] Cullmann, 'This, Our Common Crisis' as cited in Mascall, *Theology and the Gospel of Christ*, 28–30.

[77] Ibid., 29.

[78] Forsyth, *God the Holy Father*, 20.

Select Bibliography

Abraham, W., *The Logic of Evangelism* (London: Hodder & Stoughton, 1989)

——, *The Logic of Renewal* (London: SPCK, 2003)

Albrecht, D., *Rites in the Spirit: A Ritual Approach to Pentecostal/ Charismatic Spirituality* (Sheffield: Sheffield Academic Press/Journal of Pentecostal Theology, 1999)

Barth, K., *Church Dogmatics* Volume 1:1 (trans. G.T. Thomson; Edinburgh: T&T Clark, 1963 [1936])

——, *Church Dogmatics* Volume 4:3 (trans. G.W. Bromiley; Edinburgh: T&T Clark, 1962 [1959])

Bartholemew, C., R. Parry and A. West (eds.), *The Futures of Evangelicalism: Issues and Prospects* (Leicester: Inter-Varsity Press, 2003)

Bonhoeffer, D., *Sanctorum Communio: A Dogmatic Inquiry into the Sociology of the Church* (London: Collins, 1963 [1927])

——, *Wordly Preaching* (ed. C.E. Fant; Nashville: Thomas Nelson, 1975)

——, *The Cost of Discipleship* (London: SCM, 2000 [1937])

——, *Ethics* (London: SCM, 1960 [1949])

——, *Life Together* (London: SCM, 1992, [1954])

——, *Letters and Papers from Prison* (London: SCM, 1971 [1953])

Bonhoeffer, D., *Witness to Jesus Christ: Selected Writings* (ed. J. de Gruchy; London: Collins, 1988)

Braaten, C.E. and R.W. Jensen (eds.), *Marks of the Body of Christ* (Grand Rapids: Eerdmans, 1999)

Brueggemann, W., *Biblical Perspectives on Evangelism: Living in a Three-storied Universe* (Nashville: Abingdon, 1993)

Buckley, J.J. and D.S. Yeago (eds.), *Knowing the Triune God: The Work of the Spirit in the Practices of the Church* (Grand Rapids/Cambridge: Eerdmans, 2001)

Capon, R.F., *The Foolishness of Preaching: Proclaiming the Gospel against the Wisdom of the World* (Grand Rapids/Cambridge: Eerdmans, 1998)

Chan, S., *Spiritual Theology: A Systematic Study of the Christian Life* (Downers Grove: Inter-Varsity Press, 1998)

——, *Pentecostal Theology and the Christian Spiritual Tradition* (Journal of Pentecostal Theology Supplement Series 21; Sheffield: Sheffield Academic Press, 2000)

Clapp, R., *A Peculiar People: The Church as Culture in a Post-Christian Society* (Downers Grove: Inter-Varsity Press, 1996)

Dawn, M.J., *A Royal 'Waste' of Time: The Splendor of Worshipping God and Being the Church for the World* (Grand Rapids/ Cambridge: Eerdmans, 1999)

De Arteaga, W.L., *Forgotten Power: The Significance of the Lord's Supper in Revival* (Grand Rapids: Zondervan, 2002)

Ellul, J., *The Humiliation of the Word* (trans. J.M. Hanks; Grand Rapids: Eerdmans, 1985)

Finney, J., *Fading Splendour: A Model of Renewal* (London: Darton, Longman & Todd, 2000)

Fee, G.D., *God's Empowering Presence: The Holy Spirit in the Letters of Paul* (Carlisle/Peabody: Paternoster/Hendrickson, 1996)

Forsyth, P.T., *God the Holy Father* (London: Independent Press, 1957 [1897])

Forsyth, P.T., *The Atonement in Moral Religious Thought* (London: James Clark & Co, 1902)

——, *Positive Preaching and the Modern Mind* (London: Independent Press, 1964 [1907])

——, 'The Ideal Ministry' in *Revelation Old and New: Sermons and Addresses* (ed. J. Huxtable; London: Independent Press, 1962 [1906])

——, *The Cruciality of the Cross* (London: Independent Press, 1948 [1908])

——, *Missions in State and Church* (London: Hodder & Stoughton, 1908)

——, *The Work of Christ* (London: Independent Press, 1938 [1910])

——, *The Church and the Sacraments* (London: Independent Press, 1947 [1917])

——, *The Soul of Prayer* (London: Independent Press, 1949 [1917])

——, *The Justification of God* (London: Independent Press, 1948 [1917])

George, T. and A. McGrath (eds.), *For All the Saints: Evangelical Theology and Christian Spirituality* (Louisville/London: Westminster John Knox, 2003)

Grenz, S.J., *Renewing the Center: Evangelical Theology in a Post-Liberal Era* (Grand Rapids: BridgePoint Books, 2000)

Guder, D.L., *The Continuing Conversion of the Church* (Grand Rapids: Eerdmans, 2000)

Gunstone, J., *Pentecost Comes to the Church: Sacraments and Spiritual Gifts* (London: Darton, Longman & Todd, 1994)

Hansen, D., *The Art of Pastoring: Ministry Without all the Answers* (Downers Grove: Inter-Varsity Press, 1994)

Hauerwas, S. and W.H. Willimon, *Resident Aliens: Life in the Christian Colony* (Nashville: Abingdon, 1989)

Hocken, P., *Streams of Renewal: The Origin and Development of the Charismatic Movement in Great Britain* (Exeter: Paternoster, 1986)

Horton, M.S., *A Better Way: Rediscovering the Drama of God-Centered Worship* (Grand Rapids: Baker Book House, 2002)

Hutter, R., *Suffering Divine Things: Theology as Church Practice* (Grand Rapids: Eerdmans, 1997)

Kavanagh, A., The *Shape of Baptism: The Rite of Christian Initiation* (New York: Pueblo, 1978)

Keck, L., *The Church Confident* (Nashville: Abingdon, 1993)

Kreider, A., *The Change of Conversion and the Origin of Christendom* (Harrisburg: Trinity Press International, 1999)

Land, S.J., *Pentecostal Spirituality: A Passion for the Kingdom* (Sheffield: Sheffield Academic Press, 1993)

Lazareth, W.H., *Reading the Bible in Faith: Theological Voices from the Pastorate* (Grand Rapids/Cambridge: Eerdmans, 2001)

Leach, J., *Living Liturgy: A Practical Guide to Using Liturgy in Spirit-Led Worship* (Eastbourne; Kingsway, 1997)

Lincoln, A., *Ephesians* (Dallas: Word, 1990)

Lindbeck, G.A., *The Nature of Doctrine: Religion and Theology in a Post-Liberal Age* (Philadelphia: Westminster Press, 1984)

Lloyd-Jones, M., *Preachers and Preaching* (London: Hodder & Stoughton, 1971)

——, *Joy Unspeakable: Power and Renewal in the Holy Spirit* (Eastbourne: Kingsway, 1984)

Long, T., *The Witness of Preaching* (Louisville: Westminster/John Knox, 1989)

Mudge, L.S., *Rethinking the Beloved Community: Ecclesiology, Hermeneutics, Social Theory* (New York: University Press of America, 2001)

Murray, I.H., *Pentecost – Today?: The Biblical Basis for Understanding Revival* (Edinburgh: Banner of Truth, 1998)

Neuhaus, R., *Freedom for Ministry* (Grand Rapids: Eerdmans, 1992[2])

Newbigin, L., *The Household of God* (London: SCM, 1953)

——, *The Open Secret: An Introduction to the Theology of Mission* (London: SPCK, 1995)

Nouwen, H., *In the Name of Jesus: Reflections on Christian Leadership* (London: Darton, Longman & Todd, 1989)

Oden, T.C., *Pastoral Theology: The Essentials of Ministry* (San Francisco: Harper & Row, 1983)

Pannenberg, W., *Christian Spirituality and Sacramental Community* (London: Darton, Longman & Todd, 1983)

Pao, D.W., *Thanksgiving: An Investigation into a Pauline Theme* (Leicester: Apollos, 2002)

Pawson, D., *The Normal Christian Birth* (London: Hodder & Stoughton, 1989)

——, *Is the Blessing Biblical? Thinking Through the Toronto Phenomenon* (London: Hodder & Stoughton, 1995)

——, *Jesus Baptises in One Holy Spirit: Who? How? When? Why?* (London: Hodder & Stoughton, 1997)

Peterson, D., *Possessed by God: A New Testament Theology of Sanctification and Holiness* (Leicester: Apollos, 1995)

Peterson E.H., *Five Smooth Stones for Pastoral Work* (Grand Rapids: Eerdmans, 1986)

——, *Working the Angles: The Shape of Pastoral Integrity* (Grand Rapids: Eerdmans, 1897)

——, *The Contemplative Pastor* (Grand Rapids: Eerdmans, 1989)

——, *Under the Unpredictable Plant: An Exploration in Vocational Holiness* (Grand Rapids: Eerdmans, 1992)

——, *Subversive Spirituality* (Grand Rapids: Eerdmans, 1997)

Ramsey, M., *The Christian Priest Today* (London: SPCK, 1999 [1972])

Reno, R.R., *Redemptive Change: The Atonement of the Soul* (Harrisburg: Trinity Press International, 2002)

Resner, A., *Preacher and Cross: Person and Message in Theology and Rhetoric* (Grand Rapids/Cambridge: Eerdmans, 1999)

Roxburgh, A.J., *The Missionary Congregation, Leadership and Liminality* (Harrisburg: Trinity Press International, 1997)

Schmemann, A., *Church, World and Mission: Reflections on Orthodoxy in the West* (Crestwood: St Vladimir's Press, 1979)

Schmidt, L.E., *Holy Fairs: Scottish Communions and American Revivals in the Early Modern Period* (Princeton: Princeton University Books, 1989)

Smail, T., *Reflected Glory: The Spirit in Christ and in Christians* (London: Hodder & Stoughton, 1975)

——, *The Giving Gift: The Holy Spirit in Person* (London: Darton, Longman & Todd, 1994)

Thornton, M., *Pastoral Theology: A Reorientation* (London: SPCK, 1956)

——, *Christian Proficiency* (London: SPCK, 1956)

Torevell, D., *Losing the Sacred: Ritual, Modernity and Liturgical Reform* (Edinburgh: T&T Clark, 2000)

Torrance, J.B., *Worship, Community and the Triune God of Grace* (Carlisle: Paternoster, 1996)

Turner, M., *The Holy Spirit and Spiritual Gifts: Then and Now* (Carlisle: Paternoster, 1996)

——, *Power from on High: The Spirit in Israel's Restoration and Witness in Luke–Acts* (Sheffield: Sheffield Academic Press, 1996)

Volf, M., *After Our Likeness: The Church as the Image of the Trinity* (Sacra Doctrina/Grand Rapids: Eerdmans, 1998)

Walker, A., *Telling the Story* (London: SPCK, 1996)

——, *Restoring the Kingdom: The Radical Christianity of the House Church Movement* (Guildford: Eagle, 1998)

Walker, A. and K. Aune (eds.), *On Revival: A Critical Examination* (Carlisle: Paternoster, 2003)

Ward, W.R., *The Protestant Evangelical Awakening* (Cambridge: Cambridge University Press, 1993)

Webber, R.E., *The Younger Evangelicals: Facing the Challenges of the New World* (Grand Rapids, Baker Book House, 2002)

Weinandy, T.G., *The Father's Spirit of Sonship* (Edinburgh: T&T Clark, 1995)

Westermeyer, P., *Let Justice Sing: Hymnody and Justice* (Collegeville: The Liturgical Press, 1998)

Willimon, W.H., *Peculiar Speech: Preaching to the Baptised* (Grand Rapids: Eerdmans, 1992)

——, *Pastor: The Theology and Practice of Ordained Ministry* (Nashville: Abingdon, 1996)

Coming next in the Deep Church Series

The Third Schism
Christianity and the
Legacy of Modernism

ANDREW WALKER

It has long been recognised that the Christian church has been divided by two great schisms between Orthodox and Catholic and between Catholic and Protestant. Andrew Walker argues Christians today face a 'third schism' between those who maintain allegiance to historic orthodoxy, with its credal basis in the Trinity, the divinity of Christ, and a high view of scriptures and those who do not. The book provides a ground-breaking study of the roots of the third schism and a prophetic call to the church.

ISBN: 1-84227-291-8

On Revival

A Critical Examination

ANDREW WALKER and KRISTIN AUNE (eds.)

'Revival' is an exhilarating word: it evokes visions of new life, the power of the Spirit, renewal and restoration, the promise of hope. Yet Revival is a diverse, multifaceted, and controversial phenomenon. The Protestant Great Awakening of the eighteenth century, the Evangelical missions and campaigns of the nineteenth century, and the Pentecostal/ Charismatic movements of the twentieth century have all been called 'Revivals'.

But what does Revival mean for the church in the twenty-first century? This collection of essays aims to address this question through a variety of perspectives: theological, historical and contemporary.

On Revival will appeal to all those who want to reflect on the meaning, significance, and future of Revival – church leaders, students and academics, and practitioners and Christians from all denominations.

Contributors include

DAVID BEBBINGTON, TOM SMAIL, MARK STIBBE, MAX TURNER, ROB WARNER and NIGEL WRIGHT

ISBN: 1-84227-201-2